Financial Openness and National Autonomy

WIDER

Studies in Development Economics embody the output of the research programmes of the World Institute for Development Economics Research (WIDER), which was established by the United Nations University as its first research and training centre in 1984 and started work in Helsinki in 1985. The principal purpose of the Institute is to help identify and meet the need for policy-oriented socio-economic research on pressing global and development problems, as well as common domestic problems and their interrelationships.

Financial Openness and National Autonomy

Opportunities and Constraints

Edited by

TARIQ BANURI *and* JULIET B. SCHOR

A study prepared for the World Insitute for Development Economics Research (WIDER) of the United Nations University

CLARENDON PRESS · OXFORD

This book has been printed digitally and produced in a standard specification in order to ensure its continuing availability

OXFORD
UNIVERSITY PRESS

Great Clarendon Street, Oxford OX2 6DP

Oxford University Press is a department of the University of Oxford. It furthers the University's objective of excellence in research, scholarship, and education by publishing world-wide in

Oxford New York

Auckland Bangkok Buenos Aires Cape Town Chennai Dar es Salaam Delhi Hong Kong Istanbul Karachi Kolkata Kuala Lumpur Madrid Melbourne Mexico City Mumbai Nairobi São Paulo Shanghai Taipei Tokyo Toronto

Published in the United States by Oxford University Press Inc., New York

Reprinted 2004

ISBN 0-19-828364-4

Antony Rowe Ltd., Eastbourne

Preface

The breakdown of the Bretton Woods fixed exchange rate regime in 1971 marked a major change in the post-war international monetary and financial system. The conventional wisdom of the time had it that the advent of floating exchange rates would introduce a needed element of automatic and continuous adjustments in external balances of payments. This would, it was argued, avoid the need for periodic changes in exchange rates, which promoted destabilizing speculation, allow market incentives greater freedom to influence the flow of investible funds, and allow national authorities greater latitude in the implementation of domestic monetary and fiscal policies to the extent that they would no longer be constrained by the possible danger to a fixed rate of exchange.

In the event, however, it became clear that these expectations were unfounded. The new regime of floating rates rapidly developed three characteristics which, together, have had a major adverse impact on the smooth growth of the world economy. First, floating rates resulted in a marked increase in the short-term instability of exchange rates, not only of key currencies in world trade—particularly the US dollar and the pound sterling—but also of the currencies of many small countries whose currencies were pegged to the key currencies. Second, far from promoting automatic and continuous adjustment to shifts in the underlying trade and payments positions, the floating of exchange rates has been associated with large and persistent misalignments of currencies, particularly among the currencies of the principal trading countries. Third, floating has resulted in the emergence of new forms of constraint on the autonomy of national economic policy-making, since national policies have now become heavily dependent for their success on favourable changes in the international economy.

A common factor behind these several—and generally adverse—effects of currency floating has been the vast expansion in the volume of speculative funds and other capital flows across national borders over the past decade. The impact of the ebb and flow of these funds on asset markets, both on domestic financial assets and on the foreign exchanges, has been greatly accentuated by the deregulation of financial markets that has taken place during the 1980s. Exchange rates, at least of key currencies, have consequently come to reflect 'market sentiment' and associated uncertainties, which influence speculative transactions, as much as—or even more than—the underlying 'fundamentals' of trade in goods and services. Equally, the persistent misalignment of major currencies has greatly intensified protectionist pressures in countries with overvalued exchange rates, and greatly increased the danger of a new global recession as the USA attempts to correct its huge trading deficit. Moreover, the greater integration of national economies, reflecting very largely the free-market philosophy of the major trading countries, has reduced still further the potential for autonomous national policy-making.

These drastic changes in the institutional framework of international economic intercourse raise a number of important issues for a fuller understanding of the nature of the present international economy, of the changing role of national policy, and of the interrelations between national policy and the constraints arising from the global system. As regards the specific issue of exchange rates, one question is whether the balance of advantage now lies in moving away from a regime of floating rates towards some arrangement which would ensure more stability, and greater predictability, in foreign-exchange markets. What would such an arrangement imply for national policy autonomy? Would greater currency stability push speculative funds into other asset markets, and so increase instability there?

Another major area of concern relates to the place of the developing countries in the international financial system. Efforts by the key trading nations to protect the exchange value of their currencies by raising domestic interest rates, for example, can have major adverse effects on the debt-service burdens of Third World countries. More generally, the operation of the international monetary and financial system is seriously asymmetric in so far as creditor countries and agencies can insist on austerity measures by debtor nations to ensure the payment of debt-service obligations, whereas debtors cannot, under the existing 'rules of the game', insist on economic expansion in creditor countries to widen the markets for developing country exports.

These and related issues have been the subject of a WIDER research project, to which contributions have been made by many experts, culminating in a WIDER conference on this subject in the summer of 1988. The present volume contains some of the major papers presented at that conference. It is hoped that, by exploring the national-autonomy issue in the broader framework of a political-economy approach, they will provide a more realistic interpretation of the recent erosion of national policy autonomy than that based on a neoclassical perspective.

Lal Jayawardena
Director, WIDER

Acknowledgements

The authors of this volume received help from a variety of sources. Financial assistance was provided from WIDER's Macroeconomics Research Project. The members of this project, particularly Stephen Marglin, provided invaluable assistance in two ways: by formulating the context of this research, and by offering constructive criticism of drafts of the chapters that follow. The authors would also like to record their appreciation for the guidance and criticism provided by Professor Sukhamoy Chakravarty, who is, sadly, no longer with us. Help was also provided by participants at two meetings held at Helsinki in 1987 and 1989, particularly by Amit Bhaduri and Bob Rowthorn.

The staff of WIDER helped in many ways in the organization of the project and the research conferences. One person whose assistance was invaluable is Anne Ruohonen.

In addition to this, Robert Zevin would like to record his appreciation of comments from Roger Alcaly, Peter L. Bernstein, David Colander, J. Bradford DeLong, Heywood Fleisig, Herbert Gintis, Robert Heilbroner, Hendrik Houthhakker, Peter Kenen, Charles Kindleberger, Lawrence Litwak, Arthur MacEwan, Nancy Pettis, Leonard Rapping, Peter Temin, Jonathan Weiner, and Jeffrey Williamson; and to thank his colleague, Heidi Soumerai, for help with collection and analysis of data.

Andrew Glyn would like to thank Wendy Carlin and Peter Kenyon.

Gerald Epstein and Juliet Schor would like to thank Amit Bhaduri, Sam Bowles, Susan Collins, and Jim Crotty for comments; and Carol Barton, Edwin Dickens, Alexandra Edsall, Emily Kawano, Trish Kelly, and Eileen Kelly for research assistance.

Gerald Epstein and Herbert Gintis wish to thank Amit Bhaduri, Sam Bowles, Jim Boyce, Carol Heim, Charles Kindleberger, Martha Olney, Manuel Pastor Jr., and Bob Rowthorn for comments and advice; Emily Kawano, Trish Kelly, and Barney Wagman for research assistance; the Department of Economics and the office of Faculty Research Grants of the University of Massachusetts for financial support; and Andrea Leibson and the Social and Demographic Research Institute for help with data.

Jaime Ros would like to thank Robert Zevin and an anonymous referee.

Tariq Banuri would like to acknowledge with thanks the comments and advice provided by Olivier Blanchard, Larry Goulder, Zvi Griliches, and Nancy Gutman.

Contents

List of Contributors

TARIQ BANURI, International Union for Conservation of Nature and Natural Resources, Pakistan.

ANDREW D. COSH, University of Cambridge.

GERALD A. EPSTEIN, University of Massachusetts.

HERBERT GINTIS, University of Massachusetts.

ANDREW GLYN, University of Oxford.

ALAN HUGHES, University of Cambridge.

ROBERT PRINGLE, *Central Banking*, London.

JAIME ROS, University of Notre Dame.

JULIET B. SCHOR, Harvard University.

AJIT SINGH, University of Cambridge.

ROBERT ZEVIN, US Trust Company.

List of Tables

1
Introduction

JULIET B. SCHOR

I. INTRODUCTION

The 1980s ushered in a sea-change in international financial markets. The most obvious transformation has been a tremendous growth in the volume, variety, and extent of international transactions. Throughout the financial services industry—from bank lending to debt for equity swaps to foreign-exchange dealings—there has been an explosion in the extent of cross-border activity.

This explosion has been accompanied by new ways of understanding the world economy. The Keynesian, or 'national', model which dominated economic thinking from the Second World War until the end of the 1970s is no longer widely accepted. The corner-stone of the Keynesian approach was the need for governments to carry out macroeconomic policy at a national level, and the importance of an international system of financial management which facilitated such policy. In particular, the unrestricted international movement of capital was seen as being incompatible with effective policy and hence with prosperity.

This view is now out of fashion. Economists, financiers, and policy-makers themselves have taken up a distinctly anti-Keynesian view, which we shall call 'global neoclassicism'. Global neoclassicism stresses the futility and even the folly of international financial regulation and discretionary macroeconomic policy. It contends that national governments or even international regulatory systems neither can nor should control the flow of capital across borders, and hence cannot regulate interest rates, fix currency values, or pursue macroeconomic policies which are at variance with the 'dictates of the international market'.

Politicians and policy-makers have been very obliging to global neoclassicism. In recent years there has been a marked shift toward governmental passivity in the face of financial markets. Large, powerful financial markets (the USA, the UK, and Japan) were deregulated at the end of the 1970s. In the USA and the UK, these measures were quite consistent with the overall economic policy orientation of the conservative governments then in power, namely an almost blind faith in the 'free markets'. Other OECD governments followed suit, either with genuine enthusiasm for deregulation, or fatalistically, believing that they could not remain out of step with the larger markets. More European deregulation is scheduled in coming years.

The South did not escape the ascendance of global neoclassical thinking. Economists, politicians, and policy-makers from the North pressed financial liberalization upon the nations of the South. The major US plan for Third World debt (the so-called Baker Plan) offered countries debt relief only if they agreed to deregulate. The International Monetary Fund conformed to the US position, after decades of tolerating, even believing in, the need for capital controls in its client countries. Although a large proportion of the developing world, such as India, China, and South Korea, have liberalized without significant international pressure, for other countries the changes have come only under duress and with considerable scepticism.

This scepticism is not unwarranted. As was argued in an earlier volume of the WIDER Global Macroeconomic Policies Project (Banuri 1991), the benefits of financial liberalization are dubious, the costs exacting. Policy-makers in the South are worried about the very real problems of capital flight, policy ineffectiveness, and exchange rate instability. At the global level, financial liberalization raises the spectre of destabilizing speculation, financial panics, and depression. There is now a massive pool of capital circulating in international markets, operating with what some observers have termed a 'hypermobility of capital'. One estimate put the daily value of foreign-exchange transactions in the mid-1980s at $250bn (Levich 1987*b*). The vast majority of these funds are purely speculative, and thus potentially destabilizing.

These developments can be attributed in significant part to the demise of the system of international monetary regulation. The Bretton Woods system, which managed international financial relations after the Second World War, disintegrated during the 1970s. Whatever its shortcomings, this system had provided a certain level of stability. Although based on the hegemony of the USA, its foundation was nationally based macroeconomic policy. In essence, it was a system of national regulation, made viable by a stable set of international linkages.

The demise of Bretton Woods has called into question the feasibility of that national regulation. Its key dimensions—stable currency parities, limited capital mobility, and restricted international linkages—have been transformed. The present alternative, an anarchic international monetary order, appears to have undermined the possibilities for national autonomy. Individual countries are caught in a classic Prisoners' Dilemma with respect to increasing growth. The present system inhibits individual action, and instead yields financial speculation and global instability.

But the current impasse does not obviously vindicate the global neoclassical view of the world. In our view, global neoclassicism—which emphasizes above all else the inevitability of market-determined outcomes and the importance of governments—is based on a serious misunderstanding of the changes now being wrought in international financial markets. Those changes are first and foremost political. They involve a thoroughgoing restructuring of the international political economy. And this restructuring can in no sense be said to have been 'caused' or 'determined' by any inexorable forces emanating from the globalization of financial markets. Its origins lie in the enhanced power of financiers, the rise of conservative politics, and the breakdown of the system of international co-ordination.

It is the premiss of this book that neither the national nor the global neoclassical model is adequate: the former is overly global, the latter overly national. What emerges from the papers collected here is, by contrast, a political-economy model of international economic relations. This model says that the world can be both global and national at the same time. International monetary markets may be opening up in some places, but this is a selective process, caused by the growing power of financial markets over states. For Mexico and Brazil, to whom financial markets are dramatically more closed today than fifteen years ago, the global neoclassical model is a fictive enterprise of the ivory tower. To understand today's developments, we need to recognize the constant dialectic between national and international forces in the world economy. We need to reject both poles (neoclassical globalism and Keynesian nationalism) in favour of a more balanced perspective.

II. NATIONAL KEYNESIAN AND GLOBAL NEOCLASSICAL MODELS

The fundamental premiss of the national Keynesian model is the need for, and possibility of, effective national policy. This model takes the nation, rather than the entire world, as its unit of analysis. Underlying this choice is a basic faith that international economic linkages are weak and the nation state is strong. Keynes himself argued the wisdom of limiting international linkages, particularly financial transactions:

> There may be some financial calculation which shows it to be advantageous that savings should be invested in whatever quarter of the habitable globe shows the greatest marginal efficiency of capital or the highest rate of interest. But experience is accumulating that remoteness between operation and ownership is an evil in the relations between men, likely or certain in the long run to set up strains and enmities which will bring to nought the financial calculation. (Keynes 1980*a*: 236)

Followers of Keynes, and perhaps even Keynes himself by the time of his death, took a somewhat more sanguine view of cross-border finance.

Nevertheless, the Keynesian model remained wedded to the idea of limited international linkages. Ultimately, the weakness of international linkages ensures the effectiveness of fiscal and monetary policy. For example, the central bank can maintain an interest rate below the so-called 'world rate of interest', either because international financial channels are insufficiently developed to prevent cross-border interest rate equalization, or because it can restrict capital mobility through direct regulation. World-wide rates of interest and profit do not equalize. Important implications of this non-equalization are the linking of domestic savings and investment, and the viability of a large number of domestic policy initiatives which alter domestic rates of savings, interest, and investment.

By contrast, global neoclassicism begins with the world as the basic unit of analysis, bypassing the nation state. Cross-border flows of capital are assumed to occur as easily as international flows in the national Keynesian model. Global capital mobility is assumed to be perfect and markets are complete. As a consequence, an individual central bank cannot maintain an interest rate which is at variance with the world rate, as offsetting capital flows will be rapid and powerful. Regulations will be ineffective, because economic agents will evade them. The novel aspect of the policy package is the desirability of financial openness. Previously, neoclassicals stressed trade openness, and laid little stress on the need for capital markets to be liberalized.

In its most extreme version, this model predicts that the law of one price will hold everywhere. Interest rates, profit rates, wage rates, and commodity prices will equalize across borders. A country deviates from the logic of the world market at its peril. If its workers demand high wages, they will lose their jobs as capital flows to places with cheaper labour. If a state enacts 'green' policies to protect the environment, capital will again flee, searching out locales where it will not be forced to internalize social costs. In financial markets, global competition will force deregulation, proliferation of financial instruments, and uniform rates of return.

In the global neoclassical model, the loss of policy autonomy is severe. However, it does promise benefits to those who willingly submit to its dictates. Gains from trade can be fully realized; cross-border flows lead to rapid technological diffusion and the survival of only the most efficient firms; and, as we have seen in the debates over Europe 1992, proponents of these ideas predict a general increase in standards of living.

III. 1949–1979: THE RISE AND FALL OF THE NATIONAL MODEL

Although individual cases differ, the nations of the capitalist world adopted some variant of the national model at the close of the Second

World War. This history has been discussed in two previous volumes produced by the WIDER research project on macroeconomic policies. These writings stressed the contribution of macroeconomic policy to the successful growth experiences of the period following the Second World War. The contributors to Marglin and Schor (1990) argued that the golden age of the advanced capitalist countries (the 1950s and 1960s) rested on the creation of a set of national institutions and policies which ensured stable and high levels of aggregate demand. Similarly, the striking difference between the experiences of East Asian and Latin American economies, analysed by the contributors to Banuri (1991), was not the result of *laissez-faire* in the former and government regulation in the latter, as many observers have claimed, but was due to macroeconomic policies, in addition to the distinctiveness of institutional structures and historical experience.

However, the national model, in both South and North, could not have succeeded without a system of international co-ordination. In the monetary area, the set of agreements known as the Bretton Woods system provided that co-ordination. Those agreements were based on the leadership or hegemony of the USA, and provided for the maintenance of stable parities among national currencies, the establishment of the International Monetary Fund, and use of the US dollar as a reserve currency. A basic tenet of Bretton Woods was the need for both nationally based financial regulation and global co-ordination.

The breakdown of the Bretton Woods system, at the beginning of the 1970s, had a profound and ultimately depressing effect on the world economy. On the one hand, floating exchange rates resulted in tremendous exchange rate instability for many currencies, including the US dollar. On the other, the erosion of US power and leadership left individual countries adrift. Without a commitment to rapid world growth from the USA, individual countries were faced with a Prisoners' Dilemma with respect to growth. Going it alone became increasingly infeasible and growth slowed as a result. The ascendance of global neoclassicism can only be understood as a response to the demise of the national model and its international system of regulation. In the absence of an effective international system, the case for no system at all was more plausible.

IV. ARE FINANCIAL MARKETS GLOBALLY NEOCLASSICAL?

While global neoclassicism has captured the imaginations of economic theorists, it is important to assess the empirical evidence. Does the world conform to this model: are international capital markets perfect? What historical trajectory have financial markets travelled? Are they more globally neoclassical now than in the past? Following Feldman (1986) and Levich (1987*a*), Cosh, Hughes, and Singh in Chapter 2 suggest three measures of the degree of integration of capital markets: legal, volume-based, and price-based.

One way the world has changed is that *legal* barriers to financial integration have declined significantly in recent years, particularly in the OECD. As Epstein and Schor show in Chapter 6, an index measuring the extent of capital controls in the OECD now stands at its lowest point in over fifty years. By 1992, all controls on capital within the European Community are expected to have been lifted. An investigation of restrictions does not validate the global neoclassical model, but it does represent the removal of a significant institutional impediment to its functioning.

Trends in the *volume* of cross-border flows appear to be consistent with global neoclassicism. Especially during the 1980s, there has been a tremendous increase in the gross volume of international financial integration, in a variety of financial instruments. Chapter 2 documents this increase for a number of large OECD countries. Banuri (Chapter 9) argues that international financial channels have been strengthened in the case of Pakistan and other countries of the South which witnessed growth in foreign remittances. Finally, Latin America in the 1970s reveals a historically very large degree of cross-border financial flows. This evidence has typically been adduced as evidence in the case for increased integration. On the other hand, the 1980s witnessed a precipitous decline in capital flows into the South, which can certainly be described as a contraction of international financial linkages and a withdrawal from capital mobility.

In either case, the gross volume of capital flows is not the crucial criterion for confirmation of the model; it is possible for gross flows to increase as a result of a common cause affecting all countries, at the same time that international substitutability of financial assets remains low. The more decisive test is the extent to which the law of one price holds in financial markets. If price differentials exist for identical financial instruments, then one may infer that a basic condition of the model fails to hold, namely, perfect capital mobility. Existing evidence supports the view that throughout the OECD, rates of return on short-term financial instruments equalize for countries which do not legally restrict capital flows. (For a discussion of the studies which measure these so-called covered interest differentials, see Chapters 3 and 6.) However, before taking this evidence as conclusive, we must confront a number of interesting paradoxes. First, it is just as clearly the case that not all assets conform to the law of one price. Profit rates, for example, show very wide differentials among nations, which cannot be accounted for by this theory.

The second paradox is raised by Zevin in Chapter 3. Zevin argues that historical evidence stretching back at least to the early eighteenth century (and perhaps even further) reveals that financial markets throughout north-west Europe were 'perfect' in the sense of the operation of the law of one price. Except during the brief Keynesian interlude in this century, nation states had little control over the vicissitudes of financial markets, communications were efficient, and investors were highly sophisticated, even in comparison to today's standards.

In view of the arguments we have put forward, what are we to make of Zevin's evidence? At least two interpretations are possible. The first is that the world has been 'globally neoclassical' for centuries, and that nothing new is happening. This claim is logically possible, but historically infeasible. One difficulty is that this view forces one to reinterpret and indeed to reject the entire experience of Keynesianism. It denies that there was (or could have been) a period of significant national policy autonomy, in which national financial markets were relatively self-contained and governments had an added degree of policy latitude. The extensive economic and policy-making literature (and evidence) which exists on the Keynesian period in the OECD countries must be judged as wrong. Thus, this extreme neoclassical position implies that the world currently is, always has been, and presumably always will be neoclassical. It is a profoundly ahistorical approach which will fail to satisfy those who are impressed by the evidence that something new is now occurring.

A second interpretation is that the degree of openness has not been constant over time, but in fact has oscillated in response to political factors. The high degree of international capital mobility of the eighteenth and nineteenth centuries did not persist throughout the twentieth. From the inter-war period until roughly the beginning of the 1970s, the major capitalist nations experienced a phase of unusually non-integrated financial markets. The combination of depression and war combined to disintegrate existing financial linkages. When world economic growth resumed after the Second World War, it was in a context of relatively contained national capital markets. Governments enjoyed a unique degree of policy autonomy—partly as the result of the establishment of institutions consciously crafted in response to the difficulties of the earlier period—which helped facilitate the acceptance and appropriateness of Keynesian policy doctrines. At the same time, Keynesianism justified three decades of governmental attempts to retain (or even strengthen) their control over capital markets. Over time, the uniqueness of the post-war period was eroded, and financial markets in the major capitalist countries began to look more as they had previously. Barriers to mobility became less potent. Even so, the gold standard may still represent the high-water mark of integration.

Zevin's argument is more inclined to this second interpretation. He provides evidence that the 1960s, for example, were a low point, and that the 1970s and 1980s both reveal higher levels of integration. He notes that there was a 'reasonably steady path' toward increasingly efficient links from the 1960s to the 1980s. Indeed, Zevin's evidence corroborates the arguments of Cosh, Hughes, and Singh, Epstein and Schor, and Glyn, by suggesting that it was not technology but a political consensus that created the oasis of political autonomy and policy effectiveness in the post-war period. It was the erosion of this political consensus rather than technological developments that brought about the greater financial openness in the subsequent years.

To some extent, this interpretation reconciles the apparently divergent views of Zevin and of Cosh, Hughes, and Singh, whose argument concerns the growth in gross flows, and by implication international integration. Cosh, Hughes, and Singh are concerned only with recent decades. However, the apparent contradictions between the two chapters also reveal real differences of opinion. Zevin believes that the rise in gross flows and the higher financial market correlations of the 1970s and 1980s were due more to common shocks affecting all countries than to an underlying increase in integration. To a certain extent these alternative perspectives are unresolved in the text, and it remains for the reader to make his or her own judgement on the evidence. On the other hand, the authors do agree that, in order to understand the genesis of the long-term changes in the degree of openness, the global neoclassical model must be rejected. For that model predicts an ineluctable trend toward globalization, at least so long as technological developments follow their usual course. Globalization is efficient, it claims, therefore it will occur.

V. THE POLITICAL ECONOMY OF INTERNATIONAL FINANCIAL MARKETS

In contrast to both the national Keynesian and the global neoclassical models, the authors in this volume are inclined towards a synthesis of the two, the political-economy model. The political-economy model begins with the recognition that financial relations, like nearly all other economic interactions, are inevitably characterized by relations of power.[1] Rich creditor countries exercise power over poorer debtor nations. Nations with economic clout have their currencies accepted worldwide, thus paving the way for seignorage gains. And finally, as Pringle argues in Chapter 4, financial markets themselves wield tremendous leverage over governments despite being dependent on government support and patronage. The recognition that international financial markets have an irreducible element of power and conflict compels us to abandon the global neoclassical model. This is the argument contained in a number of the chapters in this volume, seen most clearly in the papers by Epstein and Gintis and by Ros. These authors have formulated new models of international financial relations which are based on fundamental asymmetries between debtors and creditors.

In Chapter 7, Epstein and Gintis argue that the nature of financial transactions has been misunderstood by the global neoclassical model because of its standard Walrasian assumption that transactions take place with perfect information and no risk. They argue that this is a poor description of the typical financial transaction, which is characterized by problems of enforcement of contract, forms of moral hazard, and strategic behaviour. The Walrasian paradigm assumes a 'wallflower' theory of finance, in which lenders and borrowers wait passively for financial opportunities. A political-economy approach recognizes that lenders may be reluctant, fearing inadequate control over borrowers and uncertainty concerning repayment. Similarly, borrowers may be reluctant, wary of ceding too much autonomy to creditors.

In either the reluctant-borrower or the reluctant-lender case, the financial transaction contains a political element. The model is thus unusual in that it sees power operating not only outside the sphere of the market, but within it. As a consequence, many of the standard predictions of the global neoclassical model fail to hold. For example, consider the operation of the law of one price and its relation to capital mobility. In the global neoclassical model, capital mobility should lead prices to equalize everywhere. Indeed, as noted above, the literature on the OECD reveals that where restrictions are absent, interest rates on identical short-term assets equalize (see e.g. Chapters 2 and 3). But does this mean capital is perfectly mobile? According to the political-economy model the answer is 'not necessarily'. As Epstein and Gintis note, there are important stylized facts about the operation of world financial markets which are inconsistent with the inference of perfect capital mobility.

First, national savings and investment rates are apparently highly correlated, whereas the global neoclassical model predicts they would be virtually uncorrelated. Second, the claim of perfect mobility predicts that investor portfolios would contain a particular nation's assets roughly in proportion to the size of that nation in the world economy. If we consider the world-wide distribution of financial assets, however, it turns out that nationals disproportionately hold assets of their own countries. Third, the equalization of short-term interest rates is not matched by the equalization of profit rates, which show considerable divergence internationally. The law of one price appears to operate only in some markets. But this is in violation of basic principles of the operation of markets on which global neoclassicism is based. These deviations from neoclassical predictions can be explained as manifestations of the reluctance of both borrowers and lenders to cede control over funds or over autonomy. This political element of financial transactions is at the core of the political-economy approach.

Capital rationing is another empirically important contravention to the global neoclassical model. Epstein and Gintis argue that financial markets typically ration capital, in violation of Walrasian predictions. Lenders secure their interests by creating a market which does not clear, as rationing ensures that only the safer borrowers get credit. Ros presents just such as an example of capital rationing, investigating the case of Latin American debtor countries in the 1980s, particularly Mexico. He finds that capital mobility is far from perfect, and exhibits instead a crucial asymmetry. The Government of Mexico cannot currently borrow on world capital markets—at any price. Capital outflows are highly responsive to prices, capital inflows completely unresponsive. If the world were globally neoclassical, the Mexican Government could offer an interest rate on its debt slightly above the world rate and an unlimited quantity of capital would appear. Yet we find that it cannot attract any capital at all. This asymmetry—which is a persistent feature of world financial markets—highlights two crucial weaknesses of the global neoclassical model. The first, that it fails because of problems of enforcement, repayment, and power between borrower and lender, has been identified by Epstein and Gintis.

The second concerns the size of actors on world financial markets. In the global neoclassical model, actors are small (relative to the market) and there are many of them. This means that cartels are difficult to organize, centralized rationing is hard to enforce, and mobility is ensured by the autonomous actions of many small players. The Latin American debt crisis should perhaps teach us otherwise. The players in this game are very large and very powerful. Mexico fails to attract capital not only because lenders are worried about its creditworthiness. It is also subject to the discipline (i.e. rationing) of an organized financial system dominated by very large banks, the G7 countries, and the IMF. This is a political process. It is an exercise of power.

The importance of big players is discussed by Cosh, Hughes, and Singh. They document the tremendous growth in the volume of cross-border flows and the potential these forces have for breaking previously virtuous links between domestic financial and industrial systems (e.g. in West Germany and Japan). They also show that the role of institutional investors in this growth has been substantial, and that large corporations are restructuring production via the linked phenomenon of international takeovers. Consideration of particular incidents (the collapse of the silver market, the October 1987 crash of the US stock-market, and the October 1989 stock-market scare) support the view that big institutions and large individual players influence market outcomes. The prevalence of big actors casts doubt on the global neoclassical description of how world financial markets operate. It seems that we have not only price-takers but price-makers, collusion as well as competition, and capital rigidity alongside capital mobility.

Our reading of the evidence suggests that the case for global neoclassicism is weak. Legal and practical barriers to the mobility of short-term capital have diminished. Among OECD countries, rates of return are very close on short-term financial instruments. But more than this it is difficult to conclude. Other evidence (rates of return on long-term investment or foreign exchange, correlations of national saving and investment, the pattern of investor portfolios, and the existence of capital rationing) is at variance with the model. In order to draw conclusions for the degree of policy autonomy, we need a different model. The political-economy approach bids us consider international enforcement of financial contracts, the actions of large financial institutions, and relations between markets and states. Without an examination of these issues, we cannot judge whether it is really enhanced capital mobility which has led to the current phase of policy ineffectiveness, or whether other forces are at work.

VI. WHY HAVE GOVERNMENTS LOST POLICY AUTONOMY?

A premiss of this volume is the claim that governments increasingly believe themselves powerless in the face of international financial markets, and that they are acting according to this belief. On the basis of the research contained in Part II of this volume, we find considerable evidence for the view that the current policy environment cannot be explained without reference to political factors. Of these, three are paramount: the assertion of financial interests against state power and regulation; the desire of states themselves to conform to the dictates of world financial markets; and the imposition of constraints on debtor nations of the South by banks, states, and the international agencies of the North. Although these do not exhaust the factors at work, they comprise the key political restructurings now occurring on a global level. We discuss them in turn.

As Pringle argues in Chapter 4, the last decade has witnessed a crucial change in the relation between financial institutions and states, or what he terms 'the bankers' bargain'. The crux of that change is that banks upset the existing bargain with the state. They are now demanding (and getting) less regulation, greater protection from insolvency, and enhanced protection of their profitability. This combination has reduced the room within which policy-makers can manœuvre: the bargain encourages more risky activity, thereby raising the likelihood of panics and bankruptcies, and rendering government ever more subject to the sentiments of the market. On this reading, the current phase of policy ineffectiveness has a political origin.

This interpretation of recent events is supported by the analysis of Epstein and Schor, who examine the political economy of capital controls. They conclude that financial interests, far more than either industrial interests or labour, are hostile to the use of controls. Indeed, they find that the propensity of governments to use controls is correlated with political-economic aspects of the economy such as the strength of Left political parties and the degree of independence of the central bank. Their analysis is consistent with Pringle's view that financial deregulation represents an assertion of financial interests.

In Chapter 9, Banuri presents a model of financial regulation which contains similar themes. Addressing himself to the effect of dollar-based remittances on the Pakistani economy, he argues that the growth of alternative remittance-driven financial networks has eroded the central bank's ability to maintain an official exchange rate. This is in part a consequence of the state's inability or unwillingness to adopt corrective measures, and to sustain institutions which facilitate the effective exercise of policy. Once again we are faced with the political-economy questions: why has the state allowed the growth of these alternative, illegal networks? How have they gained such protection and power?

The second development we identified, the desire of states themselves to conform to the dictates of world financial markets, is taken up by Glyn in Chapter 5. Glyn's paper considers the abolition of exchange controls in Australia by a Labour government. Glyn questions the view that decontrol was an economic exigency. While the Australian case has its own peculiarities, it shares a basic outline with many European and Third World nations now abandoning systems of financial regulation which have operated for decades. This thrust of governments towards divesting themselves of responsibility for policy cannot be explained without reference to the currents of political conservatism and economic liberalization which became dominant in the 1980s throughout much of the world.

The third development is the imposition of constraints on debtor countries. Here we note the paper by Ros, who shows how the constraint on inward flows of capital has created a situation in which the Mexican Government no longer has any space for effective macroeconomic policy, either fiscal or monetary. The result is tremendous economic hardship for an already poor country. Ultimately, we must acknowledge the irreducible political element in the Mexican case. The demands of Northern creditors have been articulated in a process which is as much political as economic. Thus, the current policy paralysis of the Mexican Government is not the inevitable outcome of its foray into world financial markets, but the denial of access to those markets by the institutions which dominate them.

VII. LOOKING AHEAD

The policy environment has changed radically. On this the political economist is in agreement with the global neoclassicist. Governments have lost a significant degree of policy autonomy. Those who cling to the national Keynesian model, confident of the ability of the state to control the macroeconomic environment, if only it had the will, are bound to be disappointed.

The political economist and the global neoclassicist part company in the interpretation of *why* policy autonomy has been eroded and *whether and how* it can be restored. For the neoclassical, the loss was impersonal and inevitable, hence irrevocable and even desirable. The market knows best. The alternative interpretation stresses that governments, under pressure from financial interests, either willingly or unwillingly have ceded power to those interests. There remains, therefore, the possibility of their recovering it.

A reimposition of government authority over financial markets seems unlikely at this point. Financial interests have gained considerable clout, and there is little support for government regulation. History is not easily reversible, especially with respect to powers the state has ceded. But we should not be blind to the difficulties of the present arrangement. The opportunities and incentives for financial panic and disarray are greater than ever. The ability of the world financial system to maintain an orderly and sensible movement of funds is far from guaranteed. If financial markets fail to fulfil their most basic functions, pressure for government intervention and regulation is likely to mount.

In both the North and the South, policy-makers will be faced with the task of designing new forms of regulation and control. One route is to reimpose national systems, along the lines of those now being dismantled. It is an open question whether national reregulation would work. The scale of cross-border activity may now be too large to regulate nationally. Financial integration may be irreversible. This is certainly the dominant view. On the other hand, the context will matter a great deal. A world-wide financial collapse, or greatly heightened trade tensions among the major countries, may create a climate for national action. There is a large reservoir of populist sentiment throughout the world which may be mobilized in the face of financial distress. What is politically unimaginable one day can rapidly become feasible if circumstances change dramatically. The political power financial markets wield today must be recognized as somewhat precarious.

An alternative route is to institute new forms of regulation based on international co-operation. If markets have gone global, then too should institutions of government. This is the direction many Keynesians advocate, and numerous schemes for international co-operation have been designed. These plans also have their drawbacks. In a world of fierce economic competition, such as our own, co-operation is difficult to secure. Without a hegemonic power to enforcc its will on weaker states, it may well prove impossible. Certainly the 1980s do not give grounds for tremendous optimism.

Whatever the form, the case for reregulation is strong. Having finally been freed from the strictures of the gold system, it is not obvious that governments should submit to a new structure which replicates its constraints. The period following the Second World War was unusual in the degree of policy autonomy available to governments; it was also unusual in the degree of economic prosperity it delivered. We would be wise to understand more fully the links between the two before treading further along the path of deregulation and policy agnosticism.

NOTE

1. Similar analyses have been done for other economic relations, such as employers and employees (so-called efficiency wage or labour extraction models) and for varieties of product market. For an example of the former, see Marglin and Schor (1990).

PART I

HOW HAS THE WORLD CHANGED?

Introduction to Part I

TARIQ BANURI

This section describes the dramatic increase in global financial linkages and the significant restructuring of domestic financial institutions that has taken place in the previous two decades.

Following Feldman (1986) and Levich (1987*a*), Cosh, Hughes, and Singh (Chapter 3) introduce three different but related measures of capital-market integration: legal, volume-based, and price-based. They show that global financial integration, measured in all three ways, was significantly higher in the 1970s and 1980s than in the 1950s and 1960s. Capital controls, i.e. legal restrictions on capital flows, which were ubiquitous in the post-war period, had almost been eliminated in OECD countries by the mid-1970s. This is corroborated by evidence presented later: Epstein and Schor show, in Chapter 6, that an index measuring the extent of capital controls in OECD countries stands at its lowest point in over fifty years. Similarly, Banuri argues, in Chapter 9, that many Third World countries introduced legal openings for international capital flows on discovering that the effectiveness of controls had diminished because of the emergence of strong and vigorous currency black markets.

The volume measure of financial integration and openness reveals similar results. Cross-border flows of debt, as well as of equity instruments, has increased rapidly since the 1960s. Cross-border trading volume in company shares is estimated to have been $400bn. in 1985 and $750bn. in 1986.

Zevin, however, argues that legal or volume-based measures are inadequate indicators of the degree of financial integration, and recommends reliance on price measures alone. By this count also, the 1970s and 1980s appear to have a much higher degree of integration compared to the 1960s—but not compared to the late nineteenth or the early twentieth century. And thereby hangs another tale.

If it is true that the degree of financial openness has not increased monotonically since the nineteenth century (or earlier), then it becomes very difficult to argue that the move towards freer markets is an inexorable process driven by history or technology. On the contrary, it can be argued that the Keynesian interlude of diminished financial openness was made possible by *political* actions, namely the agreement between policy-makers of a number of industrialized countries to construct institutions of global governance through an act of political will. Likewise, the recent era of flexible exchange rates and financial openness is best seen as the result of a new set of political actions—this time the passivity of national decision-makers, and their inability to forge a consensus to balance the growing political power of financial interests. These issues are taken up in more detail in Part II.

Another important aspect of recent developments is the change in the domestic regulatory environment. As Cosh, Hughes, and Singh demonstrate, regulation of financial institutions has become weaker in industrialized countries, the nature and variety of financial instruments has mushroomed, and the pattern of asset ownership has been remarkably transformed, in the sense that organizations (such as pension funds) rather than individuals have become the predominant owners of financial assets. All this had contributed to, and in turn derives from, the increased political power of financial institutions.

2

Openness, Financial Innovation, Changing Patterns of Ownership, and the Structure of Financial Markets

ANDREW D. COSH, ALAN HUGHES, AND AJIT SINGH

I. INTRODUCTION

The financial markets of the advanced industrial economies have undergone far-reaching changes since the mid-1970s. These changes essentially stem from the following interrelated factors: the progressive deregulation of financial markets both internally and externally in the leading countries; the internationalization of these markets; the introduction of an array of new financial instruments allowing riskier and bigger financial investments; and the emergence and the increasing role of new players, particularly institutional investors, in the markets. The main purpose of this essay is to provide an analytical description of these transformations and to outline some of their broader economic implications.

In addition to the questions of the macroeconomic vulnerability of an economy to such financial-market developments and the issues of national economic-policy autonomy, which are the main focus of this book, these changes also have extremely important repercussions for the savings and investment behaviour of individuals and firms. Specifically, a growing proportion of household savings are being directed towards financial institutions—insurance companies, pension funds, mutual funds, unit and investment trusts. Institutional investors have an increasing influence on the national and international stocks and bonds markets. The important question, then, pertains to the effect of these two changes—increased institutional investment, and growing international integration of the capital markets—on the financing of real investment by industrial companies. Similarly, one may analyse the nature of the relationship between institutional investors and the domestic and foreign companies in which they hold shares.

In principle, changes in financial markets could have a considerable impact on corporate control and performance. To provide a simple illustration, consider just three forms of corporate finance: shares, marketable debt, and direct bank lending. Each involves the problem of asymmetric information and gives rise to different principal-agent relationships. Shareholders have the choice of passive or active reaction to information (i.e. simply selling shares or attempting directly to intervene). It can be argued that the concentration of shares in institutional holdings will result in more informed and more active involvement by the shareholders or their representatives. On the other hand, the institutional investors may themselves be subject to short-term performance pressures which limit their desire or capacity for long-term involvement. Furthermore, the globalization of equities may have created a large class of marginal (and therefore volatile) shareholdings by foreign institutions.

With respect to debt, the debt-holders are more concerned about the immediate creditworthiness of companies. There is no doubt that the development of specialist credit-rating agencies has lowered the information cost in this area and given some large companies cheaper access to wider markets. However, the stability of these new markets is not ensured, and a danger exists of undue dependence on them. Direct bank lending has traditionally involved a close relationship between the lender and borrower. This relationship can be both active and long-term as, for example, in Japan and Germany. New financial instruments to make credit more secure would represent a move away from this close relationship. It is a moot question whether the net result would overall be beneficial for industrial investment and performance.

II. THE INTERNATIONALIZATION OF CAPITAL MARKETS AND THE DEVELOPMENT OF NEW FINANCIAL INSTRUMENTS

Since the demise of Bretton Woods and the introduction of floating exchange rates, there has been an increasing internationalization of capital markets, which has led to the expansion of international lending and security dealing and to the development of new instruments to cope with the associated risk. Floating rates have encouraged the adoption of new instruments. The large savings and investment imbalances, reflected in large current-account and payments imbalances, have expanded international bank lending and built up the Euro-currency markets. The dismantling of exchange controls by West European countries, beginning in the late 1950s and culminating in October 1979 with the abolition of remaining exchange controls by the UK, has freed international currency flows. This, together with the internationalization of trading activities, has permitted companies to seek out the cheapest sources of finance, and investors to spread their risk by diversifying their portfolios internationally.

The dismantling of exchange controls has been augmented by the deregulation of domestic financial markets. This had come about as a response both to the deregulation of other domestic markets and to international competitive pressures. Financial markets have been amongst the most regulated of markets, partly to ensure investor protection and financial stability and partly to form part of the monetary policy tools available to governments. These markets had developed as compartmentalized institutions with constraints on both their assets and liabilities. Competition was restricted not only between these different types of institutions but also within these compartments (due both to regulation and to concentration and entry barriers).

The last decade has seen significant changes in the regulatory climate, leading to the promotion of competition as well as internationalization. These changes have been in response to the growth of an unregulated financial sector both internationally and domestically. A notable example was the Big Bang in the UK markets in October 1986. The underlying cause was the removal of exchange controls in 1979 and the resultant opening of the domestic capital market to international competition. This and the deregulation of the New York market in 1975 led to the fear that the London market would lose business overseas (since its commission rates were too high and capital resources of security firms too small). Along with regulatory changes came major technological improvements and a merger of the domestic and international securities markets in London.

Elsewhere, changes have reduced the compartmentalization of financial companies, and have led, through deregulation, to increased capitalization of their securities business. Deregulation of financial markets has therefore involved opening up the markets internally (decompartmentalization) and externally (by removing obstacles to the entry of foreign financial companies). This represents a shift in policy from the protection of domestic ownership and financial prudence towards the promotion of free competition and market efficiency.

The marked growth and the change in the structure of international capital markets is shown in Table 2.1. The growth has been stimulated by, and has itself stimulated, the development of new financial instruments, designed to increase the marketability and risk-diversification of funds raised. Initially, the growth of international capital markets was largely associated with bank lending, which, at its peak in 1978–9, accounted for two-thirds of the total funds raised on international capital markets. Since that time the debt crisis, the reduction in banks' credit rating, and the pressure to raise their capital ratios have led to a reduced attractiveness of bank lending both for banks and for borrowers (who were not able to borrow directly as cheaply as banks). The decline in syndicated bank lending has been more than outweighed by the rapid growth of bond, particularly Eurobond, issues, as can be seen in Table 2.1.

TABLE 2.1. *Funds raised on international markets, 1972–1986 ($USbn.)*

	1972	1977	1982	1986
Bonds	11.2	36.1	75.5	228.1
Equities	—	—	—	11.7
Syndicated loans	8.7	34.2	98.2	52.8
Note issuance facilities	—	—	5.2	24.8
Other back-up facilities	—	—		4.5
Total securities and commited facilities	19.9	70.3	178.9	321.9
Euro-commercial paper programmes	—	—	—	59.0
Other non-underwritten facilities	—	—	—	8.6
Total uncommited borrowing facilities	—	—	—	67.6
TOTAL	19.9	70.3	178.9	389.5

Source: OECD, *Financial Market Trends* (various issues).

The use and spread of new financial instruments is shown in Table 2.2. These instruments are used for hedging against and distributing risks, and their popularity is a response to the greater scale and volatility of financial markets in recent years. New instruments, such as floating-rate notes (FRNs), interest rate options, and interest rate futures, provide borrowers and lenders with the possibility of hedging against the risk of interest rate movements. The underlying trend in the use of the new instruments has been the gradual replacement of traditional bank loans with marketable security issues (equities and bonds) on which virtually all the new instruments are based. Marketable securities have turned out to be an effective funding instrument for industrial riskspreading. Unlike direct bank loans, these securities allow risks to be split among a large number of investors, who can manage them in a more dynamic and flexible manner because of their liquid character.

The table shows that floating-rate notes have grown from insignificant levels at the end of the 1970s to $51bn. in 1986, when they represented about one-quarter of bond issues. Another significant development supporting disintermediation and the credit-security has been the growth of note issuance facilities (NIFs) and other back-up facilities (e.g. revolving underwriting facilities (RUFs)). The development of new markets leads in turn to the expansion and development of others. There has been a marked increase in the use of swap techniques and of financial futures and options. The use of swaps was important in the growth of bond issues, and tended to tie the domestic and international markets even more closely together. 'Because of their depth and greater efficiency, or because of fiscal and regulatory advantages, an increasing proportion of the credit flows between domestic savers and investors is intermediated directly or indirectly via the international markets' (BIS 1986: 92–3).

TABLE 2.2. *International capital markets: major instruments, 1984–1988 ($USbn.)*

	1984	1985	1986	1987	1988[a]
Straight bonds	58.4	94.7	141.4	124.0	162.8
Floating-rate notes[b]	38.3	58.7	51.0	10.7	19.3
Equity-related bonds	10.9	11.2	26.9	39.1	44.5
Other bonds	3.9	4.5	8.8	3.5	2.7
Equities	—	2.7	11.7	18.2	5.8
Syndicated loans	45.8	36.0	52.8	79.4	108.4
'Managed' loans[c]	11.2	7.0	—	9.4	6.7
Note issuance facilities	17.4	34.4	24.8	28.1	20.7
Other back-up facilities	11.4	8.5	4.5	1.8	1.8
Euro-commercial paper programmes	—	12.6	59.0	55.3	58.0
Other non-underwritten facilities	—	10.6	8.6	14.3	18.9
TOTAL	197.3	280.9	389.5	383.8	449.6

[a] First three-quarters annualized.
[b] Including medium-term floating-rate CDs
[c] Syndicated loans extended in connection with restructuring agreements.
Source: OECD, *Financial Market Trends* (various issues).

For banks, the new instruments have provided fee income (through providing guarantees, stand-bys, back-up facilities, etc.) at a time when they feel constrained against increasing their conventional lending. Banks actively engage in managing their assets and liabilities by trading in these new financial markets so as to ensure an appropriate balance sheet structure. Another response of banks, particularly in the USA, to the rise in cost of borrowing resulting from the downgrading of their credit rating and the tougher capital requirements imposed by supervisors, has provided another example of increased security. This has involved the repackaging of conventional bank loans for sale as marketable securities, and the fast growth of mortgage-backed securities (e.g. CMOs).

Corporate borrowers have become major borrowers on international markets via these new instruments, and non-bank institutions have become major investors on these markets. For investors and borrowers the international market and these new instruments provide a cheaper, more flexible, and less risky source of borrowing or investment. Table 2.2 shows that another growth area has been international issues of equities and equity-related bonds (warrants and convertibles). This is associated with the globalization of equity markets, a subject which will be discussed in section IV below.

In 1986 about 85% of international market activity was accounted for by security-related funding. After the stock-market crashes of October 1987, straight bond issues (particularly those denominated in dollars) and equity-related issues came almost to a halt. There was a revival of the syndicated bank loan, but this cannot be interpreted simply as a move away from increasing securitization, since it was associated with the development of new instruments such as the multi-option facility (MOF). Interest and exchange rate volatility, which hit the bond market, probably stimulated bank lending. The bond market was also hit by the stagnation of the FRN market. The collapse of this market was a major event. For borrowers it meant the elimination of a major source of international finance. For intermediaries it meant losses on the investment in staff and resources in this type of activity. 'Finally, recent events have dealt a major blow to FRN investors who not only have incurred significant losses but, more importantly, who have had a tangible proof of how ephemeral the liquidity of negotiable financial assets can become if suspicions arise about the capability of trading houses to maintain an orderly market' (OECD, *Financial Market Trends*, No. 37).

When the Euronote market was first established, borrowers typically used NIFs. More recently, as shown in Table 2.2, borrowers have tapped the short-term note market by issuing Euro-commercial paper (ECP), which is placed by dealers on a 'best-efforts' basis. At times of financial volatility, borrowers may find that the ECPs cannot be placed at favourable rates, and so they wish to have alternative sources of committed finance. The MOF can potentially offer both greater flexibility and security to the corporate borrower, particularly when doubts arise about the liquidity of some of the new markets. The MOF can be thought of as a securitized instrument with a back-up line of credit.

1988 has seen some recovery on the Eurobond market, and the ECP market has continued to grow; but the main source of growth has been the continued revival of the market for syndicated bank loans. Equity-related bonds have started to recover, but the FRN market has remained in a slump.

III. HOW INTEGRATED ARE INTERNATIONAL CAPITAL MARKETS?

Following Feldman (1986), Levich (1987*a*) has proposed three approaches to measuring the degree of integration of capital markets. The *legal* approach focuses on the extent to which the law provides the right and opportunity for cross-border capital flows. The *quantity* approach posits that a larger volume of cross-border transactions is associated with greater internationalization. The *price* approach is the most exacting. It suggests that the internationlization of a market is complete when its prices are brought into an international equilibrium. Feldman takes the interest rate parity relationship as his standard; when deviations from covered-interest parity are small, markets are assumed to be integrated under the price approach.

Levich (1987*a*) provides evidence of the increasing integration of the capital markets on all three counts. On the price test, for example, a study by Mahajan and Fraser (1986) examined 92 matched pairs of offerings in the Eurobond and US bond markets between 1975 and 1983. Mahajan and Fraser concluded that once they had standardized for issuer, maturity, rating, and coupon, they could not reject the hypothesis that yields were similar in the two markets. This suggests an integration and harmonization of terms between the two markets.

TABLE 2.3. *Aggregate open interest in major world financial futures and options contracts ($USbn.)*

	1975	1980	1984	1985	1986:3
Futures	0.2	81.0	190.7	253.7	439.9
Interest rate contracts	0.0	78.8	182.1	236.0	412.4
Bonds	0.0	35.9	25.0	49.5	104.3
Money market	0.0	42.9	157.1	186.5	308.1
Stock index contracts	0.0	0.0	4.6	9.7	18.1
Currencies	0.2	2.2	4.0	8.0	9.4
Options	0.0	0.0	40.3	138.2	239.6
Interest rate contracts	0.0	0.0	21.5	88.8	161.9
Bonds	0.0	0.0	21.5	41.4	45.8
Money market	0.0	0.0	0.0	47.4	116.1
Stock index contracts	0.0	0.0	14.7	37.1	38.9
Currencies	0.0	0.0	4.1	12.3	38.8
Aggregate open interest[a]	0.2	81.0	231.0	391.9	679.5

[a] Measured by dollar par or index value of outstanding positions on the last day of the period.

Source: Levich (1987*a*: 47)

Finally, in relation to new financial instruments, Table 2.3 presents data on aggregate open interest in major world financial futures and options contracts. The aggregate open interest in financial futures and options, a measure of speculative capital at risk in the market, has increased at a phenomenal rate in recent years—more than eightfold since 1980. Over the same period, the daily trading volume in futures and options contracts has increased sevenfold. Levich (1987*a*) reports that in 1984 and 1985 the volume of average daily trading in the US treasury bonds futures was about four times greater than in the underlying cash market; the same was true of stock-index futures in relation to the purchase of equity shares. All this raises important questions whether increasing internationalization of the capital markets, and the growing role of financial futures, make the underlying spot markets more volatile.

IV. THE ROLE OF FINANCIAL INSTITUTIONS IN SAVINGS AND INVESTMENT

Table 2.4 summarizes the main changes over the last decade in the portfolio composition of the private non-financial sector in the leading industrial countries. These data highlight the significant increase in institutional investment which has occurred in all industrial countries since the mid-1970s. This is in part due to financial deregulation and financial innovations, which have helped to make non-bank financial intermediaries attractive to savers, usually at the expense of the traditional banks. As a consequence, the share of institutional investment in the financial portfolios of households and non-financial enterprises has risen by 15% (Canada) to 50% (the UK) in the leading industrial countries over a period of under ten years.

In the 1980s the fastest-growing financial institutions in the USA and the UK have been mutual funds or unit trusts. The sales of mutual investment funds in the USA increased from about \$10bn. in 1981 to over \$100bn. in 1985; their assets increased over the same period from about \$75bn. to over \$250bn. The number of funds and the numbers of shareholders nearly tripled between 1981 and 1985. (In 1985 there were over 20m. shareholders in US mutual funds[1]) (OECD 1987*b*). Similarly in the UK, as the last row of Table 2.5 indicates, the assets of unit trusts have increased more than eightfold between 1978 and 1986.

The main part of Table 2.5 reports on the investment portfolios of the UK financial institutions over 1978–86. The data indicate that, in the UK domestic equities loom very large in the portfolios of all types of institutional investor: they comprise more than a third of the assets of insurance companies and about half the assets of pension funds, unit trusts, and investment trusts. The table also shows the very large increase in the holdings of overseas company equities by all financial institutions since the abolition of exchange controls by the UK Government in 1979.

In 1986, the unit trusts held 40% of their assets in foreign company shares; the proportion was higher still for investment trusts. By 1986, even pension funds had increased their holdings of foreign equities to 15% of their total portfolios. The question of foreign equity holdings will be discussed further below.

Table 2.6 provides further information on the UK equity holdings of these financial institutions. These statistics suggest that institutions now

TABLE 2.4. *Portfolio composition of the private non-financial sector* [a] *(as % of gross financial assets)*

Country and items	1976	1977	1978	1979	1980	1981	1982	1983	1984	1985
USA										
Deposits	33	34	35	33	32	33	33	32	34	32
Bonds[b]	10	10	10	10	9	9	9	9	10	11
Shares	20	18	17	18	20	18	18	18	16	17
Institutional investment[c]	20	20	20	20	21	21	22	23	24	25
Japan										
Deposits	51	53	53	52	51	51	52	51	49	49[d]
Bonds[b]	4	5	5	5	5	6	6	6	7	6d
Shares	9	8	9	8	8	8	8	9	10	12[d]
Institutional investment[c]	7	7	8	8	8	8	9	10	11	11d
Germany										
Deposits	57	57	58	57	55	55	54	53	51	48
Bonds[b]	9	9	9	10	10	11	11	11	13	13
Shares	12	12	12	10	10	10	10	11	11	15
Institutional investment[c]	9	9	9	10	11	12	12	12	12	12
UK										
Deposits	33	32	32	32	32	33	31	30	29	29[e]
Bonds[b]	6	6	5	5	5	4	5	4	4	4e
Shares	12	14	13	12	12	11	11	12	13	12[e]
Institutional investment[c]	19	21	23	23	25	25	28	29	30	30[e]

Country and items	1976	1977	1978	1979	1980	1981	1982	1983	1984	1985
Canada										
Deposits	31	32	32	32	32	31	31	29	29	29[d]
Bonds[b]	8	8	8	7	6	6	7	8	8	9[d]
Shares	17	17	18	17	18	17	17	17	16	16[d]
Institutional investment[c]	15	16	15	15	15	16	16	17	18	18[d]

[a] On the basis of non-consolidated balance sheets for the household and business sectors; in the case of the USA, except for sole proprietors and agriculture. The sum of the subtotal does not add up to 100 because some items, such as commercial credit and direct investment abroad, are not included.

[b] Except for directly held mortgage debentures.

[c] Mutual funds, pension funds, asssets management funds, and insurance company funds not classed as deposits.

[d] Estimates.

[e] 3rd quarter.

Source: National balance sheets data, BIS and OECD (1987).

TABLE 2.5. *Asset distribution of portfolios of financial institutions, 1978–1986*

Type of asset	Insurance companies			Pension funds			Unit trusts			Investment trusts		
	1978	1980	1986	1978	1980	1986	1978	1980	1986	1978	1980	1986
UK public sector	27.7	29.4	19.8	22.8	22.6	15.1	1.0	1.6	1.8	3.6	3.2	1.3
UK company securities	35.7	34.5	47.0	50.7	48.4	53.1	81.6	73.9	57.3	60.5	57.5	45.2
Ordinary	27.4	28.0	35.2	47.5	45.9	51.1	78.6	72.5	54.1	57.8	55.3	42.4
Unit trusts	2.8	2.6	8.5	0.6	0.7	1.3	—	—	—	—	0.6	1.4
Other	5.6	3.8	3.3	2.6	1.8	0.7	2.9	1.4	3.2	2.7	1.6	1.4
Overseas company securities	3.2	3.9	10.3	5.0	8.4	16.2	17.4	23.7	40.3	33.3	52.1	50.3
Ordinary	3.1	3.8	9.8	4.8	—	15.8	17.1	23.4	38.9	32.0	49.1	46.8
Other	0.1	0.1	0.5	0.2	—	0.4	0.3	0.3	1.4	1.3	3.0	3.5
Overseas government securities	0.4	0.2	1.4	0.2	0.2	0.6	—	—	—	0.6	0.3	2.5
Loans, mortgages, land, property, and property unit trusts	31.2	30.3	16.8	20.9	18.9	8.5	—	—	—	—	0.2	0.2
Other (net)	1.9	1.6	4.7	0.3	1.5	6.5	0.1	0.8	0.6	2.0	1.2	0.4
Total investments	100.0	100.0	100.0	100.0	100.0	100.0	100.0	100.0	100.0	100.0	100.0	100.0
Value of total investments (£ m.)	36,760	52,130	158,551	29,584	51,886	190,044	3,474	4,625	30,344	6,460	8,352	20,422

Source: HMSO, *Financial Statistics* (various issues).

hold nearly 60% of the shares in companies quoted on the UK stock-markets. In 1985 the pension funds alone controlled about a third of the market value of all listed companies; this compares with a figure of less than 20% just ten years earlier.

TABLE 2.6. *Beneficial holdings of UK equities by financial institutions, 1976–1985*

	1976		1980		1985	
	£m.	%	£m.	%	£m.	%
Insurance companies	6,671	16.3	16,248	18.9	47,508	19.4
Pension funds	7,414	18.1	23,650	27.5	78,163	31.9
Investment trusts	2,584	6.3	4,327	5.0	7,377	3.0
Unit trusts	1,705	4.1	3,357	3.9	11,138	4.6
Total holdings	18,374	44.8	47,582	55.3	144,186	58.9
Market value of all listed securities at year end	40,997	100	85,910	100	244,711	100

Source: Cosh *et al.*, (1989).

TABLE 2.7. *Share of financial institutions in total corporate stock, USA, 1952–1974 (%)*

Year	Personal trusts[a]	Pension funds[b]	Investment companies	Life insurance companies	Other[c]	All financial institutions[d]
1952	11.4	0.9	3.0	1.1	2.5	18.9
1958	11.4	3.1	4.6	1.1	1.5	22.7
1968*a*[e]	9.1	5.6	5.7	1.3	2.3	24.0
1968*b*	8.6	6.4	6.1	1.4	2.3	24.6
1974	11.1	9.9	5.4	3.5	3.3	33.3

[a] Personal trust funds managed by commercial bank trust department and trust companies.
[b] Private non-insured pension funds.
[c] Includes commercial banks, mutual savings banks, property insurance companies, common funds.
[d] Excludes 3 categories of fund managed by commercial bank trust departments: estates, agency accounts, and employee benefit funds other than pension funds.
[e] The series for 1952–68*a* is compiled on a slightly different basis from that for 1968*b*-74. In the absence of a single consistent series, data for each is shown for 1968 for comparative purposes.

Source: Kotz (1978).

Table 2.7 provides corresponding information for the USA for 1952–74. It shows a similiar picture of the increasing ownership of corporate equities by financial institutions in the USA. During the last decade, the domination of institutions over US corporate stock has increased very much further.

In view of the quantitative importance of equity ownership, both domestic and foreign, by financial institutions, their decisions with respect to portfolio choices, takeovers, and the degree of participation in corporate governance will all have a significant influence on real corporate investment and performance.

V. THE GLOBAL EQUITIES MARKETS

A global market in equities and bonds is an age-old phenomenon in the history of capitalist development. In the first decades of the nineteenth century, US securities accounted for a large proportion of trading on the London Stock Exchange. It is estimated that, at the beginning of this century, US investors held $600m. of foreign securities (Lambert 1987). However, the growth of the international equities market in the 1980s has been extremely rapid. This is due to a number of proximate causes as well as to structural features. The most important among the former, already referred to in section II, include the following: the outright abolition or lowering of exchange controls in several countries; deregulation of financial markets which has often taken a competitive form among the leading financial centres; and permitting foreign financial institutions to become members of national stock exchanges. The main structural factors are (*a*) the desire of some multinational companies to become truly global by having shareholders from several countries to match their business interests, and (*b*) the increasing role of the financial institutions, and the desire of fund managers to diversify their portfolios and to seek the highest risk-adjusted rates of return.

Let us briefly consider both (*a*) and (*b*). Taking (*b*) first, there is prima-facie evidence that fund managers can in principle improve their returns by diversifying into foreign equity markets. The correlation coefficients between the national stock market indices of leading industrial countries with Japan over 1960–80 are given below.[2]

	Japan	Germany	France	Italy	USA	England
Japan	1.000	0.302	0.361	0.307	0.216	0.171

The degree of correlation in the share price movements in different markets is quite low. Although the 1980s witnessed a growing convergence in the indices of leading stock markets, they are still far from being perfectly collinear (IMF 1988*b*). Hence there is considerable scope for usefully including foreign equities in institutional fund managers' portfolios.

With respect to (*a*), a company can reap many advantages from foreign listing. Naslund (1984) and Wallgren and Karlsson (1988) have referred to factors such as publicity, prestige, increased interest in the company's products, and a demonstration, to the foreign financial community and to competitors, of the company's commitment to its activities. In addition, there is evidence that companies that obtain a foreign listing experience, *ceteris paribus*, a rise in share prices. This is especially so for companies from small countries (Sweden, Denmark, Australia) quoted on larger markets such as London or New York (see Schwartz 1987; Alexander and Eun 1985). No doubt this reflects the segmentation of small-country markets from those in the UK or the USA. The main disadvantage of a foreign stock-market listing is that the company might be required to disclose more information than in its national market. Depending on the nature of the institutional and legal constraints on takeovers in the home country, an international stock-market listing may also make a company more vulnerable to acquisition by foreign predators.

The development in technology has also clearly played a part in the globalization of stock-market trading, but its role should not be exaggerated. It is also not a new phenomenon. The opening of the Atlantic Cable in 1896 cut the communication times between London and New York from several days to a matter of minutes, and thus significantly improved the arbitrage between the two financial centres. In comparison, the current improvements in information technology seem less significant. The main impetus for the globalization of stock-markets has come, not from technology, but from the other factors outlined here. What technology has done is to facilitate the process, so that for shares of about 200 leading companies there is truly an international market which, according to John Tagino, head of global equity trading at Merrill, 'gives the customer the ability to have instant liquidity any time of the day or night he (or she) wants it' (*Financial Times*, 21 Oct. 1987). Whether this new capacity is necessarily good for the company in the long run—or, more importantly, for the real economy—is an open question.

Although equity markets of leading capitalist countries have taken important steps towards internationalization in recent years, the global equity market is still in its infancy. There is a large degree of segmentation among the national stock-markets. For the market to be truly global, each and every investor should have access to all possible asset claims (Schwartz 1987). Information barriers, transaction costs, legal impediments, varying national tax regimes may mean that many investors are obliged to limit their investments to a subset of the universe of assets (e.g. the shares of companies in their own stock-market or a small number of markets).

Such considerations lead Nicoll (1987) to observe: 'In a sense the global equities market could be said not to exist at all. It remains essentially an agglomeration of national markets and depends on their individual strengths.' Table 2.8 shows that during the last decade, in part because of the structural and other factors mentioned earlier, there was an enormous increase in the activities of major stock exchanges in OECD countries. Turnover on the New York and Tokyo stock exchanges increased sevenfold between 1975 and 1985. Table 2.9 provides complementary information to that in Table 2.8; it reports on the size of the secondary (resale) markets for securities in relation to the primary markets (original issues). The much greater size of secondary market is due to the intense level of activity among financial institutions (OECD 1987*b*).

TABLE 2.8. *Turnover on major stock exchanges 1975–1985($USbn.)*

		1985	1984	1983	1982	1981	1975
USA	New York SE	970.5	755.9	751.3	459.4	395.0	133.7
Japan	Tokyo first section	321.2	267.1	213.8	141.2	217.8	51.2
Germany	All exchanges	75.5	29.7	32.9	14.0	13.5	11.1
UK	London	70.2	48.4	42.5	32.3	32.7	19.6
Canada	All exchanges	39.3	25.3	28.7	16.5	23.6	5.4
France	Paris	17.8	10.2	12.4	8.9	12.1	7.3
Netherlands	Amsterdam	17.1	11.9	10.0	4.8	3.9	2.5
Australia	All exchanges	15.6	10.8	9.3	5.1	8.2	0.7
Italy	Milan	14.3	3.8	3.8	2.8	9.7	2.1
Hong Kong	All exchanges	10.0	6.2	5.2	7.6	18.9	2.1
Sweden	Stockholm	9.9	8.5	9.9	4.3	3.6	0.5

Source: *Euromoney*; OECD (1987*b*).

To digress slightly from the discussion of internationalization of equity markets, it is useful to note here the important point made by Mayer (1988) with respect to the role of the stock-market in the financing of investment in plant and machinery. Using flow-of-funds sectoral accounts, Mayer shows that between 1970 and 1985, in the two leading stock-market economies of the UK and USA, new issues made a negative contribution (i.e. there were net redemptions of shares due to takeovers) to net investment in the non-financial corporate sector. In these two countries, the non-financial corporations financed most of their net investment from retentions (in the case of the UK, more than 100%). Nevertheless, the secondary market significantly influences company behaviour through the take-over mechanism (Hughes and Singh 1987).

Returning to international stock-markets, Table 2.10 indicates the declining relative importance of the US stock-markets in the world equity index. The USA represented about half the capitalization of world equity markets five years ago. By August 1987, before the crash, the US

TABLE 2.9. *Domestic corporate securities markets:*[a] *largest share of secondary transactions ($USm.)*

	1982 primary markets				Secondary markets		Secondary transactions/ primary issues	
	Gross new issues of shares		Gross new issues of corporate bonds		Domestic[b] share trades	Domestic[b] corporate bond trades	% values	
	No. of issues	Amounts	No. of issues	Amounts	Value	Value	Shares	Bonds
Australia	260	2,601	25	1,658	(8,179)	(38)	314	2.3
Belgium	12	492	0	0	1,034	—	210	—
Canada	70	846	110	5,442	17,988	—	2,126	—
France	66	533	—	1,309	(8,403)	—	1,576	—
Germany	35	535	2	49	(13,470)	360	2,517	735
Japan	192	3,288	149	6,361	(266,426)	(5,710)	6,852	90
Netherlands	2	15	17	667	4,826[c]	8,946	32,173	1,341
Switzerland	109	276	103	3,372	(15,537)	—	5,629	—
UK	80	3,108	39	1,687	32,737[c]	2,131	1,053	126
USA	1,320	23,399	552	42,296	603,861	7,073	2,580	17

[a] All amounts have been converted to $ at the respective average annual exchange rates.
[b] Traded on the stock exchange(s): figures in brackets represent 1981 results, at 1981 end-of-year exchange rates.
[c] Netherlands and UK trade values represent one-half of reported figures, to make them conform to other country reporting practices, and also include foreign shares in the case of the UK.

Source: International Finance Corporation, World Bank, (1981); OECD (1987*b*).

TABLE 2.10. *World equity markets: national markets by capitalization as percentage of world total.*

	Aug. 1987	Aug. 1986	Dec. 1985
Australia	1.52	0.94	1.25
Austria	0.06	0.06	0.06
Belgium	0.57	0.55	0.48
Canada	2.15	2.15	3.00
Denmark	0.18	0.18	0.23
France	2.01	2.19	1.71
West Germany	3.36	4.51	4.90
Hong Kong	0.91	0.69	0.81
Ireland	0.10	0.06	0.07
Italy	1.49	2.47	1.44
Japan	35.48	31.82	22.85
Malaysia	0.08	0.05	0.07
Mexico	0.09	0.05	0.06
Netherlands	1.31	1.41	1.51
New Zealand	0.21	0.20	0.16
Norway	0.06	0.12	0.18
Singapore	0.16	0.11	0.11
South Africa	0.81	0.52	0.64
Spain	0.87	0.67	0.44
Sweden	0.32	0.33	0.33
Switzerland	1.15	1.34	1.31
UK	9.67	8.50	9.48
USA	37.43	41.07	48.93
World	100.00	100.00	100.00

Source: *FT* Actuaries World Indices: © *Financial Times*, Goldman Sachs & Co., Wood Mackenzie & Co. Ltd., 1987. *Financial Times*, 21 Oct. 1987.

markets accounted for less than 40% of world equity. On the other hand, the share of Japanese and East Asian stock-markets has greatly increased in recent years. It is mostly due to the rise in Japanese share prices and the strength of the yen.

One measure of the globalization of equity markets is the size of the cross-border trading volume in company shares. Salomon Brothers estimated this volume to be about $400bn. in 1985 and $750bn. in 1986 (*Financial Times*, 21 Oct. 1987). Table 2.11 reports on gross and net transactions in US equities by foreigners in 1986 and 1987. The gross trading volume rose from $277bn. in 1986 to nearly $500bn. in 1987 but, as a consequence of the stock-market crash, the net purchases of US equities in 1987 amounted to just over $16bn., significantly below the expected level of $30bn. Table 2.12 provides information on cross-border flows for equities for the leading industrial countries during 1987 as a whole and in the last quarter. The table indicates an enormous sale of foreign equities following the October crash: a net $46bn. in the last quarter. The British investors, particularly the financial institutions, were the biggest net sellers in both the US and the Japanese stock-markets. Despite the crash, the Japanese seem to have increased their net purchases of US shares by nearly $2bn. in the last quarter of 1987. As far as foreign selling of shares is concerned, the Japanese stock-market seems to have suffered the most in the post-crash period, much more so than the US market.

TABLE 2.11. *Foreign activities in US equities, 1986 and 1987 ($USm.)*

	1986 gross activity	1986 net transactions	1987 gross activities	1987 net transactions
Europe	141,811	9,559	232,283	1,864
Belgium–Luxembourg	8,525	633	11,708	435
France	9,581	459	19,920	903
Germany	9,992	341	16,204	(74)
Netherlands	6,246	936	11,267	890
Switzerland	36,982	1,560	59,493	(1,162)
UK	64,608	4,826	103,820	517
Canada	34,584	816	49,524	1,116
Latin America and Carribbean	39,192	3,031	46,870	1,318
Bermuda	11,836	794	10,428	(101)
Netherlands Antilies	11,606	226	15,551	224
Asia	55,285	4,851	142,349	11,535
Hong Kong	8,574	403	12,500	658
Japan	26,904	3,305	102,554	11,365
'Other Asia'	16,269	976	20,545	(1,361)
TOTAL	277,509	18,719	481,500	16,273

Source: *Financial Times*, Survey on US banking and finance, 24 June 1988.

As noted before, the financial institutions are the big players in the global equities market, with the UK institutions being particularly important. The UK pension funds, for example, on average hold 20–25% of their equities in foreign stocks. This compares with about 5% for the US pension funds. How much foreign exposure should financial institutions have? Some purists argue that fund managers should take a purely global stance so that their exposure in the domestic market should be in proportion to its contribution to capitalization of the international market. On this criterion, the US financial institutions need to invest 60% of their funds abroad and the UK institutions should have under 10% in the domestic market (see Riley 1987). In practice, institutions adopt a variety of approaches to decisions concerning foreign holdings in their portfolios. (US institutions tend to consider the problem in terms of risk and return effects.) However, with progress towards free trade in services and greater integration of national financial markets (e.g. as a result of 1992 in Europe, the Uruguay Round at the international level), the share of foreign equities in institutional fund managers' portfolios in most countries is bound to increase appreciably from its current levels.

TABLE 2.12. *International equity flows, net transactions,*[a] *leading industrial countries, last quarter 1987 and total 1987($USbn.)*

Market 4th quarter 1987	Investors from					
	USA	Japan	Britain	West Germany	Rest of world	Total
USA	—	1.9	- 5.0	0.4	- 4.5	- 7.2
Japan	- 2.8	—	- 6.0	- 0.4	- 13.1	- 22.3
Britain	0.5	0.2	—	0.0	1.0	1.7
West Germany	- 0.5	0.0	- 1.4	—	- 2.1	- 4.0
Rest of world	- 0.8	- 5.4	- 4.2	0.7	- 5.0	- 14.7
Total	- 3.6	- 3.3	- 16.6	0.7	- 23.7	- 46.5
Market 1987						
USA	—	11.4	0.5	0.8	3.5	16.2
Japan	- 6.0	—	- 8.0	- 1.4	- 27.0	- 42.8
Britain	3.0	1.5	—	0.2	5.7	10.4
West Germany	- 0.2	0.3	- 1.9	—	0.9	- 0.9
Rest of world	2.2	3.7	- 7.4	0.6	10.0	9.1
Total	- 1.5	16.9	- 16.8	0.2	- 6.9	- 8.1

[a] Minus sign denotes repatriation.
Source: *The Economist*, 23 Apr. 1988.

The discussion of the global equity markets would be incomplete without some reference to the emergence of Third World stock-markets. At present there are over 35 equity markets in developing countries, with a market capitalization of over $130bn. and close to 8000 listings. In 1986 the five largest—Brazil, India, Malaysia, Korea, and Taiwan—ranged in size from $42bn. to $13bn. (see Table 2.13). This makes them bigger than many of the medium-sized European stock-markets. A number of Third World stock-markets enjoyed spectacular boom conditions in 1987 until the Black Monday crash. In the first nine months of 1987, share prices on the Mexican stock-market rose six fold (*Financial Times*, 21 Oct. 1987). However, following Black Monday, prices fell to a tenth of their pre-crash level. The World Bank and the International Finance Corporation are encouraging the development of Third World stock-markets. They are also promoting foreign equity investments in these markets in order, among other things, to facilitate 'debt–equity swaps' as a part of the solution to the Third World debt problem.

TABLE 2.13. *Emerging equity markets in the Third World: market capitalization 1980–1986($USm.)*

Country[a]	1980	1982	1984	1986
Brazil	9,220	10,260	28,990	42,084
India	10,350	—	12,550	18,000[b]
Taiwan	6,080	5,080	9,870	15,366
Malaysia	12,397	13,905	19,401	15,065
Korea	3,830	4,410	6,220	13,924
Mexico	12,992	1,719	3,661	5,952
Chile	9,400	4,530	2,110	3,027
Thailand	1,238	1,257	1,720	2,878
Jordan	1,605	2,845	2,222	2,549
Nigeria	3,119	1,457	3,190	2,138
Philippines	2,096	1,236	—	1,991
Pakistan	643	878	1,157	1,710
Argentina	3,865	974	1,171	1,591
Greece	3,016	1,923	766	1,129
Colombia	1,605	1,322	762	710
Turkey	477	952	957	97

[a] Table in order of 1986 market capitalization.
[b] Estimate.

Source: International Finance Corporation, Washington, DC, and *Banker*. Reproduced from *Financial Times*, 21 Oct. 1987.

VI. THE GLOBAL MARKET FOR CORPORATE CONTROL?

In their survey of mergers and acquisitions in the industrial countries in the post-war period, Hughes and Singh (1980) observed that the 'golden age of capitalist development' (i.e. 1950–73) was 'also attended by another extremely important phenomena—a merger wave that occurred more or less simultaneously in several countries and that in a number of them, again by past standards, was immense'. In explaining this simultaneity of merger movements in industrial countries, particularly in the 1960s, Hughes and Singh emphasized among other aspects the important role of international factors, namely the liberalization of international trade and the impact of multinational investment. Nevertheless, they were surprised to observe that the overwhelming proportion of this huge merger activity—the largest ever recorded in the Anglo-Saxon countries—was confined to mergers among national firms. There were relatively few international mergers, i.e. those involving firms of more than one country. Table 2.14 reports on international mergers in the six original EEC countries during 1966–73. These numbers were minuscule compared with those involving mergers between firms in the individual countries themselves. As Jacquemin and De Jong (1976) pointed out, such mergers evidently encounter a number of legal, institutional, and psychological obstacles.

TABLE 2.14. *International mergers in the EEC, 1966–1973*

	West Germany	France	Italy	Netherlands	Belgium	Luxembourg
1966	22	19	13	16	24	6
1970	24	22	12	13	22	7
1971	22	24	11	12	24	7
1973	16	26	7	13	22	16

Source: Jacquemin and De Jong (1976).

The liberalization of financial markets in recent years has coincided with cross-border merger and takeover activity on a far larger scale. This is clear from the data in Table 2.15 on national and international mergers involving the largest 1000 EC firms from 1982/3 to 1985/6. The financial Press reports, if anything, a further big rise in international takeovers over the last two years. According to W. T. Grimm and Company, in the first half of 1988 the number of cross-border acquisitions involving a US company increased by 12%, to 1032, over the same period of 1987. This represented an increase in the value of the deals of 42%, or $129.4bn. The much larger increase in value can be attributed to the greater number of big acquisitions. In the first half of 1988, there were 195 deals valued at over $100m., compared to 166 in the previous year; and 30 deals of over $1bn. compared to 17 earlier. In the first nine months of 1988, there were 283 purchases by British companies in the USA worth $18bn. In 1987, there were only 134 such acquisitions, totalling $1.25bn.[3]

In a recent survey of cross-border takeover activity, based on newspaper reports of deals involving a shift of majority control, it was found that, in 1987, the countries making the most transnational acquisitions were: Britain, 427; France, 194; USA and Canada, 167 (only with European sellers); West Germany, 137; the Netherlands, 126; and Switzerland and Austria together, 120. The countries in which the most companies were acquired by foreign firms, according to the study, were the United States and Canada, 417 (only from European buyers); West Germany, 269; France, 178; and Britain, 138.[4]

Obviously, financial liberalization is not the only factor responsible for this large increase in international takeovers. There are, for instance, good product market reasons for the merger activity—e.g. the creation by 1992 of a single European market and protectionist pressures in the USA. However, financial deregulation in the non-Anglo-Saxon countries and the international integration of capital markets have undoubtedly played a significant role in facilitating this process. As financial deregulation proceeds further (e.g. as national obstacles to foreign takeovers are removed), international takeover activity is likely to increase in the future.

TABLE 2.15. *Industrial mergers involving the largest 1000 community firms, 1982/3–1985/6*

	All	Intranational		Intra-community[a]		Extra-community	
		No.	%	No.	%	No.	%
1982–3	117	59	50.4	38	37.5	20	17.1
1983–4	155	101	65.2	29	18.7	25	16.1
1984–5	208	146	70.2	44	21.2	18	8.6
1985–6	226	144	63.7	52	23.0	30	13.3

[a] i.e. international but involving companies in member states.

Source: Commission of the European Communities, *13th Annual Report of Competition Policy in the European Community* (Brussels, 1986), table 2, p. 18.

In relation to industrial performance, the question arises whether the presence of international predators affects the efficiency of the stock-market selection process by, for instance, increasing the supply and quality of raiders. However, it may also be the case that cross-national mergers serve to strengthen oligopolistic market links in international markets, and to worsen problems of regional or national autonomy and economic performance as a result of the geographical redistribution of headquarters staff, R&D personnel and local sourcing connections, including in particular financial and professional services. All these are important policy issues which require systematic exploration.

VII. CONCLUSION

This paper has traced developments over the last fifteen years of increasing integration of international capital markets, deregulation and financial liberalization in domestic markets, and the emergence of new financial institutions in domestic as well as global equity markets. In addition to the questions of national vulnerability and autonomy, we have suggested here that these trends have very important implications for savings and investment behaviour of economic agents as well as for industrial performance. With respect to the latter, our conclusion is that the relationship between financial and industrial capital is becoming more expert, more technical, more international, and more informed. By the same token, it is also likely to become more short-term, more 'arm's-length', and more diffuse. There can be no doubt that many of these changes have been beneficial, stimulating a more competitive atmosphere in capital markets and facilitating the management of risk. A large, high-risk project like the Eurotunnel could not have been financed, in the absence of these new forms of financial arrangements, without significant public-sector funding. However, these changes have a direct effect on only the largest companies. Exclusive access is given to these companies in the new markets, and so the market power of these companies may be reinforced. In addition, the changes seem to encourage a distant relationship between borrowers and investors and an environment in which institutions seek to reduce their exposure to a problem rather than tackle it directly. This 'marketization' of industrial problems, as well as the readier access to both short- and long-term debt, is reflected in the huge increase in mergers, takeovers, and sell-offs in recent years. These may be inimical to investment in plant and equipment and to long-term industrial performance.

Finally, it has been suggested to us that the international financial market trends which we have outlined in this paper coincided particularly in the 1980s with the US current-account deficit. This raises the interesting question of how much of what is going on is just being driven by the US deficit, and how much is an independent trend which would have occurred if the USA had maintained external balance. In our view, two factors have been fundamental to the processes we have described: the abolition of exchange controls in industrial countries in the 1970s, and internal and external financial deregulation. In general, both factors have preceded the US balance of payments difficulties. The US deficit and, since 1985, the fall in the relative value of the dollar have of course affected the nature and degree of globalization—e.g. the incidence of takeovers from Japan and other countries in the USA. However, it is also important to recognize that the US deficit has most likely also contributed *indirectly* to these trends—in particular by hastening the process of financial liberalization in some countries. To counterbalance its deteriorating international position in manufactured products, the USA has pressed for freer trade in financial services and financial liberalization in countries like Japan and, more recently, Korea. The continuing liberalization of the Japanese financial market in the 1980s has been particularly significant in the global integration of the capital markets.

NOTES

1. Not surprisingly, the growth of mutual funds and unit trusts has suffered a sharp set-back following the stock-market crash of Oct. 1987.
2. These figures are quoted in Brunello (1988).

3. W. T. Grimm counts as an acquisition any deal involving an American company in which at least 10% of another company's stock is being purchased, or in which the purchase pricc is likely to be at least $10m. See further *International Herald Tribune*, 10 Nov. 1988, special financial issue on mergers and acquisitions.
4. The survey was carried out by ALW/MA International—France, a Paris-based mergers consultant. See further *International Herald Tribune*, 10 Nov. 1988.

3

Are World Financial Markets More Open? If So, Why and With What Effects?

ROBERT ZEVIN

I. INTRODUCTION

It is generally considered all too obvious that the world's financial markets have become continuously, dramatically, and unprecedentedly more open since the end of the Second World War. And—often in the same breath—the equally obvious explanation is provided that these facts are the consequences of advances in computers and high-speed communications.

In this essay I demonstrate that, while financial markets have certainly tended toward greater openness since the end of the Second World War, they have reached a degree of integration that is neither dramatic nor unprecedented in the larger historical context of several centuries.[1] Moreover, as is strongly suggested by the latter observation, today's openness is not in any important way a consequence of today's information technology.

Here, as in other chapters of this volume, financial openness is of interest because of its consequences for the autonomy of national economic policy. How shall we define financial openness? If our concern is constraints on policy freedom, then our measure of openness might be the dependence of a nation's interest rates, stock-market prices, or exchange rate on events in the rest of the world. If a nation's interest rates converge towards, or move in common with, world interest rates, that nation may have lost control of its interest rates and/or money supply to the world. Of course, it may also have lost control of its interest rates along with the rest of the world to some common cause.

Since it is especially in the nature of financial-asset prices to adjust swiftly to important developments, it is particularly appropriate to examine their prices rather than the flow of funds across national boundaries 'into' or 'out of' assets. The necessary price adjustments in interdependent financial markets will in theory—and sometimes do in practice—take place without any transactions occurring. That is, financial-asset prices can change to incorporate new information before any new transactions take place, or can eliminate the profit of arbitrage before any arbitrageurs have traded.[2]

Exactly what behaviour of financial-asset prices shall we look for to confirm the existence of relatively open or closed financial markets? The question is not trivial: geographically separate markets can be integrated in two theoretically distinct but empirically overlapping senses.

If news of hostilities between two countries caused bond prices to fall in all the world's major markets, we could conclude that these markets were part of a single, efficient system for disseminating and responding to the information concerning a new war and its presumed impact upon aggregate demand. Similarly, if we could show that changes in the expected depreciation of sterling against the dollar in three months' time are directly matched by changes in the difference between interest rates on three-month UK and US treasury bills, this again would demonstrate the efficiency of the transatlantic markets for treasury bills and foreign exchange.[3]

Now suppose that the US Government embarks on a course of higher budget deficits, with a concomitant increase in the issuance of treasury bills. The London and New York financial markets are integrated in the second sense if this increase in US treasury bills causes identical increases in US and UK treasury bill rates. That is, the two markets for treasury bills are actually one market, not just because of rapid communications but because the two treasury bill instruments are perfect substitutes in all investor portfolios, in the sense of having infinite cross elasticities of demand.[4]

Assets in transnational markets that are perfect substitutes for each other are the pure case of a more general phenomenon. Equities of different issuers and bonds of different qualities and maturities are clearly close but imperfect substitutes in well-integrated national markets. It is reasonable to look for the same degree of international substitution as a measure of international integration.

Both types of integration—induced by efficiency and by substitutability—will be characterized by high cross-market correlations between asset price movements. The two types of integration differ less in the fact of the correlations than in the reasons for them. Efficient markets will move synchronously in response to events with supranational effects on classes of assets. Crop failures, the beginnings and ends of wars, or oil price shocks will produce common consequences for similar assets in different markets, whether or not they are directly substitutable.

In these cases, the extent of observed correlation will depend not only on the degree of cross-market efficiency but also on the frequency and severity of the exogenous shocks. If two assets are perfect substitutes, their prices and price changes will necessarily be identical. Efficiency is a necessary precondition for observing systematic correlations; substitutability and common shocks are alternative additional conditions, either one of which is a sufficient addition.

International substitutability of assets encompasses most of what we mean by financial openness as a factor in economic-policy autonomy. If domestic financial assets are perfect substitutes for foreign financial assets, then domestic policy-makers can only exert influence over the effective stock or price of those assets to the extent that the domestic share of the relevant world total is large. Thus, for a relatively small country, control over domestic interest rates or money supply might be lost, and with it control over ultimate targets such as investment, real growth, and inflation.[5]

In conclusion, if two financial-asset prices are highly correlated, it follows either that they are close substitutes or that the same events typically move both their prices. However, the latter is tantamount to saying again that they are substitutes in as much as investors have no reason to expect different results from holding one or the other.[6] Conversely, if two assets exhibit no price correlation, they are necessarily neither substitutes nor subject to even infrequent common exogenous shocks.

We can take the serial congruence of asset price movements as a first approximation of market integration in the sense of high substitutability, subject to episodic exaggeration by exogenous events with common consequences.[7] Section II below employs measures of price conformity to explore transnational market integration at various times over the last 300 years.

Section III approaches the same problem from a different point, more specific to the possible impact of financial openness on domestic economic autonomy. I estimate reduced-form macroeconomic functions describing financial and real variable determination, and examine cross-sectional data and other studies to distinguish better the substitution and common-shock explanations of financial-market correlations observed in Section II. I argue that the two oil shocks and the general conditions of capitalist world inflation and disinflation in the 1970s and 1980s were important common sources of synchronous asset market behaviour. Section IV concludes this study with a more explicity political examination of international relations, financial innovations, and the oil price shocks.

I find no trend toward financial openness over the last century, or over the last three centuries. There is, partly as a consequence, no evidence that the microelectronic revolution has caused a qualitative transformation of international financial markets. Finally, while the existence of a hegemonic power in the international order of nations has coincided with stable exchange rate regimes, the consequences of those regimes for national autonomy have not been uniform.

II. HOW OPEN HAS THE WORLD BECOME?

II.1. In the Beginning

In our modern myopia, we usually forget that a world of separate national monies was not the primeval economic garden from which we evolved. It could as well be argued that the intermittent attempts of nations to impose their sovereign control over money have waxed and waned. The century from 1870 to 1970 was an episode in which national governments briefly held the high ground in their struggle to control money.

For a thousand years before that, the large-denomination coins of many nations circulated in international trade, and substituted freely for local money. The same can be said for the bills of exchange issued by well-known banking houses from northern Italy to north-west Europe. A local authority that might have wished to make money dear or plentiful was thwarted by direct and effective financial openness (Cipolla, 1967: 13–26).

Individual states were able to achieve independent influence despite the collective weakness of states. A country that supplied a great deal of other nations' imports as producer, carrier, or entrepôt, and that simultaneously provided a large market for their exports, might be in a strong position to insist on being paid, as well as paying, in its own coin. An issuer with great military power and a disposition to use it would also achieve enhanced acceptance (Cipolla, 1967: 23–6; Hicks, 1969: 65–8, 89–90).[8]

However, even such countries did not—and presumably could not—confine legal tender within or across their boundaries to their own issue. Cipolla (1967: 14) says: 'As late as the nineteenth century no western state enjoyed a complete monetary sovereignty.' National monies were close substitutes. Why should they have been otherwise? The important thing about a coin was that it contained so many grammes of gold. Whether the gold was stamped with the picture of King Louis or King Henry could have mattered only if one or the other picture was a better guarantee of the gold content, or if superstition at the periphery of the market economy granted one or the other some special acceptance.[9]

We shall see below that, compared to the high gold standard in the late nineteenth and early twentieth centuries, today's world may be less integrated. First we shall glance at the scanty data available for the few hundred years before the gold standard system. We do know that the international network of financial markets in the late seventeenth and early eighteenth centuries, especially the Amsterdam–London–Paris triangle, was efficient as I have used the word (Neal 1985; 1987*a*).[10]

Substantial international capital movements relative to wealth and income constitute additional indirect evidence of cross-country integration of financial markets. Goldsmith (1985) provides information about the ratios of net foreign debt to total domestic assets and GNP for several countries that developed early. In 1760, long after Britain's greatest indebtedness to Dutch and other foreign investors, her net foreign debt was still 23% of GNP. By 1800, Britain's net foreign-investment position had improved to a modest + 5% of GNP; and by 1830 and 1850 to the high positive levels of + 32% and + 38% of GNP (Goldsmith 1985: 232).[11]

Considering the size of the British economy in the world, these percentages represent substantial flows of capital from the Netherlands to eighteenth-century Britain, and from early and mid-nineteenth-century Britain to many parts of the world. France, too, was a net international creditor, by 4% of GNP in 1815 and 6% in 1850. Among other destinations, investments flowed to the USA, which owed 13% of GNP in 1805 and 8% in 1850, to India, owing 8%, and to Italy, owing 3%, around 1860 (Goldsmith, 1985: 216, 242, 250, 297).

These ratios of net foreign debts to GNP grew substantially larger during the high gold standard. In the last quarter of the nineteenth century, India, Italy, and Japan all owed foreigners amounts between 20% and 30% of GNP. In 1913, Japan and Russia owed more than 20%, India and Denmark more than 30% (Goldsmith, 1985; see also Chapter 7 below). These numbers are close to the ratios for the largest debtor LDCs today. Subsequently, India, owing 43.5% of GNP in 1939, and Canada, owing 37.5% in 1955, were about the same on this score as contemporary Argentina, Brazil, Korea or Turkey (see Chapter 7).

Creditor country positions also expanded relative to GNP during the high gold standard, to 153% of British GNP and 97% of French GNP in 1913–14. These creditor ratios have declined quite continuously over the past 75 years. Today, no creditor nation comes close to these pre-First World War heights (see Chapter 7). Moreover today's ratios of foreign-asset and liability positions to GNP are considerably less than those that apparently prevailed 150–300 years ago.[12]

In the seventeenth and eighteenth centuries, specie and bullion still served as ready means of exchange in all countries, regardless of origin. Privately or publicly issued bills and notes typically served the same purpose, but less reliably, and often with limited application to a particular bilateral or other narrow trade pattern (Cole, 1929: 385–9).[13]

Eagly and Smith (1976) studied the dependence of London money market interest rates for most of the eighteenth century on other London market rates and on Amsterdam rates. They found equally large effects for the domestic and foreign rates, concluding that their results demonstrate the efficiency of the London money market and the dominance of Amsterdam in the determination of London interest rates.

The process of securitization (the interposition of uniform, marketable securities between assets and their ultimate owners) discussed by Cosh,

Hughes, and Singh in Chapter 2 above was also very much under way from the early 1600s. The beautiful stock exchange, visible through the window in the background of so many seventeenth-century Dutch portraits and duplicated in so many other European cities with the patronage of monarchs, is a clear enough record of the process.

This evidence provides a strong, albeit circumstantial, case for believing that financial markets were strongly integrated across north-west Europe by the early eighteenth century, if not earlier. Money itself of different national origins was certainly fungible. Holdings of foreign loans or debts were very large compared to total wealth or income by contemporary standards.

Speculative money moved swiftly from one country to another as early as 1720 (Neal 1987*b*). Prices and interest rates moved together internationally according to all standard accounts of the period. Markets behaved efficiently. A growing multinational class of portfolio investors perceived securities of different national origin but similar characteristics as close substitutes because of comparable transaction costs, low information costs, and the absence of serious currency exchange impediments.

II.2. The Gold Standard

Historians of the gold standard disagree about much, including whether it was in fact a gold standard, a gold exchange standard, or a sterling standard. The salient characteristic of the international gold standard regime about which there is no disagreement is that it 'succeeded, to a unique degree, in preserving exchange-rate stability' among 'the more advanced countries' without restrictions on the movement of capital or goods (Triffin, 1968: 13).[14]

This suggests that we should expect to find a large degree of financial-market integration in the gold standard period. Unrestricted capital mobility fulfils an important set of conditions for inter-market efficiency, and exchange rate stability does the same for substitutability (see Section III.5 below).

Panel A of Table 3.1 provides a condensation of various indices of financial-market integration and real integration calculated by Morgenstern (1959) for the high gold standard and for the inter-war period. Panel B displays similar calculations that I have performed on data starting in 1960.

Entries in Panels A and B cannot be directly compared because A uses monthly and B annual data; Panel A covers substantially larger samples; and Panel A mixes two unusual indicators of synchronization with the more conventional correlations used throughout Panel B. The data in Panel A that average percentages of correspondence for phases are most directly comparable to the data in Panel B that correlate year-over-year rates of change: that is, nominal long rates, the yield curve, and real activity—(4) and (12), (5) and (14), (7) and (16) or (17).

TABLE 3.1. *Measures of international financial integration*

(a) France, Germany, UK, USA

	1876–1914	1925–38
(1) Nominal short rates[a]	.54***	.56***
(2) First differences[b]	.11**	.15*
(3) Central bank discount rates[a]	.56***	.56***
(4) Nominal long rates[c]	.65	—[d]
(5) Yield curve[c]	.71**	.53
(6) Stock price first differences[b]	.17***	.12
Real variable:		
(7) Phase of business cycle[c]	.76***	.64

(b) West Germany, Japan, UK, USA

	1960–70	1971–80	1981–7
(8) Nominal short rates	.15	.59*	.78**
(9) First differences	.01	.66**	.05
(10) Real short rates	−.04	.34	−.10
(11) First differences	.06	.18	.22
(12) Nominal long govt.	.19	.41	.91***
(13) First differences	.25	.63*	.58
(14) Yield curve	−.10	.53	.03
(15) Stock-market change	.35	.44	.39
Average of 8 financial correlations	.11	.47	.36
Real variables:			
(16) Change in GDP	.15	.75***	.49
(17) Industrial production	.21	.80***	.72*

***, **, and * indicate a value of the statistic that would be significant at the 1%, 5%, and 10% levels respectively for a single application with this many degrees of freedom.

Panel A

All data are from Morgenstern (1959), as are all the references below. The data Morgenstern uses are monthly. The length of the series varies. I have indicated immediately after the page reference for each line the number of months, or the range of months, included in the pre- and post-war samples respectively. The table presents average of all unique pairs of the statistics of correspondence described in more detail below.

[a] In these rows Morgenstern has calculated simple correlation coefficients.

[b] Morgenstern (pp. 106–9) has computed a 'sign correlation' statistic that he developed for this purpose with Abraham Wald for which he supplies measures of significance. The statistic depends on whether pairs of serial 1st differences have the same or different signs. It is most comparable to the 1st-difference measures reported in Panel B.

[c] Here Morgenstern has calculated the % of months for which a pair of series were in the same 'phase', based on NBER methods for determining cyclical turning-points in time series. The same phase represents the same position between peak and trough. Significance levels for these statistics have been estimated from a randomly generated standard reported by Morgenstern on pp. 53–60.

[d] Data not available in Morgernstern.

(1) p. 105 (463, 168). Private discount rates for prime paper in Berlin, London, and Paris and the prime commercial paper rate in New York.
(2) p. 106 (462–511, 167–8). The same data as in (1).
(3) p. 395 (463, 168). Central-bank discount rates. The pre-First World War figure does not include the USA, and is thus an average of only 3 correlations.
(4) p. 456 (426). Nominal long-term bond rates selected by Morgenstern to be as comparable as possible. They are discussed by him on pp. 448–51.
(5) p. 505. (4)–(1).
(6) p. 536 (151–27, 120–68). The data are % changes in stock price indices for Germany, the UK, and the USA only before the war, and for all 4 countries after. Morgenstern also uses a stock index for France beginning in 1899, and reports %s of phase overlap for all 3 samples on p. 535. Using the shorter pre-war period that includes French data or the phase overlap measure does not change the general pattern of a small, irregular decline in stock-market correspondence from before to after the First World War, and a general absence of significance for the post-war correspondences.
(7) p. 49 (419, 157).

Panel B

For all but row (17), the panel presents averages of the 6 unique correlations among the 4 country time series.
(8) Annual averages from IMF (1988*c*) and Morgan Guaranty Trust Company, *World Financial Markets*, June 1987 and Jan. 1988. 'Money market' rates for Germany and Japan, 3-month treasury bills for the UK, and federal funds for the USA.
(10) (8) converted to real rates with the consumer price index reported in IMF (1988*c*) for all 4 countries. 1987 data from Council of Economic Advisers (1988: 372) and *Datadisk* (1989).
(12) Annual average from IMF (1988*c*).
(14) (12)–(8).
(15) A moving 1-year price change in the calendar-quarter average level of a comprehensive, market-weighted equity price index. From *Datadisk*.
(16) Annual change in real GDP from IMF (1988*c*).
(17) % changes from 1 year earlier of quarterly average industrial production indices for the EC, Japan, and USA. Quarterly averages of monthly levels from *Datadisk*. The numbers reported are averages of 3 correlations.

Each of these entries for the gold standard period tend to be larger than their counterparts in the next column or in Panel B, and of equal or greater significance. The sole exception is the large and significant average correlation of long-term government bond yields in the 1980s.[15]

The comparison can be extended by looking only at the significance of the statistics as tests of the hypothesis that the national series are independent. We can then compare the levels and changes in short-term rates and changes in stock prices—(1) and (8), (2) and (9), (6) and (15). Again, the three gold standard entries equal or exceed the significance of all comparisons.[16]

The data confirm the high degree of international capital market integration that we expected to find for the gold standard era. We have already seen that Goldsmith's (1985) data on international assets and liabilities relative to domestic assets and income tell a similar story: higher in the mid-nineteenth century than today, highest by far in the gold standard era.

Morgenstern (1959) provides an additional data set reflecting the extent to which securities were listed, traded, and owned transnationally before 1914. By one estimate, the total value of foreign securities traded in London in 1874 was £3.6bn., exceeding the £2.2bn. value of British and colonial government securities listed in London (p. 524). At the end of the nineteenth century this 62% foreign share had fallen slightly to 59%, £4.7bn. out of £8bn. total (p. 514). At the same time, in France an estimated 53% of all domestically traded securities were non-colonial foreign issues (p. 514).[17]

Morgenstern also presents data on the numbers of foreign and domestic securities listed for trading in various principal cities.[18] In Amsterdam, the proportion of all issues that were neither Dutch nor Dutch colonial was a staggering 82% in 1855, and 77% in 1875. This ratio declined steadily to 53% in 1900. In 1987, the comparable Amsterdam number for equities was 54% (Morgenstern, 1959: 514; Neal, 1985: 226; Salomon Bros., 1987: 95). In the principal German financial centres of the 1880s, Berlin, Frankfurt, and Hamburg, 27% of all bonds and 8% of all stocks actually traded were of foreign issue. The comparable number for stocks in 1987 was 43% (Morgenstern 1959: 513; Salomon Bros. 1987: 112).

Finally, the Salomon Bros. source gives data on the relative number of foreign common stocks traded in the UK and France (1987: p. 108, 84) at 20% and 29% respectively, well below the value proportions given above, 59% and 53%, for the same two countries respectively at end of the nineteenth century.

All these measures of transnational-securities trading and ownership are substantially greater in the years before the First World War than they are at present. More generally, every available descriptor of financial markets in the late nineteenth and early twentieth centuries suggests that they were more fully integrated than they were before or have been since.

II.3. The Role of Technology

We have not found much evidence of increased financial openness compared to a century ago. Therefore I shall not spend much time considering whether what I have *not* found is caused by improved techniques for the transfer and exchange of monetary assets.

Computers and related paraphernalia have made it possible to convert a large balance of funds in one currency and location into a different currency in a different place, all in a moment. Many think these new devices have forced the opening of financial markets. Such thinking credits the cart for the arrival of the horse. The essence of money is that it is an idea. It exists within and between human minds. 'You cannot ride on a claim to a horse' wrote Schumpeter, 'but you can pay with a claim to money.' For as long as there has been money, and longer, it has been possible to create any amount of it as fast as one could preface the amount with, 'I owe you . . .'. It did not take a Renaissance prince much longer to say these three magic words than it does an IBM mainframe. Nor is there anything about the computer, or the motley collection of entities that speak through it, to make its promises any more valid than the prince's. Money being an immaterial idea, those who developed and dealt with it have always shown a keen interest in the most rapid possible communication of ideas. The mail packets and express riders of the eighteenth century who bound Amsterdam to London, Philadelphia to New York, carried cargoes of words. The words were orders, bills of exchange, promises, demands—that is, the money or conveyors of money.

It is doubtful if the computer has created a class of transactions and orders that are conceptually more complex than those invented by the Dutch in the seventeenth century. It is more the case that the computer has increased the volume of transactions that can be processed or data that can be analysed. It represents a massive substitution of capital for labour. A merchant's counting-house was full of people collectively processing as many transactions in a year as a computer might handle in minutes. These are only questions of scale and cost; they had been sufficiently resolved before the eighteenth century to establish the reach and dominance of money institutions and merchant activities.[19]

If integration means, however abstractly, one market with one price, then the critical constraint is not processing capacity but communication velocity. People in two different places can be part of the same market only if they have the same information at the same time. The international transfer and exchange of money is a very old reality. The speed of such transfers has always depended only on the speed of communication. Since money is essentially immaterial, only the idea of a debit, credit, or exchange need be transported.

Eighteenth-century Amsterdam, London, and Paris were nearly the same market in this sense, if we interpret 'the same time' to mean the same week or couple of days. After the transatlantic telegraph in 1866, 'the same time' between New York and London financial markets became a matter of minutes. The spread of telephone and telegraph communication a hundred years ago was the decisive event in unifying financial markets. The essential ideas of finance were well established before, and have been little changed since.[20]

II.4. Recent Times

If international financial openness has declined since the eve of the First World War it has nevertheless increased since the end of the Second. One difference between this and several other chapters in this volume is that I place more emphasis on the lack of change in the historical long run, while other authors pay more attention to the recent trends toward integration. A second difference which will become apparent is that I see less loss of independence from recent increased integration because of the offsetting influences of floating exchange rates and lost US hegemony. A third difference is that I do not attribute many characteristic recent features of financial markets to the effects of openness.[21]

Panel B in Table 3.1 contrasts the three periods 1960–70, 1971–80, and 1981–7.[22] Before 1971, there were surprisingly low levels of cohesion among all manner of financial (and real) variables in four of the world's largest and most developed nations. In the next ten years (1971–80) average correlation increased for each of the ten financial and real series analysed, and in every case but stock prices the increases were quite dramatic. In the 1980s, seven of the ten series have exhibited less congruence than in the 1970s. However, all but one still evidenced more international correlation than in the 1960s.

A substantial literature on international capital markets provides confirmation for these findings and illuminates their decomposition into changes in efficiency and changes in substitutability. Assets traded in different markets that are otherwise essentially the same and therefore strong substitutes will be more or less perfectly correlated, as the respective markets are more or less integrated in the efficiency sense of having available, inexpensive information, low transaction costs, and low institutional barriers.

The extent of these international efficiencies can be tested by measuring levels of movements of interest rates on domestic and Eurocurrency instruments of identical maturity and issuer; or the coherence of rates fully hedged for exchange rate changes on intrinsically similar instruments in different countries and currencies.[23]

Such tests of what Frankel (1986) calls closed and covered interest parity, respectively, confirm a reasonably steady path toward increasingly efficient links between major country capital markets from the 1960s through to the 1980s, and especially from before 1974 to the subsequent period.[24] Most of the increase and most of the remaining inefficiencies are due to dismantling or retaining controls and taxes on international capital movements, rather than to changes in technology.[25]

If efficiency has increased while the conformity of asset prices and yields has not, it follows that international financial-asset substitutability has declined in the 1980s, or that ubiquitous, exogenous impacts have diminished.[26] It is not too difficult to understand how broadly fluctuating exchange rates have diminished substitutability among assets denominated in different currencies.[27] This would perhaps account for the small decline in apparent cohesion from the 1970s to the 1980s. However, the more dramatic increase in exchange rate volatility from the 1960s to the 1970s corresponds to an equally strong increase in cohesion. The only surviving explanation is an increased influence of common shocks in the 1970s.

I shall argue that the two oil price shocks and the simultaneity in the developed nations of the problems of high inflation and unemployment followed by successful disinflation provided just such a set of common forces to distinguish the 1970s (strongly) and the 1980s (less vividly) from the 1960s.

On the whole, economists have been bedazzled by the visible progress toward less political interference and more efficiency, at the expense of seeing what was really happening to financial openness and why.[28] Table 3.1 suggests a rank order of international financial-market cohesion as follows: (i) the forty years before the First World War, followed closely by (ii) the 1970s, (iii) the inter-war period, again followed closely by (iv) the 1980s, and (v) the 1960s, far behind. A progression toward more financial interdependence is hard to find in this record.

Fischer (1988: 14) writes that 'Capital flows . . . are a major and extraordinarily rapid mechanism for transmitting shocks in the international economy.' A footnote (p. 39) acknowledges that capital flows played 'this role too in the heyday of the gold standard'. Fischer argues convincingly (pp. 14–15) that floating exchange rates, and interest rates in a world of capital mobility, transmit effects internationally because they adjust more rapidly than prices and wages.[29]

Fischer also argues (p. 15) that world economic recovery 'in 1984 and 1985 under the impetus of an expansionary US fiscal policy despite restrictive European and Japanese fiscal and monetary policies' constitutes 'commonsense evidence' that interdependence is important.

Isn't this pursuit of opposite policies equally common-sense evidence for the increased independence that the current international regime affords for national economic policies?

III. HAVE POLICY OPTIONS CLOSED?

III.1. What Has Changed?

How can we best measure the degree of constraint on the freedom of domestic economic policy? The principal targets of a national economic policy include the level and growth of output and employment, the proportion of product invested, the composition of investment and production, the distribution of income, and the rate of inflation. In this section I will look directly at how the ability of nations to achieve their targets has been impaired by financial openness. I will also consider the effects of the current regime of floating exchange rates on national autonomy. As we have seen, exchange rate volatility is the principal source of disintegration in the world economy; and it has emerged in step with the increased similitude of financial prices that can be, and are, fully insured against exchange rate risk.

In theory, financial openness in general and floating exchange rates, in particular, could enhance economic independence (i) by making domestic saving and investment independent of each other; (ii) by disjoining both domestic inflation and real growth from their international counterparts; or (iii) by introducing manipulation of a country's own exchange rate as a new policy instrument.

Independence could be diminished for the following reasons:

(i) If the domestic interest rate becomes essentially the world interest rate, or, equivalently, if domestic money and liquid assets become perfect substitutes for their international counterparts, control over a policy instrument, the domestic interest rate or money supply, has been lost.

(ii) To the extent that exchange rate risk, or political-policy risk, differentiates a country's financial assets so that they are not perfect substitutes for their external equivalents, then the possibility exists that policy deviations from prevailing international standards will be 'punished' by more severe and precipitous flights of capital, increases in own-currency interest rates, or depreciations of exchange rates than would have occurred with fixed or pegged exchange rates.

(iii) As in (ii), a country's exchange rate itself and financial assets denominated in its currency become new dimensions of speculative activity. Financial markets may be subjected to increased buffeting by speculative bubbles or irrational expectations with both domestic and external origins.

The rest of this section considers these potential enhancements and reductions of independence.

III.2. The Independence of National Investment from Saving

The extensive recent literature on this subject finds that, far from going their separate ways, national saving and investment have been strongly linked from 1960 to 1985.[30] And, if anything, the link has been growing stronger (see Ch. 7 below; Gintis, 1986: 26; Feldstein and Horioka, 1980; Feldstein, 1983; Frankel, 1986: 40–7).[31]

Table 3.2 offers some additional calculations of the Feldstein–Horioka (1980) type which cover the gold standard era and the aftermath of the First World War. Summary statistics for the 1960s and 1970s, from Feldstein (1983), are added for comparison.

If regressions of this type are measures of effective capital market integration, then the results in Table 3.2 can be interpreted as confirmation of our finding that the gold standard era was one of particularly effective capital mobility facilitated by financial openness. Coefficients of the savings ratio are not significantly different from zero in 1870, 1890, and 1910. The adjusted R^2s, plausible alternative measures of investment/saving autarky, are uniformly lower in the gold-standard years than in the 1960s and 1970s.[32]

This regression specification provides a powerful test of the hypothesis that openness makes domestic savings irrelevant to domestic investment. That hypothesis is decisively rejected by the contemporary results and also rejected for the gold standard years.[33] However, regressions of the type reported in Table 3.2 are a meaningless test of the hypothesis that international capital flows are also relevant to domestic investment, a hypothesis which cannot be rejected as an explanation of the remaining differences between investment and saving in many countries.

Epstein and Gintis (Ch. 7) provide and test a model of the agency considerations that would cause creditor and debtor nations to act to balance current accounts, at least of the debtor nations. Their model explains quite well why we observe limits on the extent to which international capital movements drive a wedge between national investment and saving rates. There are plenty of reasons why saving and investment rates might tend to equality, thus reducing the demand for and supply of equalizing international capital flows.[34]

Capital movements that remain after the pull of external accounts toward balance, and of internal saving and investment toward each other, might be small relative to saving and investment in the receiving and sending countries. Their fluctuation as a share of investment will be due to changes in the mobility of capital, including, in the Epstein–Gintis framework, possible shifts in global rules and attitudes towards inter-

TABLE 3.2. *Regressions of investment ratios against savings ratios, 1870–1920*

Time span	Constant	Savings ratio	Adjusted R^2
1870	.013	.836	.23
	(.064)	(.50)	
1880	–.027	1.179	.65
	(.048)	(.34)	
1890	.045	.668	.26
	(.052)	(.36)	
1900	.049	.603	.35
	(.045)	(.28)	
1910	.051	.625	.00
	(.109)	(.64)	
1920	.043	.767	.60
	(.040)	(.26)	
1960–9	.059	.779	.82
	(.022)	(.19)	
1970–9	.047	.843	.67
	(.036)	(.19)	

The dependent and independent variables throughout are the ratios of gross saving and gross investment, respectively, to GDP or GNP. Standard errors are in parentheses.

The data for 1870–1920 are from Green and Urquhart (1976: 239, 241): gross capital formation and gross saving as a % of GNP for GB, Canada, France, Italy, Sweden, the USA, and Australia. For Germany, only net saving data were available, and this was matched with net domestic capital formation. Both the saving and investment data are centred averages of periods ranging from 1 to 10 years. The data are incomplete for France in 1870, Canada in 1880, France and Germany in 1920. Otherwise, there are 8 observations for each regression.

Data for 1960–79 are from Feldstein (1983).

national debt. Notwithstanding theoretical and econometric results, capital movements are substantial today, and have apparently grown modestly since the 1960s and 1970s.[35]

The USA has used flexible exchange rates and international capital movements to finance a very substantial excess of investment over saving in the 1980s. Even so, the USA, Canada, and Australia, as well as Argentina, Brazil, and South Africa, all financed comparable or larger excesses in the nineteenth century under fixed exchange rates.[36]

III.3. Inflation and Real Growth

The observed degree of cohesion among international growth and inflation rates may reflect a similar degree of policy cohesion. Alternatively, it may reflect the common effects of global events on growth and inflation or the common appearance of similar domestic causes. My primary concern in this section is to identify the degree of cohesion and how it has changed.

To the extent that exchange rates under Bretton Woods were firmly pegged, they should have imposed tight constraints on national economic policies. While there might have been some room for variations with respect to the microeconomic or social aspects of policy, and for different mixes of policy instruments, the aggregate effect of the small number of fiscal and monetary policy instruments available to a government should have been closely harmonized with the external norm.[37]

How was the norm established? Partly by the leadership of multinational bodies such as the IMF and OECD; partly by the equilibrating effects on the system of individual country responses to balance-of-payments or capital-market disturbances; and mostly through the hegemony of the USA. The USA exercised dominant influence over the multinational institutions. The USA sought to enforce the rules of the fixed exchange rate system. And the USA used trade, aid, military power, covert activity, and overt persuasion to influence the composition of governments and the choices made by governments in the whole domain of its world influence.

The dollar crisis of 1971 and the advent of floating exchange rates in 1973 were symptomatic of a decline in US hegemony, and were perceived as such at the time. In addition, the principal argument for floating exchange rates was, and has remained, that they would increase national economic autonomy by removing a rigid constraint on policy. In theory, under floating exchange rates, each country has the option of departing from the international policy norm. A country could choose, for example, deliberately to experience higher inflation than the rest of the world, with an offsetting currency depreciation.

However, as we have already seen in Table 3.1, the reality is that growth rates of major-country domestic product and industrial production have been much more synchronous since 1971 than they were before.[38] Fig. 3.1 (*a*) illustrates a similar phenomenon for year-over-year Consumer Price Indices (CPIs). The US rate is compared with a simple arithmetic average for Germany, Japan, and the UK. The lower part of the figure shows US inflation minus 'rest of world' (ROW) inflation, the difference between the two upper lines in the figure.

From the first quarter of 1953 up to the end of 1970, the correlation between US and ROW inflation was only .47. US inflation averaged

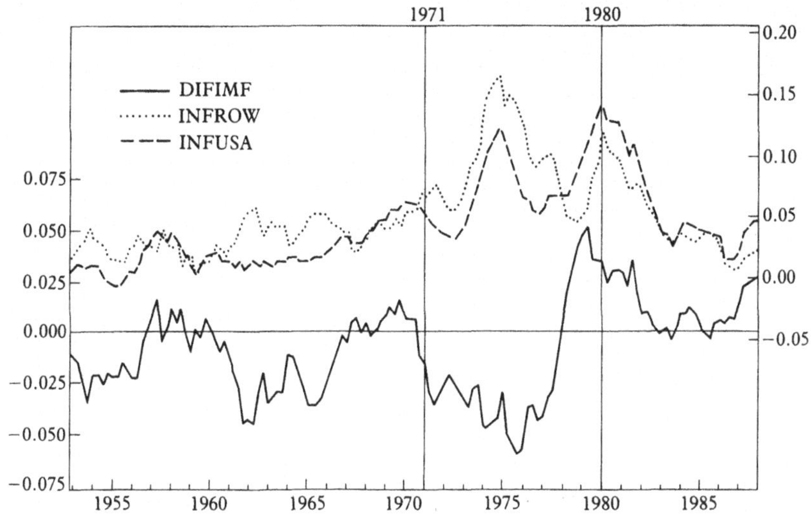

Fig. 3.1(*a*) CPI inflation: USA versus ROW, quarterly at annual rates, 1953–1987.
INFUSA = US inflation; INFROW = Rest of World inflation; DIFINF = INFUSA minus INFROW.

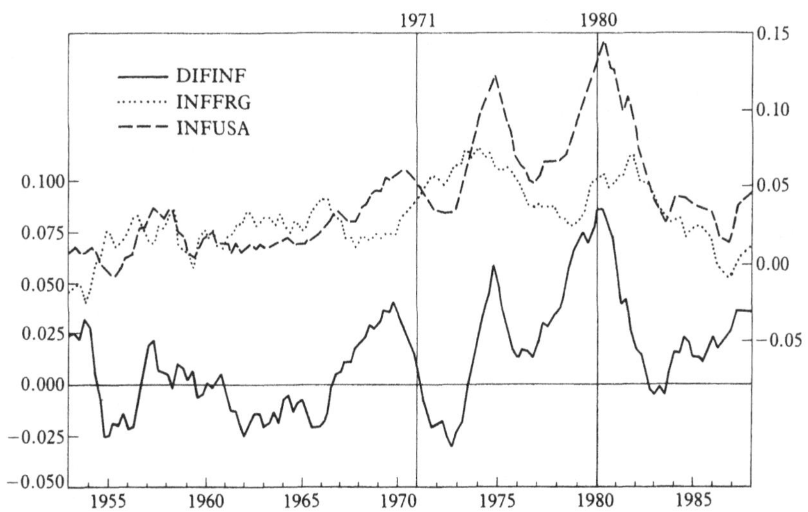

Fig. 3.1(*b*) CPI inflation: USA versus FRG, quarterly at annual rates, 1953–1987.
INFFRG = West German inflation; DIFINF = INFUSA minus INFFRG.

about 1.15% a year less than ROW inflation. In 1971–80, the correlation between US and ROW inflation was little changed at .49, and US inflation averaged 1.50% a year less. In 1981–7, the inflation correlation increased substantially to .94, while US inflation averaged 1.05% more than the ROW. After the dollar floated, US inflation remained low relative to the ROW, and ROW inflation remained semi-independent of US inflation. Beginning in 1978, US inflation became distinctly higher than ROW inflation, and after 1980 the two rates were much more correlated.

There were no dramatic signs to distinguish US relative inflation before President Nixon ended the convertibility of the dollar into gold in 1971. In fact, during the first phase of floating rates, dollar depreciation, and US temporary import surcharges and price controls, the USA achieved its most dramatic improvement in relative inflation performance —the declining line in the lower half of Fig. 3.1(*a*) from 1970 to 1976.

This evidence that US inflation was relatively low before floating and lower thereafter, and that inflation rates were relatively independent under Bretton Woods, does not support the common belief that floating rates in the 1970s and 1980s, as in the 1920s, are due to fundamental differences in willingness or ability to combat inflation.[39]

With respect to the individual ROW countries, US inflation was consistently less than UK inflation throughout the thirty-five years from 1953 to 1987, while the correlation increased gradually after 1970 and dramatically after 1980 (.42, .53 and .95 respectively). The USA–Japan comparison is almost identical to the USA–ROW comparison.

West Germany is the exceptional case. Its inflation rate was already an average .2% lower than the USA in 1953–70, with a low correlation of .31. By 1971–80, the average German inflation advantage had increased to 2.75%. And German inflation was independent of US inflation, with an average correlation of only .11. This can be seen in Fig. 3.1(*b*), which compares the inflation rates of the USA and West Germany only. The sharp increase in US relative inflation under President Carter that is visible at the bottom of Fig. 3.1(*a*) is anticipated by a sharp relative increase in 1973–5. Both episodes are at least partly accounted for by German restraint as well as American excess.

Then, in 1981–7, the German inflation advantage narrows to a still large 1.95%, and German inflation becomes highly synchronous with American inflation (.85). It is arguable that the Bundesbank was freed to pursue stricter anti-inflation policies after the end of Bretton Woods, and that German policy took good advantage of this opportunity.[40]

Although the possibility of divergent inflation rates has increased, the actual divergence, at least in the 1980s, has diminished. We saw in Table 3.1 that the real growth rates of developed countries in the 1980s were less divergent than in the 1960s, more diverse than in the 1970s or under the high gold standard, and about the same as during floating exchange rates in the inter-war years.

In the late 1960s, US inflation and lack of resolve to combat it were symptoms of domestic strains on the welfare state and international strains on the warfare state. In the 1970s, world-wide inflation was partly a continuing hangover from the success of post-war Keynesianism, but primarily a consequence of the two oil price shocks.[41] Inflation, real growth, and policies that affected both all responded in common to the oil shocks and their consequences.[42] For most of the 1980s, inflation and interest rates have generally declined because of common political and private responses to the previous inflation experiences.[43]

III.4. Domestic Policies and the International Economy

Cohesion of financial-asset prices is evidence of financial-market integration in the sense of efficiency, substitution, or both. If cohesion were caused by common responses of efficient markets to internationally significant events, such as the OPEC price increases, then further investigation should yield no additional evidence of international interdependence in direct measures of the responsiveness of one country's economic instruments or targets to the values of similar variables in another country. This suggests ways of distinguishing between substitutability and efficiency as causes when high transnational financial-market correlations are observed.

The size of the coefficients of foreign variables relative to domestic variables in the explanation of domestic outcomes is a general test of the degree of interdependence (Bryant 1980: 135–83).[44] This measure might be strengthened by increased trade or political integration as well as financial-market integration. Table 3.3 reports some regression results designed to test the strength of international impacts on domestic policy and the extent to which they have changed since 1971.

The first four regressions estimate central-bank reaction functions in setting short-term rates, which are viewed as policy instruments. The dependent variables are Di, the annual change in the US federal funds rate, and Di^{w}, the annual change in the average short-term interest rate in Germany, Japan, and the UK (hereafter ROW). Central banks were modelled to vary interest rates positively with inflation and negatively with changes in the labour unemployment rate. These are the two domestic variables which throughout the table have been kept to the right-hand side of the independent variables.

The first independent variable in equations (2)–(4) captures international effects. The Federal Reserve varies interest rates to achieve target levels for the exchange value of the dollar. ROW central banks close differences from US interest rates. All the coefficients are significant.[45]

TABLE 3.3. *Foreign and domestic response coefficients for the USA and the ROW viewed as a two-country world*

Dependent variable	Sample	Independent variables			Adj. R^2	%F
(1) *Di*	60–70		+.636 *DP2* (4.08)***	−.583 *DU* (−2.28)**	.73	0
(2) *Di*	71–87	−.082 US$ (−1) (−3.49)***	+.537 *DP2* (3.55)***	−1.90 *DU* (−6.10)***	.75	26
(3) Di^w	60–70	.288 Dii^w (−1) (5.79)***		−1.82 DU^w (−8.00)***	.93	45
(4) Di^w	71–87	.271 Dii^w (−1) (1.97)*	+.176 $DP2^w$ (2.33)**	−2.17 DU^w (−4.25)***	.62	23
(5) *D$R*	60–70	.384 Dii^w(−1) (1.32)	−.292 *CA/W*(−1) (−1.09)		.52	100
(6) *D$R*	71–87	3.00 Dii^w(−1) (3.68)***	+2.09 *CA/W*(−1) (3.29)***		.52	100
(7) *DGDP*	60–70		−.722 DPP^w (−1) (−3.80)***	−.770 *Di* (−1) (−2.72)**	.77	58
(8) *DGDP*	71–87	+.417 $DGDP^w$ (−1) (2.22)**		−.782 *Di* (−1) (−5.12)***	.61	30
(9) $DGDP^w$	60–70	+.451 *DGDP* (−1) (1.40)	−1.410 DP^w (−1) (−3.58)***		.54	28
(10) $DGDP^w$	71–87	+.149 *DGDP* (−1) (−1.33)	+.263 CAP^w (−1) (1.74)	−.778 Di^w(−1) (−5.02)***	.60	16
(11) *DP*	60–70		+.860 *DP* (−1) (6.27)***	+.161 *CAP*(−1) (2.78)**	.96	0
(12) *DP*	71–87		+.418 *DP* (−1) (3.92)***	+.746 *CAP*(−1) (5.92)***	.86	0

(13) DP^w	60–70	.366 DPM (− 1)		+ 1.77 CAP^w (− 1)	.41	62
		(2.75)**		(1.72)		
(14) DP^w	71–87		+ .440 DP^w(− 1)	+ 1.05 CAP^w (− 1)	.71	0
			(2.42)**	(3.17)***		

This table considers the relationship between the US economy and the rest of the world (ROW), defined as an arithmetic, equal-weighted average of West Germany, Japan, and the UK. Averaging is the first operator in each multi-step process. So, e.g., ratios are ratios of averages, not averages of ratios. All data are from IMF, 1988, or *Datadisk*, Jan. 1989. All data are initially annual averages or year-over-year changes. (− *n*) indicates a variable lagged *n* years. *t*-statistics are in parentheses under coefficients. ***, **, and * indicate coefficients significantly different from zero (2-tailed test) at 10%, 5%, and 1% significance levels, respectively.

CA/W: US current account balance divided by current dollar value of world exports.

CAP: ratio of US real GNP to capacity real GNP. Capacity real GNP is taken equal to actual real GNP/.999 in 1953 and 1968. Passing through these 2 points, it is assumed to grow at 3.38715% from 1952 to 1968, 3.0% until 1973, and 2.75% thereafter.

CAP^w: 1− ROW average labour unemployment rate.

D$R: change in the average annual real dollar exchange rate, computed from the average annual nominal price of the dollar in each of the 3 ROW currencies and average CPI inflation in ROW and the USA.

$DGDP\ (DGDP)^w$: growth rate of real US (ROW) GDP.

Di: $i - i(-1)$

Di: $i^w - i^w(-1)$

Dii^w: $i - i^w$

where $i =$ US federal funds rate and $i^w =$ ROW money market rate (Table 3.1).

$DP\ (DP^w)$: change in average annual US (ROW) CPI.

$DP2\ (DP2^w)$: 2-yr. change in the rate of US (ROW) CPI inflation: $DP - DP(-2)$ *or* $DP^w - DP^w(-2)$

DPM: $\{(1 + DP)/(1 + DP(-1))\}$ (1 + change in US/ROW exchange) − 1

DPP^w: $DP - DP^w$

$DU(DU^w)$: the 1st difference of annual average US (ROW) labour unemployment rate.

US$: Federal Reserve 12-nation, trade-weighted dollar index.

%*F*: $\Sigma c_f s_f / (\Sigma c_f s_f + \Sigma c_d s_d)$, where the *c*s are regression coefficients, the *s*s are the sample standard deviations of the associated regressors, *f* ranges over all international variables, and *d* over all domestic variables.

All but equations (1), (4), (5), and (6) were estimated with constant terms which are not shown. Equations (3), (4), (5), (11), and (12) were estimated with corrections for 1st-order moving average error terms. The error terms in all 14 equations are not significantly serially correlated on the basis of Durbin–Watson statistics for (1)–(10) and Durbin's *h*, for (11)–(14).

The last column in the table, %F, is a measure of the proportion of the variance explained by the international independent variables (see notes to table). For the USA, the exchange value of the dollar plays a role only after 1971, raising the importance of foreign influences from zero to about 26%. In the ROW, the tendency to close about 28% of any gap with US rates was persistent from the 1960s to the 1980s. However, its relative importance is only half as great after 1971 as before, accounting for about 23% of explained variance.

This convergence of the international sensitivity of the USA and ROW is consistent with the view that the ROW was obliged to pay more attention to pegging exchange rates before 1971, and consequently yielded the determination of interest and inflation rates to the USA. Conversely, the USA was free to set interest and inflation rates without great concern for international repercussions. In a floating-rate, multi-centred world, international considerations are equally important to the USA and ROW, and in both cases much less important than domestic determinants of interest rate policy. On this evidence, we should attribute the increases from the 1960s to the 1970s and 1980s shown in Table 3.1 for lines (8) and (9) and generally for the other six financial variables to increased transnational market efficiencies or increased significant common shocks, not to increased substitutability, which would by definition be observed as increased interdependence.[46]

Equations (5) and (6) describe movements in the real exchange rate. They are included here for completeness, since exchange rates are potentially important consequences and causes of the interest rates, inflation rates, and real growth rates considered in the rest of Table 3.3. In fact, the real exchange rate proved fruitless as an explanation of growth or inflation.

Again, I look only at the USA compared to the ROW. The dependent variable, *D$R*, is the change in the arithmetic average of the three pairs of real dollar exchange rates using CPIs. *D$R*, which is plotted in Fig. 3.2, is generally congruent with broader measures of the movement of the real dollar exchange rate. *D$R* is modelled in the regressions as responding to the previous year's average difference between US and ROW short-term, nominal rates, *DFi*, and a measure of the previous year's increase in the relative supply of US liabilities in the world financial-asset portfolio, *CA/W* the ratio of the US balance of payments on current account to the value of world exports both in current dollars. When *CA/W* is positive, dollar-denominated assets are becoming relatively scarce.[47] Real exchange rates are intrinsically international, and are here explained with two international variables. Accordingly, %F is 100 by definition.

In Equations (5) and (6), each coefficient has the anticipated sign. While each equation explains about the same fraction of real exchange

FIG. 3.2. Changes in D$R, the real dollar exchange rate versus Germany, Japan, and the UK, 1960–1987.

rate variance, there is a dramatic shift between the two periods in the amount of variance to be explained.

For the eleven years ending in 1970, nominal exchange rates were relatively fixed. The variation in real exchange rates is due almost entirely to differences in US and ROW inflation rates. The standard deviation of *D$R* is only 1.75% a year. It is not surprising that relatively high US inflation (which means an appreciating real dollar with fixed nominal exchange) is associated with relatively high US interest rates and relatively poor US current-account performance. While these variables account for half of the small variance, they do so fairly imprecisely.

For the post-1971 floating-rate period, the standard deviation of *D$R* increased to 10.6% a year. Again, interest differentials and *A/W* explain about half of this much larger variation, and do so with precision.[48] The very large amount of real exchange rate fluctuation that is left unexplained can be attributed to the seemingly inexplicable speculative component of foreign exchange markets.[49]

Equations (7)–(10) account for the growth of real GDP in the USA and the ROW. Real GDP growth was originally regressed against two lagged international effects, *D$R* and the change in the foreign country (USA or ROW) real GDP (*DGDP* or $DGDP^w$). Domestic monetary policy is measured by the previous year's change in short-term interest rates, *Di* or Di^w. The real exchange rate variable was surprisingly weak, and has been replaced by the difference between US and ROW inflation (DPP^w) in Equation (7), nothing in Equation (8), ROW inflation (DP^w) in Equation (9), and ROW capacity utilization (CAP^w) in Equation (10). The middle regressor thus has an international dimension in Equation (7) and is domestic in both ROW equations.

Each coefficient has the expected sign in Equations (7)–(10). Overseas growth has a positive impact through net exports; high absolute or relative inflation depresses real growth; low interest rates and high capacity utilization increase real growth via autonomous private spending. Each equation explains a good deal of real growth. A substantial part of that explanation is due to domestic rather than international effects.

Moreover, the importance of international effects declines after 1971 in both the USA and the ROW. For the USA, this decline may be overstated or even wrongly stated.[50] This result suggests again that the higher correlations in lines (16) and (17) of Table 3.1 for the post-1971 years are due to the greater global importance of efficiently transmitted events, rather than to the increased transnational substitutability of assets or goods.

Equations (11)–(14) regress inflation rates against lagged measures of effective foreign inflation, *DPM*, domestic inflation, and capacity utilization (*CAP* or CAP^w). *DPM* is the US inflation rate compounded with the appreciation of the US dollar against ROW currencies. In the US equations, (11) and (12), the equivalent term for ROW effective inflation, and numerous substitutes, added no explanatory power. Foreign influences on US inflation were approximately nil before and after 1971.[51] For the ROW, effective US inflation was the dominant determinant of inflation before 1971, but had no significant role thereafter.[52]

From the evidence in Table 3.3, we can conclude that there was no general increase in sensitivity to international variables after 1971 in central-bank reaction functions, real-income multipliers, or the determinants of inflation.

Loss of control over domestic monetary policy instruments was the first of three potential losses of independence from openness that I listed at the start of this section. For the four major countries considered in this analysis, no such loss is apparent. The post-1971 loss of autonomy suffered by the USA is offset by increased independence for the FRG, Japan, and the UK. Although short-term interest rates differ less among countries than at many times in the past, they still change in response to plausible domestic concerns. This result reinforces the idea that the recent correlation of international interest rates is more a result of responses to common factors than an indicator of increased interdependence.

Moreover, in the contemporary developed world the growth of domestic real product is highly sensitive to these autonomously determined changes in domestic interest rates. At the same time, domestic inflation appears insulated from all but domestic price expectations and domestic real constraints. If floating rates were provoked by the desire of the ROW countries and others to insulate themselves from US inflation, the evidence presented here indicates that they were successful. In the previous section I have argued that this success was not robustly utilized because of strong, common, external influences.

III.5. 'Small' and Developing Countries

The other two reasons that I listed for potential loss of independence had to do with floating rates rather than any other characteristics of openness. While the advent of floating rates may have implied only a redistribution of autonomy among four of the major economic and political powers of the capitalist world, it may have entailed a systematic loss of independence for weaker countries, either through exchange rate crises as mechanisms for disciplining countries or through exchange rate volatility as a new barrier to achieving desired trade and investment flows.

If, as is apparently the case, potential transnational investors attach specific-country risks to investments—exchange rate risks, political risks, or geographical/technological risks—then this very differentiation that prevents the loss of control to a world interest rate, inflation rate, and growth rate may promote another type of loss of independence. Especially in conjunction with floating exchange rates, countries may have become more subject to ill effects of international capital flows or the judgements of investors. Under a perfect fixed-rate standard, the only reasons to invest in the bonds or stocks of one country rather than those of another would be identical to the sorts of reason one might invest in one stock or bond rather than another within a single country. Under floating rates, an investor must add exchange rate risk (and prospective return) to his or her usual list of default risk, potential profit, labour 'conditions', raw-material availability, and the like.

Two investments might appear to be identically priced and actually offer very different yields to an international investor because one or the other is denominated in an appreciating or depreciating currency. The lowliest of risk-free investments in bank deposits or treasury bills is exalted to a promising speculative vehicle by the prospect of fluctuations in the exchange rate of the underlying currency. Intrinsically riskier assets have the same degree of additional risk added by the advent of floating exchange rates.[53] If a new market appears in which a variety of exquisitely liquid objects, namely currencies themselves, are traded with all the price volatility that liquid and efficient markets produce, then speculators will be attracted until the capacity of that market to entertain, enrich, and impoverish has been fully utilized.

Floating exchange rates have made it clear once more that the aspect of 'liquidity' of interest to the speculator is not in fact proximity to cash but fluidity of price. In the words of Keynes (1964: 155):

> Thus the professional investor is forced to concern himself with the anticipation of impending changes [by which] the mass psychology of the market is most influenced. This is the inevitable result of investment markets organized with a view to so-called 'liquidity'. . . . The actual private object of the most skilled investment today is to 'beat the gun', as the Americans so well express it, to outwit the crowd, and to pass the bad, or depreciating, half crown to the other fellow.

So, in the language of the 1980s, when a nation's currency floats it is subject to violent fluctuations due to speculative bubbles—what Keynes aptly described as a game of snap or musical chairs. There is some suggestive, almost anecdotal evidence of increased speculation in foreign exchange. Dornbusch and Frankel (1987: 1) conclude that

> the foreign exchange market is characterized by high transactions-volume, short-term horizons, and an absence of stabilizing speculation. As a result, the exchange rate at times strays from the equilibrium level dictated by fundamentals, contrary to theory.[54]

They estimate the 1986 volume of foreign-exchange trading at $50bn. a day in New York, $48bn. in Tokyo, and $90bn. in London. These are very large numbers. Daily volume on the New York Stock Exchange was approximately $8bn. in 1986. Over 90% of currency trading is among banks and speculators. Neither party has an interest in acquiring exchange for a capital or current-account transaction (Dornbusch and Frankel, 1987: 22). Fischer (1988: 31) shows that exchange rates have been generally more volatile than commodity prices since 1973, although somewhat less variable than equity prices.

All this in turn can have untoward consequences for foreign trade and capital flows. Real exchange rates fluctuate substantially around purchasing-power parity (see Fig. 3.2; De Grauwe and de Bellefroid, 1987: 199–204; IMF, 1984: 39–52; and, for the inter-war period as well as the 1970s, Aliber, 1980: 88–95). There is a large literature which purports to have found some substantial effects of this volatility on trade.[55]

There is also the more sinister possibility that public policy departing from the norm of the speculating public (banks) will provoke a bubble or irrational expectation in the form of a flight from the currency of the deviant regime. Floating rates, and increased capital mobility of all kinds, create the prospect that speculators or investors can 'punish' an offending regime with depreciating currency or capital flight, perhaps more effectively than may have been the case under pegged rates and more hierarchical relations among nations. Such private flights may also be encouraged by public officials.

The flight of capital from France after the socialist victory in 1981 is the example most frequently cited. After the fact, at least, this would seem to be a clear example of irrational expectations, primarily on the part of French citizens who now populate the upper east side of Manhattan. This episode of weakness in the franc resembles the American experience of the late 1970s. Fiscal and monetary policies may have been no more important than a political reading with respect to the security of private capital. Certainly, neither Mitterrand nor Carter are revolutionaries; but we live in conservative times.

More to the point, the French and US exchange rate crises of 1982–3 and 1978–9, respectively, each succeeded in provoking large changes in the direction of domestic economic policy. In France there were deficit reduction measures along with the third devaluation in three years and a return to the European Monetary System. The US crisis evoked Paul Volcker's seemingly monetarist anti-inflation policy. The French moves were politically difficult; the change in American policy contributed to the change in presidents from Carter to Reagan.

An OECD (1988) study, *Why Economic Policies Change Course*, considers eleven episodes, between 1975 and 1985, in eleven different countries, including the two just mentioned. In ten of these eleven episodes, dramatic foreign-exchange movements were (p. 16) an 'important', 'major' or the 'crucial' cause of the change. However, since eight of the eleven examples concern countries that were members or, in the case of France, sometime members of the EMS, it could be argued that these are more examples of exchange rate discipline under a fixed-rate system.

An adequate answer to the question of the relative severity of policy discipline administered by the market under fixed and floating rates requires a case-by-case catalogue and narrative comparison that is beyond the scope of this essay. However, it certainly appears true that the sterling crises of 1949 and 1964–7 were at least as grave in their policy-disciplining consequences as any runs on the pound, lira, franc, or dollar since 1971.[56]

Thus far we have considered the policy independence of a handful of developed countries. Can we say anything about openness, floating exchange rates, and the LDCs?

The developing countries of the nineteenth century were 'opened' as the century progressed if they were not already open at the outset (Lipson, 1985: 1–62). For LDCs, it is nothing new to be exposed to the consequences of international capital movements. The innovation has always been for a revolutionary Mexico or Peronist Argentina to restrict the free movement of capital.

The notion of policy autonomy has limited relevance for LDCs. Currencies that are not acceptable in international trade have always left domestic monetary policy independent but ineffective. 'Excessive' domestic monetary expansion, inflation, and exchange rate depreciation resolve the mismatch between limited domestic capacity to mobilize savings and urgent investment, social overhead, and redistributive projects.

TABLE 3.4. *Exchange rate depreciation for twelve LDCs, 1950–1987 (%)*

	1950–5	1955–60	1960–5	1965–70	1970–5	1975–80	1980–7
Total	− 20.6	− 20.2	− 18.9	− 13.4	− 19.0	− 24.4	− 52.7
Per year	− 4.5	− 4.4	− 4.1	− 2.8	− 4.1	− 5.5	− 10.1

All data are from IMF (1988*c*). The 12 countries are Algeria, Columbia, Egypt, India, Iran, Korea, Mexico, Nigeria, the Philippines, Turkey, Zaïre, and Zambia. They were selected for availability of data and for geographical, political, and historical diversity. They accounted for about 20% of LDC exports and GDP in 1970. Exchange rate data is the SDR (or, before 1969, $US) value of the domestic currency. The 1st line is the arithmetic average of the 12 exchange rate changes over the period. The 2nd line is computed directly from the 1st.

Exchange depreciation was common under pegged rates, as is illustrated in Table 3.4. The accelerating declines in the 1980s have more to do with the debt crisis and world disinflation than with floating rates. The consequences of the debt crisis for developing countries are deadly serious, as illustrated in Jaime Ros's chapter in this volume. From the perspective of the present discussion, the debt crisis is not a direct consequence of international financial openness. It is a natural sequel to the lending binge of the 1970s, which in turn may have been a consequence of financial openness.[57] Certainly, the debt crisis is also another result of the errant course of US fiscal policy. In 1987, LDCs produced an extraordinary aggregate surplus on current account, and developed countries other than the USA also experienced an aggregate surplus at unusually high levels. Some 15% of this total was offset by unrecorded transactions, the other 85% by America's anachronistic gluttony for capital imports (IMF 1988*c*: 142).[58]

When contrasted with the large and persistent capital exports of France and Britain in the nineteenth century and American policy at the time of the Marshall Plan, or even the Dawes Plan, the debt crisis appears also as the symptom of a lack of leadership, hegemonic or otherwise.

III.6. Recapitulation

With respect to the three ways in which financial openness might increase national economic autonomy, we have seen:

(i) Savings and investment ratios were more independent of each other in the 1970s than in the 1960s, but less so than under the gold standard.

They are again less independent in the 1980s for most countries, especially LDCs; but the US current-account deficits and the German and Japanese surpluses are extraordinarily large.

(ii) Real growth rates in the 1980s are correlated to an average extent and inflation rates to an extraordinary extent. However, if we measure interdependence directly through reduced-form equations, real growth interdependence appears weak and non-increasing.

(iii) There is no support from the econometric estimates, but some from a casual understanding of recent American experience, for the belief that a floating exchange rate gives domestic policy-makers an effective new instrument.

With respect to the three ways in which openness may restrict independence, we have found:

(i) Despite increased correlations of interest rates, four major developed countries have not lost control over interest rates and monetary policy by comparison with the past.

(ii) Although exchange rate movements can act, and have acted, to constrain deviant national economic behaviour in the 1970s and 1980s, there is no convincing evidence that the policy/political 'discipline' of the capital markets is greater than it ever was.

(iii) The spectacular volatility and speculative ferment in foreign-exchange markets may have negatively affected real growth for all countries. The LDCs remain open to foreign capital, and are deprived of it to their detriment, for reasons not directly related to floating rates or openness.

IV. CONCLUSION: THE POLITICAL ECONOMY OF OPENNESS

IV.1. Shocks

The striking conformity of real growth, interest rates, and inflation in the 1970s was not, according to all the econometric results in Table 3.3, caused by a sudden strengthening of international interdependence. Rather than looking for increased international cross-elasticities in goods or financial markets, we must search for 'shocks' with strong and ubiquitous consequences.

Two shocks that clearly fit the bill are the oil price shocks of 1974 and 1979. The relative price of energy changed dramatically; and it changed everywhere because petroleum was a major commodity in world trade. Capital utilization was reduced to conserve expensive energy, causing capital and labour productivity to slacken or fall and unemployment to rise at the same time (Whitman, 1979: 168–72; Zevin, 1983: 38–51;

Tatom, 1987).[59] Higher energy prices, existing wage momentum, and reduced productivity combined to accelerate inflation. Faced with these unpleasant, unexpected, and poorly understood problems, developed countries responded with policies that had little effect on GNP, unemployment, or inflation, but did allow interest rates to rise dramatically.

So, at least after 1973, the international cohesion we observe is best explained by common effects of external shocks. The differences between US inflation and inflation in each of the three ROW countries grow larger and more volatile. In late 1979, US monetary policy swings sharply back toward ROW and specifically German policies. Consequently, much of the observed international financial market cohesion in the 1980s reflects a genuine convergence of policies.[60] I believe this convergence can be explained by common responses to the inflation and perceived policy errors of the 1970s.

IV.2. Hegemony Lost

A number of commentators have suggested that the 'final breakdown of the fixed-parity system nearly three decades after its inception at Bretton Woods' was caused in large part by "the growing mass of potentially destabilizing funds flowing through virtually uncontrolled 'Eurocurrency markets' "(Leonhard Gleske in Kenen 1987: 16).[61]

Euro-currency markets developed in response to capital controls, particularly the US Interest Equalization Tax and Foreign Credit Restriction Program in the early 1960s. At that time, American multinationals sought to maintain growth by investing overseas. Bank credit was required to finance new plants or often new customers for the same reason they were sought: because profits were lagging (Zevin, 1983: 29–37, 101–5).

These events gave the appearance of conflict between the US government and major US banks and multinationals. The conflict was not too intense. The bank regulators did, and still have done, almost nothing to prevent the creation of a huge, unregulated, offshore monetary system. The less ambiguous conflict was between the banks, who would have been happier to stay home, and their influential corporate customers, who insisted that they go international.

An additional stimulus to the spread of the current international banking system came from the oil price shocks. Private banks in the Euro-currency system were available to extend balance-of-payments adjustment loans that were larger and more prompt than government or multilateral institutions could or would provide. They also recycled the tremendous new flow of dollars that went to OPEC countries in payment for oil, returned to the banks as deposits, and was lent to the importing countries for additional purchases. These activities substantially cushioned the price shocks.

The emergence of a powerful OPEC was itself symptomatic of intensifying fissures between governments and oil companies in major capitalist countries. In particular the US government, which had laboured valiantly to establish the world position of the Seven Sisters, lost touch with its oil industry alliance and began instead to compete with the companies for control of the world oil market (*Forbes* 1976: 69–83; Keohane 1984: 202–6).[62]

The coalition of private and state interests that had constructed the era of American hegemony was pulling apart. In part for this reason, in part because of its defeat in Vietnam, American dominance was being eroded. As a matter of logic, developed nations in the non-socialist world should have experienced increased autonomy from the early 1970s. This is the consistent finding for Germany, Japan, and the UK in Table 3.3.

Why don't these countries proclaim their new independence as loudly as the USA complains about its increased openness to foreign influences? First, subservience to the USA has been replaced by perceived impotence in the face of new, intractable problems such as the LDC debt crisis. Second, in Europe subservience to the USA has been replaced by subservience to the EC. Third, American deficits in the 1980s present these countries with a choice between accommodating to their own benefit or resisting and causing potential harm to the world economy. Naturally, they see this choice as coercive. Fourth, these countries know that America is still a giant economy compared to any one of them, and an awesome military power.

If the 1920s and 1930s are united with the 1970s and 1980s by a common theme, it is less a divergence of national economic objectives than something like Charles Kindleberger's analysis of the absence of leadership (Kindleberger 1973, esp. 291–308; 1978).[63] Kindleberger argues that will and imagination are the heart of international economic leadership, as of any other kind. I agree. The belief that capitalists act to defend and promote their class interests does not imply that they cannot sometimes do so with skill and daring while at other times not. Moreover, except in some *ex post* tautology, there is no necessary proportionality between the stakes of the game and the finesse with which capitalists play it.

Henry Wallich, former Governor of the Federal Reserve as well as an economist, put it this way (1985: 38):

> The importance [of US foreign trade] having risen in recent years, one might assume that the United States would be increasingly concerned with its impact on the world. . . . By and large, the United States was more concerned about the state of the world when the feedback was smaller but it was an unchallenged leader and felt strong responsibilities. Leadership has been diluted; responsi-

bility, or so it seems to me, has tended to yield to expediency. . . . if this has been the trend, it has been going against our own self-interest.

Having made this distinction between hegemony and leadership, I will revert to hegemony for convenience, although I really mean leadership. The prime relevant observation is that 'One of the most important features of American hegemony was its brevity' (Keohane 1984: 139) Floating exchange rates and OPEC shocks are symptoms of this loss of power. Lost hegemony is the common thread in our tale of oil price shocks, floating exchange rates, and LDC debt crises. The historical relation between hegemony and exchange rate regimes is straightforward. The world has experienced stable exchange regimes under British hegemony in the gold standard period and American hegemony in the Bretton Woods period. Floating rates have characterized the polycentric distributions of power after the First World War and after Vietnam.

However, the record does not indicate nearly as clear a connection between this dual description of regimes and the resulting degree of autonomy for nations (other than the hegemon). Based on our analysis, the two polycentric, floating-rate eras, after the First World War and after Vietnam, were both periods of greater economic autonomy for developed countries than in the Bretton Woods period and of less autonomy than under the gold standard.

More directly, the dilemma is that the two periods of hegemonic domination and stable exchange-rate systems appear to have had opposite implications for national autonomy. The gold standard and Pax Britannica were structures within which many nations achieved rapid, relatively autonomous economic development. Trade and financial flows were very large relative to national incomes. Persistent current-account surpluses and deficits enabled many advanced countries to invest unprecedented proportions of their wealth and income in developing countries, while the latter succeeded in sustaining levels of investment above domestic saving in proportions unequalled before or since. High financial-market cohesion was symptomatic of the enabling conditions.

The Pax Americana began, at the time of the Marshall Plan, with a similar, brief episode of capital transfer from the USA to nations in strong need of dollars and of consumer and capital goods. Japan and the ravished countries of Europe were redeveloped and in some cases went on to new heights of relative economic standing.

By the 1960s the Bretton Woods system should have been in full bloom. Major-country currencies were convertible; many post-war capital controls had been removed. Yet we observe a system with less financial-market cohesion than either of the floating-rate periods, and with far less than the gold standard (Table 3.1). International capital flows were apparently quite constrained (Table 3.2). Outside of the USA, comparing the 1960s with subsequent decades, monetary-policy decisions were more influenced by the USA, income multipliers on trade with the USA were larger, and the US influence on domestic inflation rates was much larger (Table 3.3).

The lower cohesion is partly because there was altogether less variation in inflation, interest and real growth rates in the 1950s and 1960s than there has been since. When there is no common tide, small waves make all the difference. Other measures of uniformity, based on the average size and variability of national differences, show more cohesion in the stable 1960s than the turbulent 1970s (Section III.3 above).

US influence on Germany, Japan, and the UK is, of course, exactly what we would have expected to find in the 1960s. When exchange rates were relatively fixed, financial assets were closer international substitutes than they are today. In the 1960s the US economy was larger relative to at least Germany and Japan than it is today. When nations were committed to pegging their currencies to the dollar, those currencies were pinned to US interest and inflation rates as well. The US was a fully fledged hegemonic power; but the exercise of its power had very different consequences from those that would have been expected from the history of the high gold standard.

Since the early 1970s the dollar has remained the principal currency in international transactions. Powerful global events have pushed financial and economic variables on common paths in many countries. If we examine only the differences among variables, the 1980s are about the same as the 1960s for cohesion. On balance, the high and rising volatility of real exchange rates which has characterized the post-1971 world economy has been a disintegrating force.

High international correlation under the gold standard may have represented the consequences of British hegemony. Today it charts the course of dissociated countries driven by common winds.

NOTES

1. I treat 'open' and 'integrated' as synonyms.
2. However, Kenen (1976: 17–18) describes a class of exogenous disturbances that require transnational stock transfers for adjustment.
3. Throughout, my convention is to say that a currency has depreciated (appreciated) against another if its price in units of the other currency has declined (increased). This is in accord with popular usage, and was common among economists as well until quite recently.
4. This distinction between integration in the sense of efficiency and in the sense of perfect substitutability is made in Allen and Kenen (1980: 13–14); see also Kenen (1976: 9–10), which defines integration as 'the degree to which participants in any market are enabled and obliged to take notice of

events occurring in other markets'. 'Enabled' is quite what I mean by efficient, while 'obliged' covers direct and transitive substitutability as well as other interdependencies.

In this 'other' category, Kenen cites the impact of the oil price shock on asset prices because of the ubiquitous importance of oil. Since this transmission mechanism depends only on openness in oil-trading rather than in financial markets, I prefer to say that the speed and uniformity of the financial-market impact reflects the efficiency of those markets. The efficiency/substitutability distinction is useful for my purposes and unambiguous, while the enabling/obliging division is not.

5. Kenen (1976: 13) objects that, if autonomy means control over interest rates and integration means international equality of interest rates, then the question of the impact of integration on autonomy has been answered by definition rather than analysis. His proposed solution is to measure autonomy by control over the monetary base. However, this raises more difficulties than it resolves, since definition of the monetary base is particularly problematic in a financially open economy (McKinnon, 1982).
6. This is precisely the meaning of perfect substitutes in the Arbitrage Pricing Theory (Ross 1976).
7. Identical prices (of yields) is a boundary case of perfectly correlated values. In addition to perfect substitution across markets, such an identity also implies that transaction and information costs for cross-market arbitrage are zero.
8. Bankers located in such a powerful country would also be in a position to win superior acceptance for their notes and issues.
9. Cipolla (1967: 14–15) describes several instances of superstitious misperception of the images of coins.
10. A standard test for efficiency is to observe whether or not presumed substitutes in two different markets trade at the same or nearly the same price. e.g. If the rates on 3-month Eurodollar deposits in London and 3-month certificates of deposit at the home office of the same bank in New York are identical up to a constant difference for taxes or reserve requirements, we may conclude that the London and New York money markets are efficiently integrated. Neal finds a degree of efficiency on this measure for Amsterdam, London, and Paris in the 18th C. that is identical to that found for international markets of the 1970s and 1980s (Frankel 1986: 47–9; Obstfeld 1986: 63–4).
11. For an account of the enormous magnitude of British borrowing from the Netherlands during the half-century after the Glorious Revolution, see Brezis (1988).
12. The course of net foreign debts or assets relative to various measures of domestic wealth is similar. See Goldsmith (1985) and Table 7.1(*a*) below for calculations of the ratios of foreign claims to total assets and reproducible capital for a number of countries.
13. As most Americans learn early in school, the still common name of 'two bits' for a quarter of a dollar is a heritage of the circulation of the Spanish pesos and similar coins in the USA well into the 1800s. The peso was divided into eight *reals* or 'bits'.

14. For additional views of the gold standard see Bloomfield (1959); Lindert (1969); [Nurkse] (1944).
15. The entries in both panels are averages, usually of 6 separate statistics, while I have used a conservative significance hurdle applicable to each of the components.
16. Dornbusch and Fischer (1986: 471–2) report additional calculations with similar data for own-currency interest rate behaviour between only the USA and the UK. They report the largest and most volatile short-term interest rate differential in 1974–83, the next largest in the gold standard years, considerably less during 1964–71, and the least reported for nominal short rates in Table 3.1, because of different periods compared to Panel B and because they consider only one of the 6 bilateral comparisons in the table. Cooper (1986*b*: 17) reproduces these results along with non-comparable data on closed interest rate parity.
17. Similar observations for many other countries are available in Morgenstern (1959: 512–28).
18. The proportion of foreign stocks traded in a country will generally understate the total market capitalization of such issues relative to all domestic issues, since internationally traded issues tend to be larger capitalization issues. On the other hand, only the smaller part of the trading in a transnationally listed issue will be overseas, and some portion of an expatriate new issue will be purchased in the home country.
19. Reductions in the cost of transmitting information and executing trades will obviously contribute to increased efficiency, and clearly have done so throughout the periods considered here. Cooper (1986*c*: 10–14) provides a number of specific examples.
20. The still sceptical reader may find that I have argued my case more convincingly in Zevin (1983: 71–107). The reverse image of the argument that technology has not created openness is that technology does not prevent controls. See Ch. 6.
21. Ch. 7 is valid, in my view, independently of any propositions about increased openness. Ch. 2 above focuses on the recent trend toward integration, and implies that salient contemporary features like the market for corporate control and securitization are caused by openness. Ch. 4 below again places primary emphasis on the period following the Second World War. As for Epstein and Schor (Ch. 6), I can fully accept their logic and their conclusions about the efficacy of national controls without having to believe that increased financial openness is the cause of dismantled controls rather than one of the consequences.
22. These periods were chosen in part because they served to maximize the inter-period differences in correlations, suggesting a 'natural' division around Nixon's new economic policy in 1971 and Reagan's new fiscal policy in 1981.
23. The historical results cited above from Neal (1985; 1987*a*) are tests of this character.
24. Frankel (1986: 47–9) contains an excellent review of the major literature up to that time. Kasman and Pigott (1988) perform a number of calculations, some quite similar to mine, on various kinds of interest rate coherence

among Canada, the FRG, Japan, the UK, and the USA. They find that the mean quarterly absolute difference of fully covered, 3-month money market rates from the mean for these 5 countries averaged 89 basis points in 1974–9, 60 basis points in 1980–2, and 26 basis points from 1983 up to the middle of 1988 (p. 35). See also Obstfeld (1986: 58–65) for another review of the literature with identical conclusions.

25. See all 3 citations in the previous note, and esp. Kasman and Pigott (1988: 42–4).
26. Kasman and Pigott (1988) display correlations for the 1960s, 1970s, and 1980s which tell the same story as Panel B in Table 3.1 for nominal short and long rates and for real short rates (p. 34). However, they express a preference for measuring dispersion by the average absolute deviation from the mean. This measure shows a very large increase (decline in integration) from 1961–72 to 1973–9, and another much smaller increase from 1980 up to mid-1988 (p. 32). The authors conclude that substitutability has steadily diminished because of increased exchange rate uncertainty.
27. One measure of multilateral exchange rate variability more than tripled from 1960–9 to 1973–84 (De Grauwe and de Bellefroid 1987: 211). For evidence of increased exchange rate volatility in the 1980s compared to the 1970s, see Fig. 3.2 and Table 3.4 below.
28. Richard Cooper (1986*c*), a respected analyst of international economics, strains to demonstrate the financial openness of the USA in the mid-1980s. He notes (p. 8) that a seemingly modest 4.5% of US equities and 7.9% of US corporate bonds were owned by foreigners in 1983. 'That appearance is deceptive, however . . . '. Why? Because the FRG, 'thought to be very open' and with 'exports over 30 percent of German GNP', nevertheless displays similarly small percentages of foreign ownership of its domestically issued financial assets (pp. 9–10). The syllogism implicit in this reasoning is as follows. Countries that are open with respect to goods and services must be open financially. The FRG is open with respect to goods and services. The FRG has similar measures of financial openness as the USA. Therefore, the USA must be financially open.

    In comments on Cooper's paper in the same volume (pp. 24–31), Peter Kenen observes that Cooper has sung the same tune before. Indeed, Cooper, (1986*a*) looks back at the 1960s, the decade we have found to show the least capital-market integration, under the title 'Towards An International Capital Market?'. He answers his question in the affirmative: 'A comparison of interest rates . . . reveals a marked tendency towards convergence following the move to currency convertibility by the major European countries in late 1958' (p. 143). The reader is referred to a table on the same page showing that the mean short- and long-term government-issue yields in 8 Atlantic-community countries increased by 150 to 200 basis points between 1958 and 1968, while the sample standard deviation of short rates also increased to a high for the decade in 1968 and the standard deviation for long rates fell from .94% to .81%. The reader is shown coefficients of variation which do reach a 1968 low for long- but not for short-term rates as a result of the secular increase in rates, not of any international convergence. A graph on the next page dramatically reaffirms that interest rates ended the 1960s as disparate as they began, with the maximum cohesion achieved in the middle.

29. For 'econometric' evidence, Fischer (1988: 16) presents a table of macro-economic impacts on the USA and the rest of the OECD resulting from fiscal and monetary expansions initiated in the other region. From the table we learn only that there are foreign as well as domestic policy effects, and that the foreign effects are usually much smaller. We do not learn how these coefficients or their relative sizes have changed over time. Table 3.3 below addresses that question.
30. In writing this section I have relied heavily on Gintis, 1986. Epstein and Gintis in this volume consider the relation between national saving and investment in more detail.
31. Frankel (1986) offers some strong evidence of an increasing savings/investment link for the USA from 1929 to the 1980s; while a look back to 1870 offers no such indication. Feldstein's (1983) evidence on an increasing link is ambiguous, since the regression coefficient of savings ratios against investment ratios rises, while the coefficient of determination falls.
32. In the 3 years centred on 1870, 1890, and 1910, Great Britain exported capital at rates between 5.5% and 7.5% of GNP, while Canada was importing capital at between 7% and 12% of its GNP (Green and Urquhart 1976: 244). Any statistical measure that makes sense and is properly interpreted would have to tell us that capital movements were larger then than now.
33. If the constant term is suppressed in the specification of the 1870–1920 regressions, all the savings ratio coefficients cluster between .89 and 1.02, and are 7–10 times their standard errors. The hypothesis that investment ratios are independent of savings ratios is strongly rejected. As discussed in the previous note, there were large and opposite international movements of capital. A constant-term specification is burdened with the task of averaging them.
34. Obstfeld (1986: 65–74) argues that both savings and investment ratios will vary positively with the ratio of working age to retired members of the population.
35. In addition to the results already cited, it is noteworthy that the mean absolute value of net capital flows as a % of GNP for the FRG, Japan, UK, and USA tripled from .85% in 1967 and 1977 to 2.75% in 1987 (IMF 1988: respective country pages). Obstfeld (1986: 86–95) also finds time series evidence of increasing capital flows. However, recent experience is dominated by the emergence of the USA as a perverse capital importer from Japan and Germany as well as from the developing countries (see section III.5).
36. See also the material in section II.1.
37. The international 'norm' should be understood tautologically as those growth and inflation outcomes that would preserve stable exchange rates. These might differ in their levels among countries, and also might require different policy choices for different countries.
38. Whitman (1979: 169–72) reviews a number of additional studies that find a sharp increase in business cycle coherence during this period.

39. The standard deviation of inflation rates for 4 major countries ranged between 6.8% and 12.6% in 1914–18, while for 7 major countries it ranged between 1.3% and 1.8% in 1968–72 (Aliber 1980: 91).
40. Informed analysts have said that the USA had a special responsibility as the reserve-currency country to maintain price stability, while other countries were obliged to defend their exchange rates (Wallich 1985: 34–5; [Nurkse] 1944: 45) A good case could be made that the USA abandoned its anti-inflation obligations in the late 1960s in a way that it had not done in the late 1950s or in the Korean War.
41. I have tried to disentangle the strands of post-war inflation in Zevin (1983: 3–68).
42. See section IV.2.
43. Epstein and Schor (1990*a*) find a pattern of policy convergence in the 1970s and the post-1972 period generally. They attribute some of the observed convergence to the oil shock and post-Keynesian success phenomena. They also argue that floating rates relieved the USA and UK from special reserve-currency considerations that had previously distinguished their policy conduct from other developed nations.
44. Bryant (1987: 92) contains a simple, formal statement of the relationship between international constraints on policy and structural or reduced-form model coefficients.
45. In Table 3.3, when a variable is omitted, as is the case for the international term in Eq. (1) and the inflation term in Eq. (3), the meaning is that none of the terms used in the same column for that block of equations, nor any other tested substitute, such as the current account relative to GDP, the level and change of the real exchange rate and cross-country growth, or inflation differentials in the current example, was able to reduce the standard error of the regression.
46. Once again, by efficiency I mean those changes in the transmission of information, the execution of transactions, and other rules and conditions of markets that enable them to reflect either the perfect substitutability of assets or the common effects of an event. By substitutability I mean the set of conditions in addition to efficiency that make assets in different countries fungible, destroying the possibility of purely domestic control over purely domestic asset supplies or interest rates. See n. 5 above.

    The focus of these particular regressions on the USA versus Germany, Japan, and the UK considered as a unit, precludes measuring consequences of the integration that has proceeded in the EC over the entire post-Second World War epoch. Basevi and Calzolari (1983) utilize a specification similar to Eqs. (1)–(4) for a number of EC countries during the period of the currency 'snake' and obtain results similar to mine.
47. 4 caveats: Perhaps what matters is the total supply of dollar liabilities in the world supply of all liabilities whether or not they are held transnationally (Frankel 1979). There is also no particular justification for supposing that either of the 2 regressors should act with a lag, let alone a 1-year lag. Since both independent series are highly autocorrelated, it is possibly the case that these apparent reduced-form specifications are actually wearing only thin

disguises over their simultaneous-equation biases. Finally, the observed correlation between interest rate differentials and exchange rate appreciation could reflect accurate interest rate forecasts of, rather than influences on, exchange markets. However, Frankel (1986: 36) and Krugman (1989: 84–96) show that interest rates are weak exchange-market forecasters.

48. Amano (1983) also reports the successful use of nominal interest rates to account for real exchange rates in the Japanese Economic Planning Agency World Model.

49. From Kenen (1987):

'With all due respect, it must be said that we, economists as well as ministers of finance, simply do not know enough to say what the "proper" or "equilibrium" exchange rate is. The modern . . . approach to the problem of exchange-rate determination under floating rates has taught us to be modest' (G. Haberler, p. 25).

'[Economists have] not been able to provide us with even a remotely satisfactory understanding of how exchange rates are determined—and in particular, of how floating exchange rates would behave in the absence of official intervention. The collapse of purchasing-power parity has not been fully understood' (A. Lamfalussy, p. 36).

'[The determinants of floating exchange rates] make up a complex system of dynamic interdependence that econometricians have not been able to estimate. I doubt that traders in the markets can do so either. I doubt they even try' (J. Tobin, p. 64).

Krugman (1989: 84–96) attempts to *prove* that exchange rates are irrational. As might be expected, he is not altogether successful.

50. Before 1971 changes in DPP^w, the real exchange value of the dollar and US inflation are highly colinear. DPP^w, the inflation differential, was clearly the most effective regressor of these 3 choices. To the extent that it has embedded in it the influence of innovations in domestic inflation, $\%F$ is overstated for the USA.

51. Among the other foreign influences tested were the real exchange rate, nominal exchange rate, and ROW inflation rate.

52. After specifying and estimating these equations, I came across virtually identical specifications for the domestic regressors and virtually identical results in Duck *et al.*, 1976. Their period is 1956–71, their data for the entire Group of Ten, and their interpretation, as well as their title, suggests that this specification and aggregation are appropriate only because of fixed exchange rates. Yet my result is that this specification and result are robust after floating rates.

53. Returns on bonds, stocks, and cash instruments from the multiple perspectives of investors starting and returning to various currencies are regular features in many publications. From *Global Finance* (Dec. 1988, p. 13) we learn that the investor who bought a world stock-market index with yen on 1 Nov. 1987 earned less than 10% over the next year; the investor who used and returned to markets earned nearly 25%, while the weighted return to stock investors in local-market currencies was just over 15%. For the year ending 1 Mar. 1989, the best local-currency return among 6 major government bond markets was 7.4% in France. For a dollar investor, the same

market returned 3.4%, among the worst of the 6 (*Wall Street Journal*, Mar. 1989).

54. See n. 47 above.
55. De Grauwe and de Bellefroid (1987) is a particularly elegant contribution to this literature, with a succinct bibliography. The problem with their results, as with all this literature and all the literature on openness itself, is that increased volatility of exchange rates occurs simultaneously with other independently significant events.
56. On the 1949 'sterling–dollar oil problem', which involved one of many post-war struggles for control of oil resources and succession to European colonial dominance, see Keohane (1984: 159–67). On the 1960s sterling crises and their implications for the maintenance of Britain's military power east of Suez, reserve-currency status, and other imperial aspirations in the world, see Robinson (1966). For the floating-rate counterparts, see OECD (1988: 25–35, 56–83).
57. Epstein and Gintis (Ch. 7) construct a model that accounts for the curtailment of the 1980s as a consequence of the large international lending of the 1970s.
58. Estimating world GNP in trillions of current dollars at 4.5 in 1972, 13 in 1982, and 18 in 1987, the respective %s of non-US developed countries' current-account surplus in world GNP were +.31%, −.10%, +.61%.
59. The latter has a good bibliography. Higher fuel costs cause both labour and capital to be used less intensively and therefore less productively; profits, profit-maximizing output, productivity, and real wages fall, while prices rise. Hence the oil price increases were a direct cause of the combination of high inflation and unemployment that bedevilled policy-makers in the 1970s.
60. Support for these conclusions can be found in Kasman and Pigott (1988) as well as in my analysis (not shown) of the data used in Table 3.1.
61. Gleske is a director of the Bundesbank. The same volume contains similar thoughts from Gottfried Haberler and from James Tobin, who particularly emphasizes the technological arguments I have rejected.
62. The Seven Sisters, 5 of them American, are British Petroleum, Exxon, Gulf, Mobil, Royal Dutch/Shell, Standard Oil of California, and Texaco.
63. Kindleberger's notion of leadership is less dependent on a preponderance of resources and the use of coercion than is Keohane's (1984) concept of hegemony. Aliber (1980) contains a useful analysis of floating rates and inflation in the 1920s and 1970s.

Part II

WHY HAS THE WORLD CHANGED?

Introduction to Part II

TARIQ BANURI

This part explores the causes of the recent changes in financial markets. Implicit in the papers is the 'political-economy' view, which holds that these changes have resulted neither from some inexorable historical trend towards the refinement of market freedoms nor from an ineluctable process of technological development which erodes the possibilities of societal regulation of finance. Rather, the changes are argued to be the result of political actions of interest groups who find themselves in particular situations.

Robert Pringle, writing on the basis of a twenty-year association with the financial world as a journalist and analyst, provides what can be called an heuristic game theoretical perspective on the evolving relationship between bankers and states. He chronicles the rise and development of financial institutions as a strategic game, driven on the one hand by the needs of states to finance politically legitimizing activities, such as wars or economic reforms and, on the other hand, by the banks' needs for state patronage in three areas: contract enforcement, lender-of-last-resort functions, and ensuring the security and credibility of financial institutions. The *quid pro quo* involved in these reciprocal needs and obligations led to what Pringle terms the 'bankers' bargain' with the state, in which the banks accepted restrictions on their freedom in return for state support and patronage. However, as he shows subsequently, the bargain has been upset in recent years, as the state has come to depend on financial institutions, not for its liquidity needs, but for the stability of the entire economic system. He also suggests that the problem is compounded by the unavoidable capture of the regulators by the regulated. The result is that the state continues to guarantee contract enforcement (even in multinational contracts, as in the Third World debt crisis) as well as liquidity and even viability (as in the US savings and loan crisis) without any return in the form of powers to monitor or regulate the activity of financial institutions. Pringle argues that technology has played a supportive, rather than a leading, role in these developments.

These arguments are corroborated further by Andrew Glyn's in-depth case study of the abolition of capital controls by the Australian Labour Government in 1983. Glyn frames the argument squarely in terms of the need for policy autonomy, i.e. the ability of national governments to pursue socially valued objectives such as growth or income distribution.

To the extent that unregulated capital flows render this pursuit untenable, they are likely to represent sectional rather than national interests. Glyn shows that, while the case for abolishing controls was made ostensibly on the technical grounds that they were, or had become, ineffective, the available evidence does not support this assertion. Indeed, the case was never made convincingly that controls could not be tightened significantly. Furthermore, a closer examination of the decision-making process reveals it to be a political rather than an economic decision, both *ex ante*—i.e. in terms of the motivations of the politicians—and *ex post*—in terms of its consequences of giving financial markets enhanced powers over the Labour Government's policies. Neither is a welfare argument persuasive. On the contrary, the abolition of controls has resulted in a slow-down of economic growth as well as increases in debt levels.

That the arguments made in the case of Australia can be generalized to other OECD countries is demonstrated by the evidence adduced by Gerald Epstein and Juliet Schor. They show that the recent anti-control ideology cannot be explained on the basis of a failure of capital controls to protect domestic financial markets from undue volatility, or to create a space for national policy autonomy, since there is no evidence of such a failure. Nor is there evidence of a gross misallocation of resources caused by government intervention in free functioning of markets. Epstein and Schor conclude by suggesting that, in the absence of any other convincing reason, the only likely inference is that the current episode of decontrol may well be politically motivated.

A somewhat related, though distinct, argument in the case of Third World countries is made in the next part by Tariq Banuri (Chapter 9). He looks at currency black markets as the institution which forced a number of governments to relax capital controls significantly, if not to abolish them altogether. The argument is that, while black markets created severe difficulties for the effective regulation of cross-border financial flows, governments did not explore the feasible range of options, unilateral or multilateral, to protect the space for national policy autonomy. These issues are taken up in more detail in Part III.

4
Financial Markets versus Governments

ROBERT PRINGLE

I. THE BANKERS' BARGAIN

Modern financial markets and nation states grew up together. The development of nation-wide banking systems in Europe in the eighteenth and nineteenth centuries gave enormous new potential power to the governments of these nation states, enabling them to borrow on a vastly greater scale—a power used mainly to wage wars of historically unprecedented cost. Increasingly, governments turned to central banks as instruments through which they hoped to centralize the control of credit and gain privileged access to it. As we shall see later, central banks then became important mediators in the political relationship between the market and governments.[1]

However, the financial markets have never been the passive mechanisms which they are often portrayed as being in the textbooks. The bankers and other financial entrepreneurs who created these markets and participate in them have always been aware of the double-edged role of the state—on the one hand a source of profitable business, protection, and support, yet on the other a potential threat to their very survival.[2] Thus banks have always been anxious to reach a *modus vivendi* with the state.

This relationship has gone through many phases, historically, but taking the period from 1950 to about 1970 for illustrative purposes, and generalizing broadly from the experience of most industrial countries in Europe and America, in terms of the economic and political relationship between banking and the state, a rough balance of power was maintained in which each side had its recognized sphere of influence—the state exercised control of monetary and economic policy while extending limited support to the banking system, whereas the banks secured freedom to exercise their business judgement and competitive impulses, subject to quite close official regulation.

This paper will suggest that in the past ten to fifteen years this balance has been upset. In brief, the potential for financing (and thus the incentive for governments to co-operate with the banks) has been vastly expanded, notably by the globalization of markets, but the markets have raised the stakes and governments have been on the retreat. Banks and other financial institutions have in effect extended their *de facto* rights to political support, notably in three respects:

(i) Support of creditors' claims: governments of the big industrial countries now provide strong (if discreet) support for banks' claims on other governments, especially in developing countries;

(ii) Safety nets for bankers: governments are now expected to provide an umbrella over the entire financial system, and to raise taxes as necessary to finance support operations, including large-scale cash support for insolvent financial institutions;

(iii) Creation of 'level playing-fields': government support for competition among banks and other financial institutions and abolition of capital controls to create global markets. It is not generally recognized how new all this is.

I.1. Support of Creditors' Claims

The principal creditor state of the nineteenth century, Britain, generally succeeded in maintaining its official tradition of non-intervention in private disputes between bond-holders and foreign governments (see Platt, 1968).[3] Thus default was able to serve as a safety-valve. Of course, default was not exactly encouraged—'moral' pressure could be brought to bear. But it was regarded as one of those facts of life with which the bond-holders had to live, an occasionally necessary purging of excesses, or a result of *force majeure*. In marked contrast, during the recent debt crisis of developing countries, this natural safety-valve was suppressed, partly at least by pressure brought to bear on developing countries bilaterally and by the IMF (representing in this regard the combined forces of the Group of Seven industrial countries). This may well have relaxed pressures operating on commercial creditors and on borrowing governments to seek a settlement, and thus have delayed a resolution of the problem. Bluntly, so long as banking creditors could count on the support of the G7 countries both financially and politically, they had no reason to settle for anything less than the full amount of their claims on developing countries.

I.2. Safety Net for Bankers

Similarly, the lender-of-last-resort function, which was traditionally proposed for use only when the stability of the entire financial system was at risk in times of 'panic', has recently been used as a cover for all manner of interventions and subsidies. In Britain, in the secondary banking crisis which erupted in 1974, the authorities panicked and bullied the big banks into recycling the deposits withdrawn from the fringe banks in trouble through the collapse of the property market (the 'lifeboat' operation); and when these fringe banks turned out to be insolvent rather than just illiquid, the Bank of England and the big banks picked up the bill. These costs would have soared further if the Bank of England had not persuaded the Government to rescue the property market and many more financial institutions by relaxing rent controls. The Bank succeeded in this in December 1974, and the *Financial Times* Property Share Index in two months doubled over its low the previous November! In the Johnson Matthey (Bankers) scandal in 1984-5, the Bank of England again took over a failing institution at public expense—this time largely to prevent the gold market moving to Zurich. Other institutions were rescued to prevent loss of Arab depositors. All these episodes had the effect of protecting the interests of the City of London. None of them were lender-of-last-resort operations in the classical sense (see Moran 1984).[4]

These operations were, however, dwarfed in monetary terms by the cost of rescuing or merging insolvent US savings and loan associations (S&Ls), estimated at up to $500bn., where the underlying problem was the abuse of deposit insurance. The bankruptcy of many S&Ls was precipitated by asset structures biased towards long-term, fixed-rate loans and liability structures characterized by short-term deposits which proved impossible to service as market rates rose. However, the scale of the collapse was due to the expectation that depositors would be protected and that risky, high-margin business could be taken on without risk. Risky business could be conducted safe in the knowledge that the bill would be picked up by deposit insurance, i.e. ultimately the US Government.

Takeovers of stock-market firms by banks raised the further question whether the state would be obliged to underwrite the underwriters and security markets as well as the bankers. Central banks' refusal to accept this earlier this century was one of the reasons for the separation of deposit from investment banking in most countries. But the Federal Reserve's actions in immediately injecting cash into the system after a stock-market relapse in October 1987, *before* evidence that the banking system itself was directly threatened, was widely applauded. It suggested at the very least an extreme sensitivity to the potential effects on financial institutions of stock-market volatility.[5] Now most bankers assume central banks will in future interpret the lender-of-last-resort function widely—to include support for firms threatened by stock-market losses.

Further, markets expect governments (through central banks or specialized agencies) to supervise banking and financial institutions to ensure that the security and credibility of participating institutions is beyond question—essentially by enforcing agreed capital adequacy tests, licensing, and 'supervision' requirements. This is not to deny that such supervision may serve to protect the consumer (albeit at some cost), but merely to point out that it is also in the interests of the firms being supervised, especially if they can in time capture the regulators and get them to interpret the rules in ways that the operators can live with. This has, indeed, been the essence of recent changes in financial regulation in several countries.[6]

Because it is easier to supervise and manage a few large banks than many smaller ones, most governments (at least European ones) in any case favour oligopolistic banking systems with high barriers to entry. The industry predictably is characterized by high levels of concentration (the world's largest 34 banks account for a quarter of the assets of all 500 top banks in the *Banker's* list), high profitability in normal times, and occasional outbreaks of cut-throat competition. These excess profits are required to provide reserves against losses incurred as a result of loans extended under the influence of moral hazard.

1.3. Global Financial Liberalization[7]

But what most upset the equilibrium between financial and political interests was governments' realization that, although they had extended further privileges to the financial sector, they had not gained greater policy autonomy. On the contrary, market processes contributed to the inexorable erosion of the effectiveness of policy instruments. To take one example, exchange rate 'overshooting' in the volatile foreign-exchange market persuaded many governments to dedicate monetary policy to exchange rate stabilization, which meant that it could not be used for other purposes.[8] More generally, many of the difficulties facing both monetary and fiscal policy could be traced back to increasing financial sophistication on the part both of individuals and of firms, and to their ability to 'see through' discretionary policy changes, due partly to growing familiarity with financial-market processes.

What has been behind the increasing influence of the financial markets? Whose interests have been promoted? In what follows, we adopt the 'political-economy' assumption that the behaviour of individuals and institutions, including official institutions, can most usefully be analysed as if they were prompted by self-interest. The answer tentatively suggested is that, although several forces have been at work, two have been particularly strong: first, the interaction between political and financial interests (the politicians' desire to underwrite new programmes interacting with the profit motive of financial entrepreneurs); and second, new interests generated by social changes which have introduced, in each decade since the First World War, a new generation of customers with rising expectations of political and financial services. The point is that an increased supply of political services required financing, and an increased supply of financial services required government support.

The processes through which market power has encroached on governments can be seen in the experience of widely differing countries in recent years: smaller European countries in the early to mid-1970s, Britain in the late 1970s, France in the early 1980s during its experiment in Keynesianism, and the developing countries in the debt crisis.

The markets have not had it all their own way. By the late 1980s, bankers were well aware of the strength of the resistance to 'financial openness'. Bankers' big worry was that a regionally based, political backlash (already well advanced in the EC) could gradually undermine the global markets from which they derived their real strength *vis-à-vis* governments. Their priority, therefore, was to stop attempts by countries to recover, through regional groups, defaults, and controls, some of their lost power. The following survey, based on twenty years close personal observation of how international banking and financial markets work in practice and the relationships between banks and governments, shows, however, that it is wrong to assume that the erosion of policy instruments is a necessary accompaniment of technological forces which neither governments nor bankers can control. The game continues.

II. WHEN THE BARGAIN WAS KEPT

II.1. The Gold Standard Era

Since the development of deposit banking, the classical gold standard from 1880 to 1914 has been the only system that has imposed tight constraints both on governments and on markets. Governments' autonomy was limited by the objective of maintaining convertibility at the fixed price. All other objectives of policy were subordinated to that aim. By linking gold flows and domestic money supplies (admittedly with some 'management' by central banks) in all countries subscribing to the standard, sustained outflows of gold could be relied upon to contract the domestic money supply.[9]

The financial markets were also constrained. Some prices, including exchange rates and the price of gold, were taken out of the market arena. Moreover, the governments' commitment to convertibility implied that market forces could never be seen to threaten that commitment. It was regarded as a moral issue. Because of such moral sanctions, including the doctrine of the balanced budget, market participants expected the fundamental parameters of policy to remain unchanged indefinitely. There was no equivalent to most present activity in financial markets, which consists in offering insurance cover against the pervasive uncertainty about future exchange and interest rate movements.

Ironically, although no system offered less formal 'autonomy' in monetary policy, the gold standard reigned at a time when European nationalism and the ideal of political sovereignty were at their peak. Countries were anxious to join the gold standard club. Among the advantages cited was the availability of commercial credit to cushion short-term payments and access to long-term capital. But above all, the system was viewed as the 'modern' monetary system, the mark of a civilized nation.[10]

Even now, it is unclear how large the costs of the sacrifice of monetary autonomy really were. The Keynesian revolution, with its stress on price–wage rigidity, emphasized the cost involved in requiring the internal economy to adjust to the balance of payments, and this, together with the experience of the 1920s, gave the gold standard a bad name, saddling it with responsibility for the international spread of inflations and depressions. Yet interpretations of how economies interacted under the gold standard continue to evolve. The traditional view, that international adjustment of payments was brought about by gold movements, with a country in payments deficit forced to deflate via a reduction in the country's money supply, followed by changes in its price level and terms of trade, has been challenged by the 'revisionist' school, under which prices of tradeable goods and relative national price levels were aligned by generalized commodity arbitrage (see McKinnon 1988; McCloskey and Zecher 1984).

What is clear is that the system was both a cause and a reflection of a greater integration of the world economy than was attained at any time between the outbreak of the First World War and the 1980s—and that it went along with the most strident assertions of political sovereignty (see Chapter 3 above).

II.2. Markets and Controls under Bretton Woods, 1947–1971

This period provides the only example of an attempt to subject the financial markets and national governments to an internationally agreed set of rules and institutions. Certainly, the system reflected American foreign policy and business interests, and was sustained by American power. Yet at least an attempt was made to justify and legitimize the rules in terms of universally accepted 'rational' norms.[11]

Governments of member countries were constrained by (*a*) the commitment to a liberal, multilateral world economy enshrined in the articles of agreement of the IMF and the GATT, (*b*) the need to justify internationally any proposed change in a country's par value, (*c*) the fact that exchange rate changes were fraught with political difficulties because any change hurt some sectoral interest, and (*d*) the programme for removing the remaining trade and payments restrictions under Article VIII of the IMF.

The instruments available to make these commitments effective in the markets included capital controls, credit controls, interest rate ceilings, fiscal policy, and limited credit facilities from the IMF. These instruments were effective only so long as financial-market activity was at a low level, domestic and international markets remained segmented, and such constraints on national autonomy were viewed as legitimate. While these conditions held, governments were in control, using central banks as the main institutional means of exerting such control.[12]

The belief that the system had legitimacy and respectability was very important in sustaining it. This was illustrated in Britain's 'Radcliffe Report', published in 1959.[13] This report (written largely by Professor Sayers) was controversial and ambiguous, in that its recommendations supported the maintenance and even extension of post-war direct controls while the clarity of its exposition forcefully suggested that rapid market developments could quickly make these recommendations invalid.

The report regarded currency and credit controls as legitimate policy instruments. But it also made clear that, even in the 1950s, before the invasion of US banks and the growth of the international money markets, these controls could not prevent large short-term capital movements. For instance, countries holding sterling could draw on their balances instead of using their currencies to make payments, multinational corporations could borrow in the UK and run down borrowing abroad, long-term investment continued on a considerable scale, and there were large and unavoidable swings in the timing of current payments, the 'leads and lags'.

The report demonstrated the close connection between contemporaries' perception of the country's international obligations and policies to secure domestic objectives of full employment and growth. The authors were aware of the possibility of inconsistency among these objectives, but felt that the international monetary system would provide enough latitude to call only for moderate sacrifices of national objectives. Membership of international organizations, notably the IMF, gave reality to the nation's duties and aspirations as a member of an international community. Any policy measures, it stated, 'not only must be reconcilable with the rules of these organizations but should foster the spirit of mutual aid that underlies them all'. Being part of this international community allowed the country 'to pursue in active co-operation with them the objectives of economic growth'.

This regime was weakened in both domestic and international dimensions by social changes and financial innovation. The 1960s saw the rise of a new class of internationally mobile individuals—notably international corporate executives and professionals involved in services such as insurance, ship- and air-chartering, civil engineering, medicine, law, banking, and the new international agencies—for whom it was increasingly a matter of choice where they called home. As these groups joined the ranks of the old rich, the pool of internationally mobile (and tax-avoiding) funds rose, swelled further by capital flight from developing countries. It was this pool that the new Euro-markets would tap, from the early 1960s, in addition to the liquid funds of the corporations themselves. Exchange control became gradually less enforceable.

The growth of multinational corporations was spearheaded by US corporations, riding the great waves of US foreign direct investment encouraged by the creation of the EEC in 1958. The 1960s also witnessed an expansion of US banking overseas on an unprecedented scale. Whereas formerly only a few American banks maintained a handful of foreign branches, mainly in London and South America, by the end of the decade they had scattered branches throughout the capitalist world, including many developing countries (see Pringle, 1966).

Everywhere, by the early 1960s, American bankers were breaking down time-honoured and hallowed traditions of their local societies. Openly flouting local conventions, they created their own financial markets along with their clubs and schools. Simply by picking up the telephone and borrowing or redepositing dollars from other US banks in Europe, they created havoc among local banks, for whom London was still two days' journey from Milan and for whom it was unthinkable to undercut other banks abroad or at home. Everywhere in Europe, cartels supporting wide differentials in interest rates collapsed. The Americans recognized a new frontier when they saw one.

Governments continually attempted to reassert control, partly by direct action on financial flows and partly through the creation of swap lines between central banks to defend the dollar.[14] But such policies, aimed at reasserting official control, only spurred further innovation. Everywhere market segmentation started to erode. In time, these market changes overthrew the post-war reliance on direct controls. Too many new and quite legal channels of financing were available.

By the 1960s, these social and institutional changes generated new markets that placed the fixed exchange rate system under strain: Germany revalued, France devalued, Britain held out for three years (partly in deference to the USA) before devaluing in 1967, and the USA itself was continually on the defensive. Whether the US experiment with capital controls was 'effective' has always been hard to determine. All that is certain is that the US controls did not succeed in their objective of preserving the existing monetary system, that they helped establish the offshore markets, and that they undermined the effectiveness of other countries' existing controls. This failure signalled not only the waning of US hegemony but also the passing of the era of government control over international finance.

III. HOW THE BARGAIN WAS UPSET: MARKETS AND POLICY SINCE THE 1970s

In terms of the relationship discussed in this chapter, Bretton Woods eventually collapsed in the early 1970s because market growth created a new set of incentives: governments saw that they could do better outside the official system, i.e. they could borrow offshore on a very large scale, an option that was not available in the 1950s. Thus from the mid-1960s the new international money markets granted President Johnson an initially ample supply of credit to finance the Vietnam War, allowing him to avoid raising taxes. However, this growth of US liabilities (from about $30bn. in 1966 to about $60bn. in 1971) fuelled a further rapid expansion of Eurodollar credit which was then used to finance massive speculation against the dollar (borrowing dollars on the market and selling them spot). This speculation was a key factor in the collapse of the Bretton Woods system, with President Nixon's decision to suspend gold sales in August 1971.

The British Government also needed little persuasion to abandon the old system: urged on by virtually all economists and commentators, Prime Minister Heath and Chancellor Barber floated the pound in 1972 in their 'dash for growth', and inaugurated an unprecedented overseas financial borrowing spree which in less than five years was to bring down the remains of the old sterling area and send Britain to Saudi Arabia, the IMF, and any other creditor it could find for official credit when market credit was withdrawn.

Governments took the market solution, i.e. borrowing and the move to floating, basically because it seemed to offer more freedom for policy, but found that they had in fact surrendered both their freedom and, in some cases, their credit also. Finance, not government, was the real beneficiary of floating. The move to floating rates was associated with a massive expansion of demand for financial intermediation and new financial services. This was for two main reasons. First, inflationary economic policies, previously held in check by fixed rates, were left more scope and needed vast amounts of financing: floating by itself was found not to give *sufficient* autonomy. International credit also was needed to stabilize exchange rates. Second huge differences in expectations about exchange rate movements, linked to rapidly shifting inflationary expectations, entailed an immediate increase in the risks of all financial contracts (especially longer-term contracts). Suddenly there was no international money, nothing that could serve as a standard of deferred payments (see Kindleberger, 1984). So the markets got into the business of creating risks, or at least financing risk-taking, and at the same time providing new techniques for reducing these risks.

Additional private and official demand for new financing created, in effect, a new banking system closely analogous to the development of domestic banking systems in the eighteenth and nineteenth centuries. Admittedly, bank reserves still had to be provided by governments; but the new markets allowed banks to economize on the use of reserves. More important was what banks did with them—to develop a world-wide lending and deposit-taking business on the foundations built, mainly by US banks, in the 1960s.

Governments made no attempt to limit cross-border financial flows. Deficit countries borrowed heavily while creditor governments went on providing guarantees to private banks in the form of deposit insurance, export credit guarantees, and safety nets for all 'big' banks—safety nets that could only be justified in the context of the more controlled system of finance of the immediate post-war era (see section I.2 above). To provide guarantees against insolvency while taking all restraints off lending and simultaneously raising the risks involved was a recipe for disaster. The new technology of the markets ensured that the débâcle would be global in scope (see section IV below).[15]

Both developing and developed countries first enjoyed and then suffered from the greater autonomy offered by floating rates and elastic credit supply. The promise was not entirely illusory. To quote Carlos Diaz-Alejandro (1988), 'probably no capital market in history enjoyed a lower degree of political interference, to the dismay of cold warriors and "strategic minds" like Henry Kissinger's'. Within the constraints of the prevailing regime, the markets of the 1970s clearly extended the options available to economic policy-makers in developing countries. But the bill was presented in the 1980s.

Developed countries began to count the costs of the new-style autonomy in 1974–5, when annual inflation rates averaged 13% in the OECD: 'Nobody knew where it would go. The last time a world system had been in inflation was in the third and fourth centuries under the Roman empire, and then it had lasted more than 100 years' (Morse, 1988). Although this inflation was curbed in the recession of 1980–2, the outcome was to give even more freedom to the financial markets. Increasingly, governments felt compelled to liberalize domestic financial markets even further by competitive and interest group pressures, such as those outlined in section V below.

Related to these pressures, these years saw a 'changing of the guard' in terms of the prevailing ideology of economic policy, with the new generation of monetarists taking over key policy-making posts. The monetarists offered intellectual legitimacy for financial deregulation. The monetarists' belief that the markets could be controlled by adopting monetary targets proved correct only in the short run. Such feeble defences against market power caused the markets much less trouble than Bretton Woods had done. Indeed, this was when the markets really started to have fun.

IV. TECHNOLOGY'S PASSIVE ROLE

To what extent was this official retreat forced by technical characteristics of the new markets? Technological advances were clearly indispensable to the development of many of the new tradeable instruments. However, the financial revolution was driven throughout mainly by demand factors. It was the political decision to remove capital controls, rather than technology *per se*, that re-created the conditions for truly global integrated markets to re-emerge (see Chapter 6 below).

The demand for particular kinds of product and the associated technology was shaped initially by the increased volatility of asset prices, the financing of mergers and acquisitions, and the pervasive uncertainty generated by fluctuating inflation rates and expectations.[16] As in previous periods of rapid innovation, financial institutions were also motivated by a desire to evade official regulations. The pressure on capital–asset ratios gave a strong impetus to the growth of off-balance sheet business.

The demand for hedging instruments and the shift from banks to securities issuing and trading was strongest in the USA and UK, partly because monetary policy was particularly volatile in those countries. These were countries also where financial resources had become highly concentrated in institutional ownership.[17] It is no coincidence that it was in the USA and UK that the breakdown in the post-war order governing relations between the market and the state also occurred.

Thus the preliminary stages of the process were dominated by domestic-market changes, especially the development of money market and NOW accounts at the retail level, and wholesale methods for underwriting bond issues in the USA. However, the fact that the process of innovation was led by institutions in the world's leading *international* financial centres greatly stimulated the international diffusion of the new techniques. The association of the innovations with New York and London and the breathless enthusiasm with which they were written up in the financial magazines made company treasurers everywhere believe that they could benefit from greater access to them. The rising demand by companies for access to these instruments clearly strengthened the lobby for deregulation and more openness at the national level.

Again, social changes influenced demand. The late 1970s and 1980s witnessed a rapid rise in personal financial-asset holdings, swollen by the stock-market boom. A new generation of savers demanded a far wider range of financial services, including particularly a better rate of interest on their bank deposits, than their parents had done. Moreover, the new generation was well aware of the case for portfolio asset diversification, and expected the institutions that looked after their savings also to diversify internationally. The impact of this group was particularly marked in Japan, where bank depositors had been strongly discriminated against ever since the Second World War (to provide low-interest loans to industry). Having grown up with the jumbo jet and the personal computer, this generation took unrestricted financial and personal mobility for granted—and they were certainly not going to go to Switzerland to avoid controls. Young professionals in developing countries, open to the cosmopolitan culture, were equally aware of the new opportunities—and often had a much greater incentive to avoid any domestic controls by maintaining foreign bank accounts and not declaring the interest. According to industry sources, Taiwan is the world's largest market for Reuter's monitor screens because it has exchange controls which everybody circumvents by gaining direct access to the markets.

By providing corporations with possibilities for direct dealing previously open only to banks, technology eroded the distinctions between them. It also afforded the potential for much greater control over risk exposure (itself monitored automatically). The enhanced sense of control encouraged rapid international diversification of security portfolios, especially by institutional investors. This institutional diversification was probably the single most important force in the financial markets of the 1980s. Several trillion dollars were diversified out of domestic portfolios. Technology also encouraged the standardization of financial services that were previously provided on a tailor-made basis, and of financial contracts. At the retail level, to the extent that loans, deposits, insurance, and brokerage services can be automated, any company with a large customer base could provide a range of financial services as cheaply as banks.

IV.1. Towards Global Markets

In response to these opportunities, financial institutions started to lobby hard for greater freedom to offer services internationally, a freedom restricted by remaining exchange controls and other restraints on openness. There were two main strands here. First, as financial expertise and capital concentrated in the major international centres, various national financial centres found they were losing not only international business but a significant fraction of their domestic corporate business as well to these world centres. Thus the German Government was informed by its central bank that unless it relaxed restrictions on capital-market business in Germany, its big banks would migrate to London. Second, governments were aware that trade in services has been growing significantly faster than trade in goods (the proportion of invisible trade in total world trade has increased from 23% in 1976 to 27% in 1986). Financial services are an integral part of the provision of invisible services generally.[18] Countries which have large financial earnings are also large exporters of other services: the City of London's invisible (financial) earnings increased from £1.5bn. in 1978 (out of the UK's total invisible earnings from services of £12.5bn.) to £14.6bn. in 1988, out of a total of £27.9bn. But most countries allowed foreign banks to operate in their countries only on the basis of reciprocity—a principle that forced openness on countries that wished to participate in the boom in financial services.

IV.2. Summary of the Influence of Technology

The markets take what they want from the 'shelf' of technology that is available in any period; carrier pigeon, cable, telephone, and real-time, world-wide, computerized dealing. But what the financial institutions take is shaped by demand from customers, and the role of technology and social changes in creating those new demands is much more important than its direct role in the hardware of the financial markets themselves. The demand of the 1980s was for international asset diversification, and protection against volatility and uncertainty—i.e. substitutes for the stability that had previously been provided by fixed exchange rates and confidence in the dollar. Their demand determined the types of financial product/service offered by banks and the markets. They stepped into the economic space vacated by governments.

V. THE LIMITED OPTIONS FACING GOVERNMENTS

With the breakdown of the Bretton Woods rules governing relations between finance and the state, the markets gained the upper hand. This can be seen as the result of the exploitation by financial entrepreneurs of the new freedoms that they had wrested from governments, assisted by technological and social changes. The market's ascendancy was reflected in, and further reinforced by, the move to floating exchange rates among major currencies in the early 1970s, after which markets (rather than official institutions) became the main mechanism for adjusting conflicts between national policies. This role further enhanced their position relative to individual national governments (through decisions to grant or withhold credit).

In the next stage, the markets and the attitudes they engendered steadily eroded traditional instruments of economic policy. Starting with smaller open countries, governments were gradually led to use monetary policy to target the exchange rate—in an attempt to reduce electorally damaging exchange rate fluctuations. This process of 'internalizing' the necessary co-ordination of policy was taken further in countries which, from 1978, decided to link exchange rates formally in the European Monetary System, but applied increasingly to others. Even in the USA, major changes in policy, such as the adoption of monetary targets in 1979, and the attempt to manage the dollar's decline in 1985–8, were prompted by exchange rate concerns.

Then it was realized that the other classic instrument of demand management, fiscal policy, had also been undermined by a number of factors related to the spread of 'market-oriented' attitudes among consumers and voters: these included a growing perception of the national debt as a 'burden', opposition to budget deficits, the popularization of supply-side economics, increased attention to incentive effects of tax changes, and resistance to taxation levied to finance rising interest payments. From this perspective, policy effectiveness has been diminished not only directly, by the integration of capital markets and 'financial openness', but also indirectly, by increased financial sophistication of individuals and corporations and the associated loss of money and fiscal illusion.

V.1. Reactions of Governments

The reactions of governments have taken various forms. Here we follow the typology outlined by Richard Cooper and Ann Hollick in their discussion of the effects of technological change on international relations (see Cooper and Hollick 1985: 235). These authors characterize the possible reactions of governments to the erosion of their traditional controls under four headings: defensive, accommodative, aggressive, and co-operative.

Defensive Responses

These 'involve attempts by governments to stop erosion of their actions by steps that reduce the openness of their national economies, for example, by reducing the mobility of firms or funds' (ibid.). In terms of the policy options discussed in this paper, this response would involve, for instance, imposing limits on capital movements.

The basic problem with this response is that the efficient conduct of a business enterprise in the 1980s requires management to have a large degree of discretion in financial policy. This extends not only to the financing of foreign trade but also to the monitoring and control of cash flow, short-term borrowing and fund placement, and longer-term capital-raising functions.

First, to remain competitive, firms have to be given some leeway in the timing of current payments (spot) and in the use of forward-market operations, and both of these vehicles must also be available for speculative transactions which provide liquidity to the markets. Moreover, governments of countries with ambitions to be exporters of capital goods allow the exporters or their banks to provide long-term export credit (ten to fifteen years) and to refinance such credits in accordance with changing market conditions. Since in practice it is not feasible to separate trade from capital transactions, any increase in trading openness tends to increase financial openness as well.

Second, given the fact that only a few countries have a viable and competitive domestic capital market, access to the Euro-capital market has become essential to finance corporate expansion at competitive borrowing costs, especially in the industrial economies of Scandinavia, East Asia, Australasia, and southern Europe. Equally, most countries allow large institutional investors, such as insurance companies, to invest part of their portfolio abroad, so that they can diversify their risks and improve overall performance. Virtually all countries also allow foreign companies to establish subsidiaries and domestic firms to operate abroad; true, conditions can be required, but these invariably permit scope for adjustment of cash and investment positions. The volume of funds that is able to flow freely across borders for such business reasons often exceeds by a large margin the country's foreign reserves.

Third, there is the exit option. This is one area where the technological revolution is of prime importance: transport and telecommunications costs have been drastically cut; thirty years of experience with commercial jets have demonstrated improvement of 30% a decade in fuel efficiency; computation charges have dropped by 90% in each of the past two decades; and communications satellite charges have dropped by nearly 90% in real terms between 1965 and 1982. This technological revolution enables companies to shift the location of production and even domicile at low cost, permitting many the option of moving out of countries that levy taxes exceeding the international norm—and capital controls are a form of taxation.

Thus, defensive responses in general carry high financial costs—which is not to deny that a particular society, if given the choice, may find those costs to be less than the benefits, i.e. worth bearing for the sake of other values which it holds dear.

Accommodative Responses

In this category, governments 'do not resist erosion of traditional policy measures, but rather adapt their measures to the new prevailing circumstances' (Cooper and Hollick 1985: 235). This has plainly been the most frequent response, and it serves the interests of the most creditworthy corporations. Several studies demonstrate that the largest multinational corporations have managed the floating system effectively, through shifting the location of production and sourcing and taking full advantage of new financing techniques for hedging exchange risk. As the case of

Europe shows, big business could have the best of both worlds—privileged access to cheap capital and protection from exchange rate risk. Governments and local authorities frequently engage in competitive bidding for new foreign investment, and for providing a regulatory environment favourable to banking services.

But this response tends to erode further the governments' position *vis-à-vis* banks, corporations, and their electorates, and gradually transforms official authorities into agents of businesses or even into businesses themselves, with the privatization of government services.

Aggressive Responses

Here, 'in the face of decreasing effectiveness in their actions, [governments] try to extend their reach to cover the escaping parties' (Cooper and Hollick 1985: 235). Examples include US claims to extra-territorial jurisdiction, German and Swiss attempts to stop their currencies being used as currencies of denomination for securities issued outside their countries, and export subsidies. But as this list suggests, the scope for such 'aggressive' responses in the economic and financial field is inherently limited. An individual state can only suppress activities of which it disapproves which take place outside its borders by gaining the co-operation of other states.

Co-operation

Alternatively, governments can seek 'to overcome the erosion of policy measures due to the greater mobility of firms and funds' (ibid.). Cooper and Hollick mention attempts at economic policy co-ordination and moves to establish minimum standards (e.g. in pollution control—but the same principle would apply to banking supervision). They note that the formation of the EEC itself was 'an attempt to surmount the limitations that individual European governments increasingly felt, or recognized that they would feel, in an increasingly interdependent world'.

Yet the defects of co-operation as a means of restoring policy effectiveness are also clear: essentially, this usually makes explicit the loss of policy effectiveness at the national level, and transfers the conflict to a supranational level where the same game is played out. This clearly does not imply, however, that it is physically impossible to reduce the degree of integration, or even to disengage from 'global confrontation'; it does suggest that the economic costs of doing so have grown as a result of the ascendancy of markets over governments.

V.2. The Dilemma of Democracy

The historical relationships between finance and the state sketchily outlined above can be analysed as components in a single 'economic system', in which both financial and political services are produced in response to changing consumer tastes driven by social and technological change (the consumer here seen as demanding political as well as economic goods and services). The relationship is interdependent, as each branch of this system depends closely on the other and they have grown up together. But over time the demand by the state for financial support, as an 'input' into the production of political services, has proved to be stronger than banks' need for political support. This has gradually ensured the dominance of markets. Governments have made repeated attempts to regain control and 'autonomy' in monetary and economic policy, and the markets have had some setbacks, notably during the world wars and their aftermaths. But the general trend towards increasing market dominance has been maintained.

Some of the underlying causes of this market ascendancy have been suggested in previous sections. First, the initial conditions favoured the markets, in that they could enjoy the benefits of the pre-existing legal and institutional structure of society as public goods (along with legal protection of financial contracts), though these were the products of a prolonged struggle for freedom from arbitrary rule, and for basic rights and civil liberties, which long pre-dated the emergence of financial markets. Governments, by contrast, had from the start to compete in the market for finance along with other borrowers, and, though they frequently tried to monopolize credit, they generally succeeded in doing so only in times of war. Second, the nature of financial-market instability and the desire to avoid big bank failures are such that the public sector has in the twentieth century in all countries provided 'backstops' to banking, in the form of the lender-of-last-resort function and other forms of support. Third, the quid pro quo for this support, in the form of supervision and regulation of banking, has seldom been tight enough to offset its insidious effects in increasing moral hazard and periodic over-expansion of credit. The US thrift and savings bank crisis is only the most dramatic present example of this unsolved problem at the heart of competitive banking systems and their ambiguous relationship to political power.

V.3. The Bias towards Big Banks

A further point is that, within the banking sector itself, the way in which central banks intervene in the markets gives a systematic advantage to the large banks. This is because central banks are bound to give priority to large banks in their lender-of-last-resort operations, since a failure of a larger bank obviously has greater macro-effects than that of a smaller bank. As Herring (1990: 40) states:

Creditors are most likely to be protected at a large bank because failure of a large bank is likely to cause a greater drop in aggregate demand, interrupt more credit relationships, and pose greater threat to the payments system than the failure of a small bank. Even more important, the failure of a large bank is more likely to undermine confidence in the banking system generally and to lead to runs on other banks.

Market rates reflect this expectation, allowing large banks to fund their assets at lower interest cost, and forcing smaller banks to take on higher-yielding and possibly riskier business to survive in competition with the large banks. As Herring comments: 'Reliance on discretionary LLR [lender of last resort] assistance gives these banks a wholly unwarranted competitive advantage. Moreover, it weakens market discipline on precisely those institutions which, by virtue of their size, pose the greatest potential threat to the stability of the banking system' (ibid.). Thus, large banks have established an ascendancy within the markets that is not warranted by their economic efficiency.

Most governments and central banks, therefore, have cultivated or tolerated an oligopolistic banking structure, but this has not helped them to resolve these dilemmas any better: European and Japanese banks have been just as caught up in the instability of international bank lending and losses from property of securities markets transactions as the less oligopolistic US banking system. Both systems have produced the same basic conditions: increased state protection and support (with some accompanying supervision) together with maximum freedom to expand and diversify. The further banks expand, however, the greater the freedom they need from any remaining restrictions in order to allow them to 'grow out' of the trouble in which they invariably find themselves.

A perfect example of this interaction between governments and markets was provided by the proposals for far-reaching reforms of US banking legislation presented to Congress by US Treasury Secretary Nicholas Brady in February 1991. These proposals, if adopted, would allow US banks to operate nationwide and to engage in a much wider range of activities, and were rightly called 'a prescription for massive financial and economic concentration'. Even more important, they provided no solution to the moral-hazard problem, since bank deposits would still be insured while at the same time banks would be induced to take on even more high-risk business. Indeed, in these circumstances, competition would force bankers to make decisions which would misallocate resources and carry huge risks for the long-term viability of the financial system, secure in the knowledge that neither their bank nor their personal fortune would be at risk. That the big banks were able to obtain such a legislative proposal from the US administration is eloquent testimony to their political influence.

Thus have the fears of the older generation of central bankers been vindicated. Certainly it is no coincidence that this whole cycle started at a time, 60–80 years ago, that also witnessed the advent of full adult suffrage in many democracies. This placed political leaders under enormous pressure to supply social services to the newly enfranchised electorates. Initially, the response was to subject banking systems to controls designed essentially to facilitate the supply of credit that the governments did not raise through taxation. In the long run, however, the markets themselves were the prime beneficiaries of governments' need for credit. This demand might have been rationed according to some mutually agreed set of rules at the international level, but this would have required a reform of the international monetary system which governments have been unable to bring about, and which is perhaps only likely to come back onto the international agenda in the aftermath of a major banking collapse. The seeds of such a collapse may have already been sown. The gold standard was aristocracy's way of keeping the financial markets in their place; democracy has yet to find a substitute.

NOTES

1. 'The species first emerged in England at the end of the seventeenth century to raise money for governments. In the nineteenth century, it began to multiply. In modern times it has spawned' (Hirsch 1967). On the use of finance to wage wars, see Kennedy (1988: 306).
2. 'The Bank [of England] and the National Debt had grown up together, and critics of both said that the prosperity of the Bank depended on the debt' (Morgan 1943: 1).
3. After a full survey of the evidence on this contentious point, Platt (1968: 41) concludes: 'It is perfectly clear, then, that official intervention was denied bondholders unless their loans were under British government guarantee, or unless some incident had transformed their claims from the level of private debt-collecting to that of an international obligation. Bondholders, as far as the British government was concerned, were individuals choosing to invest abroad for their own profit; in doing so, they were acting independently of the interests of the nation and gambling merely on a higher return on their capital.'
4. As Moran (1984: 111–12) points out, the true costs of these rescue operations in the UK has never been satisfactorily established.
5. The following is an account by Martin Feldstein, former chairman of the President's Council of Economic Advisers: 'How shall we judge what the Fed did at the time? I think the Fed basically had learned the lesson of the 1930s. They knew it was important to provide liquidity . . . But there was something else that has received a lot less attention . . . : the problem of

the securities firms. Some of the securities firms were in trouble and they came to the Federal Reserve and asked for credit. The Federal Reserve quite properly said to them that they were very sorry, but they were in the business of lending to banks and couldn't lend to securities firms; such firms didn't have the privilege of the discount window. However, the Federal Reserve said that it would do some leaning on their friends at the banks to make sure that the banks were receptive when the brokerage firms came along. So the brokerage firms went to the banks, the Federal Reserve stood behind the banks, leaned on them, and the two parties managed to make a deal that would not otherwise have been possible . . . Now we have to ask ourselves, how will the securities firms behave in the future? What kind of risks will they be willing to take? Will they take more excessive risks in the future because they have seen that when the crunch comes, the Fed, while not prepared actually to lend to them, is prepared to do something which is equivalent?' (quoted in Feldstein *et al.* 1988: 339).

6. On the capture of regulators by the regulated, see Goodhart (1988); Stigler, (1971).
7. This process is explored in more detail in sections IV and V.
8. Most central bankers would probably claim that monetary policy can still be made effective, even in integrated financial markets, by improving techniques of control over bank reserves, and especially through greater flexibility in short-term interest rates; but in practice, policy is increasingly geared to external objectives, and even where it is not, the political resistance to interest rate flexibility reduces the authorities' freedom of action.
9. For a description of the institutional mechanisms of the gold standard, see Kindleberger (1984); Platt (1968). A monetarist perspective is presented in Bordo and Schwartz (1984).
10. In his authoritative account, Leland Yeager (1984) quotes Dr Foregger, deputy in the Austrian Parliament, as saying in the debate on the issue that the 'scrap-of-paper' economy of Austria degraded the country economically to a second-rate power: 'We demonstrate that our Empire does not have the strength to introduce among us, too, the means of payment, hard money, that holds sway in the civilized world. We thereby incessantly damage our credit, our economic flexibility and competitiveness.'
11. The classic work on the origin of the Bretton Wood system is Gardner (1956; see pp. 299–305). But see also Gilpin (1987) and Keohane (1984).
12. See Sayers (1952) for a contemporary view of the function of a central bank: 'The fundamental business of a central bank is to control the commercial banks in such a way as to support the monetary policy directed by the State.'
13. Report of the Committee on the Working of the Monetary System, Aug. 1959.
14. The support credits of Basle banished the speculator as master of currency fortunes (Hirsch 1967: 356). (This is a reference to the swap network of reciprocal central-bank credits organized through the Bank for International Settlements in Basle to support the dollar and the pound in the 1960s.)
15. For instance, before the globalization of markets it is not clear that the suspension of debt payments by Mexico in 1982 would have led to that of Brazil a few months later, since the latter was precipitated by panic with-

drawals of bank credit: indeed, some have argued that the Mexican crisis itself was produced partly by nervousness about East European credits. See Williamson (1985).

16. The variance of inflation rates increased from 0.6% in the 1960s to 6.7% in the 1970s. See IMF (1988*a*: 40). On the increased frequency of mergers and acquisitions, see Ch. 2.
17. By the early 1980s, institutions owned about 90% of long-term government bonds in the USA and 75% in Britain, compared with 55% in Japan. For more details on this issue, see Ch. 2.
18. The other services closely linked to banking are insurance, the stock exchange, commodity markets, ship and air brokerage, portfolio management, and investment income.

5

Exchange Controls and Policy Autonomy: The Case of Australia, 1983–1988

ANDREW GLYN

I. INTRODUCTION

The case for exchange controls under contemporary conditions is simple; they assist national governments in undertaking macroeconomic policies which may diverge from the norms deemed acceptable by international financial markets. Specifically, they allow a government committed to expansionary financial policies to limit the extent to which outflows of capital force excessive currency depreciations or interest rate increases. Part of the case in favour of abolishing exchange controls is that such policy independence is actually undesirable: in the context of the current debate in Sweden on the issue, Calmfors (1985:91) has put the point particularly sharply:

> in my opinion, free movements of capital appear desirable from the standpoint of stabilisation policy. A stabilisation policy that accommodates domestic inflationary disturbances becomes untenable if it rapidly results in capital outflows that threaten the foreign-exchange reserves. As a result, greater discipline is imposed on both monetary and fiscal policy; accordingly, fundamental imbalances need not arise. Thus, currency flows should function as a clear signal that policies need to be changed.

In contrast, the starting-point for this paper is that capital flows motivated by expectations in capital markets as to the results of expansionary policies may *ensure* the failure of such policies, even when they would otherwise stand a good chance of success. If it were the case that only *actually* unsustainable expansionary packages are judged by the markets to be unsustainable, then a capital outflow which forces the premature abandonment of such a package could be judged to be in the interests of society as a whole. If, however, there is a real chance that growth and employment objectives could be met, perhaps at the cost of a higher inflation rate but without accelerating inflation, then the power of capital outflows to abort such a package simply serves the sectional interests (and reflects the fears) of financial capital.

Consideration of a single example of abolition of exchange controls can never definitively settle such fundamental issues. Nevertheless, the case of Australia is particularly interesting because an extensive set of exchange controls were abolished in 1983 by a Labour Government committed to expansionary policies which were out of line with the general trend of the OECD countries. Australia also represents a case study for the other central question in the exchange controls debate—can they work? If exchange controls are ineffective given current levels of international economic integration (extent of trade and ownership links), then their costs in terms of micro-inefficiencies may well outweigh the benefit in terms of policy autonomy, even assuming that such autonomy is desirable.

Section II of this paper describes the exchange control system operating in Australia in the early 1980s, the arguments for its abolition, and the course of events which precipitated its being scrapped. It looks, therefore, at the effectiveness of control and the political economy of decontrol. Section III charts the course of macroeconomic policy under the Labour Government, the trend towards restrictionism, and the role of the foreign-exchange markets in dictating the periodically chaotic pattern of events. The conclusion attempts to draw some broader lessons.

II. CONTROL AND DECONTROL

At the beginning of the 1980s, Australia still had an unusually controlled and regulated financial system, described by a foreign critic as 'a rigid structure often unresponsive to market opportunities, market segmentation impeding the flows of capital amongst sectors and administered prices and quantitative controls that failed to clear markets' (Carron 1983: 195). The extensive system of controls over foreign exchange was, therefore, part of a wider system of control which came under detailed scrutiny by the Campbell Committee of Inquiry into the Australian Financial System (Campbell 1981).[1]

The details of domestic financial regulation, and the process of deregulation which unwound it, is beyond the scope of this paper, and I shall not attempt any kind of critique of the principles underlying the Committee's deregulatory recommendations. Nevertheless, the fact that the abolition of exchange controls and the floating of the dollar took place in this broader context is important. These particular changes were quite widely seen as part of a more or less inevitable process of modernization of the financial side of Australia's economy. The *Australian Financial Review* (*AFR*—the respected daily newspaper concentrating on finance, politics, and economics) greeted the decision to abolish exchange controls and float the dollar with the banner headline 'A Brave New World' and the claim that 'The revolutionary changes implemented today in foreign exchange markets take Australia into the penultimate stage of deregulation of the financial system . . . Nine months into office the Hawke Government has achieved much of the brave new world outlined two years ago in the Campbell Committee's report on the Australian Financial System' (12 December 1983).

The previous Conservative Government of Malcolm Fraser had instituted a number of important changes on the domestic financial front, including the removal of interest rate ceilings (save for the important home loan sector) and quantitative guidance for trading banks, the relaxation of portfolio controls on savings banks, and the introduction of a tender system for treasury bonds. International financial relations, however, were still heavily controlled. I shall first describe the fixing of the exchange rate and the system of exchange controls before providing some evaluation of the circumstances surrounding their abandonment.

II.1. The Exchange Rate

The value of the Australian dollar was fixed in terms of the trade-weighted index (TWI) under an adjustable peg system; this had evolved (in 1976) out of earlier attempts to manage a fixed rate first against the US dollar and subsequently against a TWI. The rate was fixed each day, with the stated intention of the authorities that 'movements in the level of the rate take place by means of frequent small shifts' (Campbell 1981: 115). In the two years before the election of the Labour Government, for example, the nominal rate had first moved up steadily by around 10% (over seven months) and then declined, again rather steadily, by about 12% over the rest of the period. Substantial Reserve Bank intervention took place, and not all 'leaning into the wind'; as Argy (1987) recounts, the authorities, worried about the current account, were selling Australian dollars in 1982 to edge the exchange rate down in the face of capital inflows.

The spot market was operated by the trading banks, acting in effect as agents of the Reserve Bank which limited their foreign currency holdings to 'reasonable working balances' (Reserve Bank 1979:s. 5, p. 8). Exporters and importers could cover on the forward market. The Reserve Bank effectively set the rates in the market and acted as the underwriter, as the banks were required to balance their books with the RB. There was also an unofficial hedge market where risks ineligible for the official market could be matched (see below).

II.2. Exchange Controls

Trade

Payment for exports had to be received within six months and prepayment was limited to one month (with corresponding restrictions on payments for imports), and the Reserve Bank attempted to ensure that reported transactions were at their 'true market value' (to limit leads and lags and to control surreptitious capital movements through under- or over-invoicing). Export proceeds had to be sold immediately to a bank in Australia, although permission could be granted to hold funds outside the country for one month if they were to be used for an approved purpose. Forward cover had to be requested within seven days of the risk being incurred (aimed at limiting to the trade flows currently taking place the swings in the amount of forward cover the authorities would be obliged to provide); forward cover was denied to capital transactions.

There is no doubt that these regulations had a substantial effect in limiting the flexibility of traders in covering their risks. For example, evidence to the Campbell Committee reported of the seven-day rule that 'the degree of protest [from companies surveyed] indicates that it has a substantial degree of effectiveness' (Syntec 1982: 63). Of course, the time period allowed for payments and receipts was quite long (by comparison with some European countries, for example), thereby allowing substantial room for the use of leads and lags for speculative purposes.

Australian Investment Overseas

(i) Such investment was banned in short-term fixed-interest assets (e.g. bank deposits) other than certain working balances.
(ii) It was limited in long-term fixed-interest securities to $A10,000 per individual and $1m. per company per year (these had been banned before 1980).
(iii) It was unrestricted in equities and real estate (restrictions similar to those still in force for long-term fixed-interest securities were relaxed in 1980 and abolished in 1981).
(iv) Direct investment was supposed to meet various conditions such as the promotion of Australian exports.

Whilst there was a fairly large amount of direct investment overseas (some $A6bn., over half of which was in ASEAN countries or New Zealand), holdings of overseas financial assets by both financial and non-financial sectors were extremely low (less than $A2bn.). This confirms Syntec's conclusion on fixed-interest portfolio investment: 'the major benefit of this control would seem to be in limiting the potential volatility of short-term capital flows. In this respect these quite rigid controls are considered effective' (1982: 41).

Overseas Investment in Australia

(i) Short-term fixed-interest (e.g. bank deposits) was unrestricted except for overseas banks (including central banks), which were permitted to hold only working balances.

(ii) Portfolio (long-term fixed-interest and equities) was unrestricted, except that on occasion (between 1972 and 1978) short-term borrowing from overseas was prohibited and a variable deposit ratio (to be deposited interest-free with the Reserve Bank) was imposed on longer-term borrowings; timing of drawings on, and repayments of, overseas loans to Australian companies were monitored.
(iii) Direct investment in Australia had to meet stringent conditions (connected to concerns about ownership and control).

These regulations had not prevented a very substantial level of overseas investment in Australia, both direct and portfolio ($A27bn. and $A24bn. respectively). But the point to emphasize here is that the low level of Australian investment abroad meant that almost all this gross investment in Australia represented *net* investment—at some 23% of GNP (book values), this net investment reflected Australia's traditional role as a capital importer with relatively little of the capital inflow being re-exported.

II.3. Campbell's Criticisms Vindicated?

The criticisms and proposals of the Campbell Committee in the field of exchange rate management and exchange controls were undoubtedly influential in framing the outcome. Moreover, the bout of speculative pressure which hit the Australian dollar at the time of the March 1983 election seemed to vindicate many of Campbell's observations. This latter episode is important because it forced the Labour Government to devalue by 10% as soon as it was elected, an incident which must have had a very substantial effect on its subsequent policy decisions. Before analysing the post-election devaluation, we discuss the Campbell Committee's arguments.

The Campbell Committee's Evidence and Arguments

The Campbell's Committee's first conclusion on exchange rate management was that 'the degree of flexibility available to the authorities would be greater under a system of managed floating' (p. 116), so that the present system of fixing the rate should be abandoned and the 'exchange rate should thereafter be determined in the market and the authorities should deal in the market if they wished to promote a particular rate' (p. 117). The Committee was careful to point out that this essentially technical decision on having a market-determined rate did not imply any particular level of intervention. Their own recommendation, however, was that 'any official intervention in foreign exchange markets (apart from technical smoothing) should be relatively light, infrequent and only for short periods' (p. 129). Their preference for a 'lightly managed rate' rested on their view that 'exchange rate targeting' would 'impede the achievement of a stable monetary environment and lead to less autonomy in domestic economic management' and would not 'necessarily produce more stable exchange rates over a longer period and may indeed add to instability' (p. 121). The latter argument was based on doubts as to the authorities' capacity to judge equilibrium rates and on evidence as to central bank losses on exchange rate interventions.

The Committee accepted that a managed float could 'coexist' with exchange controls. They argued, however (p. 139), that continued use of exchange controls would be justified only if:

(a) there are significant macroeconomic benefits to be derived from maintaining an exchange rate substantially different from the free market rate for long periods;
(b) exchange controls are effective in regulating short-term capital flows, and therefore assist the authorities to manage the exchange rate with less monetary disruption; and
(c) the macroeconomic benefits of exchange control outweigh the costs.

As we have seen, the Committee did not accept the first proposition. In the event, the Reserve Bank was forced by speculative flows into much more active intervention than the Campbell Committee (or indeed the RB at the time of floating) envisaged. In any case, the disastrous swings in exchange rates during the 1980s have so shifted the tide of official international opinion in favour of managed rates (as evidenced by the Louvre accord, Chancellor Lawson's conversion to intervention, etc.) that the relevant issue now is rather whether exchange controls can make a significant contribution to exchange rate management.

The Campbell Committee took the view that the costs of exchange control were substantial, especially in respect of 'restrictions on the flexibility of business and its capacity to take initiatives and grasp investment opportunities' (p. 143). Not surprisingly, the evidence they received emphasized the heavy administrative burdens involved, but it is hard to imagine that these could be of the same order of magnitude as the benefits from a markedly improved macroeconomic performance (a possibility Campbell discounted). It should also be noted that such complaints ignore the microeconomic costs of any greater exchange rate instability which could follow from abolition of controls. The complainants looked at the impact of controls on the costs and flexibility of the foreign-exchange transactions they would have liked to undertake in the existing situation, ignoring the additional transactions that they might feel obliged to undertake in conditions of greater instability.

But the issue of the effectiveness or otherwise of exchange controls in limiting short-term capital movements cannot be sidestepped so easily. The Committee's basic conclusion was that:

in today's world of closely interrelated financial markets, exchange controls could not prevent appreciable movements of capital into and out of Australia in pursuit of interest arbitrage or speculative foreign exchange gains, if the exchange rate is markedly out of line with market expectations. (p. 121)

The Committee believed that most studies suggested that 'while controls may affect the transactions categories directly covered, they are (after a time) largely or completely offset by compensating adjustments elsewhere' (p. 141). Whilst this view was widely held, Argy's recent review concludes: 'there is no hard evidence on this'. He also points to the work of Carland and Valentine (1982) showing that controls did drive a wedge between domestic and foreign interest rates, and adds that 'from about mid 1978, after controls over inflows were removed, until end 1983 the covered differential significantly and persistently favoured overseas investment' (Argy 1987: 43). The surge in outflows that was observed after abolition of controls (see below) also suggests that the controls had had a very considerable effect.

It would be foolish to write off the almost unanimous view of market participants, both official and private, that controls had a tendency to erode as the private sector found ways around them and learned how to dress up its applications more plausibly. The Reserve Bank appears also to have relaxed some of its formalities in 1979 (see Syntec 1982:45). Nevertheless, the case for a *necessarily* fatal erosion of the effectiveness of controls was certainly not convincingly demonstrated by Campbell.

All this is not to claim that the controls *then in force* could prevent major short-term speculative movements. The Campbell Committee used the obvious fact of gaps in the existing framework of controls as justification for abolishing those controls. Its reason for advocating the removal of controls on overseas investment in Australian deposits and Australian investment in overseas securities and deposits (the latter described in the Syntec Report as the 'lynchpin of the set of controls which are designed to govern short-term outward movements of capital') is instructive:

The Committee is conscious of the concern of the authorities that these types of accounts could accumulate over time and become a source of potential speculative 'overhang'. It notes, however, that privately held foreign exchange balances can at times act as a stabilising force in the market. Moreover there is already a large volume of ongoing and accumulated overseas equity and interest-bearing investments in Australia. There can also be substantial 'leads and lags'. These funds can be extremely mobile and can also be viewed as a potential overhang. Finally, it should again be pointed out that under a more market-oriented exchange rate system, the potential capital flows would generally impact on the exchange rate rather than on domestic monetary conditions. (p. 148)

Sandwiched between their optimism that destabilizing speculation might not happen and their complacency about the domestic impact of exchange rate changes if it did happen, there is a significant argument: that controls aimed at preventing short-term capital flows were pointless because such flows could happen quite legitimately under the existing controls. In particular, it has been argued, although not emphasized in the Campbell Report, that private-sector financial innovation was ineluctably increasing the extent of such legitimate flows (in which case the effectiveness of the old controls would be undermined). This line of argument is exemplified by the growth of the private hedge market (for forward transactions) and overseas markets for the Australian dollar. We examine these rather technical issues in the Appendix to this chapter, concluding that the effects of such innovations may have been exaggerated.

This examination of the evidence about capital flows and interest rates and our discussion of the new financial markets leaves a verdict of 'not proven' on the Campbell Committee's judgement, quoted earlier, that exchange controls *could not* have a sufficient impact on short-term speculative movements. However, their view that *existing* controls were insufficient was clearly demonstrated by the events surrounding the election of March 1983, to which I now turn.

The 1983 Post-Election Devaluation

The key macroeconomic policies promised by Labour during the 1983 election campaign were the creation of half a million jobs in three years and a growth rate of 5% by the third year. This would involve increasing the budget deficit by $A1.5bn., whilst the programme promised the monetary policy would 'accommodate the stimulus without crowding out the private sector'.

A few days before the poll, fears that Labour would pursue expansionary policies and increase controls over the financial system led to capital outflows totalling several hundred million dollars a day. The *Financial Review*'s editorial on 2 March 1983 sounded the alarm:

> Let there be no mistake. The Labour Party's policy does include greater regulation of the banks than is at present in force and greater federal regulation of the non-bank financial intermediaries . . . It is true however that the policies of a Labour Government would be more likely to require more regulation than has hitherto been in place. This is the inevitable result of expansionism with little attention to inflation, to capital outflows and currency fears.

After the election result was known, the pressure continued. Two days before it formally assumed office, the new Labour Government devalued by 10%. Four days later, $2bn. of the $2.5bn. estimated to have left the country during the election campaign was thought to have returned. Indeed, the authorities immediately revalued by over 1%, a much bigger jump in the managed rate than customary. This had the aim, according to the *AFR*, of reassuring 'the financial community that the 10 per cent devaluation was at least in part a merely political response to a crisis which was not justified by the underlying trade situation, or relative inflation and interest rates' (15 March). The March devaluation, therefore, seems a classic case of a devaluation forced by market expectations of possible adverse effects (on inflation in particular) of the Labour Government being elected. After pointing out that sales of foreign exchange had been $2.3bn. in the first week of March, the Reserve Bank's *Bulletin* for April 1983 (p. 669) states:

> It is difficult to be precise about the nature of these outflows. The key factor was clearly the widely held view that the Australian dollar might be devalued to a significant extent. That prompted many transactors to take action to avoid the possibility of loss and some others to position themselves to profit from a devaluation if it occurred. Exporters sought to delay their receipts from abroad and importers sought to bring their payments forward. These leads and lags were a substantial contributor while another important factor was the extent to which overseas borrowings were replaced with domestic borrowing.

That banks may themselves have been involved is suggested by the fact that the Reserve Bank 'reminded' banks that they should not be trading in foreign currencies on their own behalf; and there were rumours that rules would be tightened so that Australian borrowers raising money overseas would have to specify in advance when the loan was to be repaid.

There was surprisingly little discussion at the time of the alternatives to devaluation; reserves were $5bn., and Australia's credit rating was AAA. A tightening up of exchange controls on trade payments and on private-sector debt repayments, plus further official borrowing to shore up the reserves, was surely a possibility. In a speech reported in the monthly Bulletin of the Reserve Bank's *Bulletin* for May 1985 (p. 726), the deputy governor described the episode thus:

> Despite exchange controls, early in 1983 intense political speculation led to very heavy capital outflows and the exchange rate was devalued discretely. This episode demonstrated that the prevailing exchange control system was not an effective barrier to short-term flows when exchange rate expectations were strong.

The decision to devalue gave the speculators a huge gain, and was reported as leaving ministers 'with the bitter taste of having lost $250 million to currency speculators'. It signalled very early how the Government would bow to market forces even in a case where it was convinced that pressures were in no sense justified by the underlying balance-of-payments position.

II.4. Abolition of Exchange Controls and Floating

There is no doubt that the immediate pressure behind the decision to float the Australian dollar in December 1983 arose from the difficulties for monetary control arising from speculative capital inflows:

> The current account was beginning to show some improvement in 1983; at the same time the interest differential moved more in favour of Australia; moreover, some confidence in the new government was beginning to surface. These forces combined to produce a dramatic reversal in capital flows. In the months that followed inflows became massive; indeed for a while they were almost double the current account deficit. As in 1980/81 they found it impossible to sterilise the inflow. During these months the money supply was overshooting its projected range (revised upwards by one point in December). (Argy 1987: 34)

But according to an apparently authoritative briefing, the 'primary reason' for the Government's decision to float was

> not the effect on the money supply although this was the factor which prompted it to act so soon . . . Mr Keating and Mr Hawke were firmly convinced a month ago that it was the managed exchange rate itself which was causing the continued speculation against the dollar. Put most vehemently by the Reserve Bank, the argument was that with the Government showing last March that it was prepared to respond to speculation by substantially devaluing the currency, the mechanism of small discretely managed shifts had been fundamentally undermined . . .
>
> When Cabinet's Economic Policy Committee met at 3.45 pm on Friday after the early morning announcement that the exchanges were to be closed for the day, the decision to float was almost inevitable. Three options were put to the committee. The first was to revalue, the second was to impose short-term currency controls to stem the inflow of capital, and the third was to float. The first option was rejected on the basis that it would merely confirm that the Government was being manipulated by the market.
>
> The second was rejected because it would undermine business confidence that the Labour Government was innovative and not locked into traditional responses. (*AFR*, 12 December 1983)

The Bank recorded its explanation for abandoning controls rather more technically: 'The authorities could have sought to deal with these unwanted flows through direct controls. The Bank saw these as a last resort, prone to create distortions in financial markets and likely to have limited and only short-run effectiveness' (Reserve Bank of Australia, *Annual Report*, 1984: 3).

This, of course, was not a line of argument which would find favour with the left of the Labour Party and the trade unions. In October 1983, the ACTU's submission to the Martin Committee, set up by the Labour Government to review the findings of the Campbell Committee, had endorsed 'the retention of existing arrangements for exchange rate fixing and the retention of controls necessary for exchange rate targeting' (ACTU 1983: 12). The *AFR* reported (12 December 1987):

Basically ministers were objecting to a managed system because it was causing speculation against the Government. They believed that if there was to be speculation, let it be among the speculators themselves. This is one argument which will help to sell the decision to the party.

Such arguments seem to have been successful. Laurie Carmichael of the Metalworkers Union offered what seems to have been a lone objection: 'the Government should have imposed foreign exchange controls to cope with the speculative inflow problem . . . the float decision was a blow to the solar plexus of the Accord' (*AFR*, 12 December 1983).

One very important issue which received little attention was the fact that the decision to float of itself did not imply the wholesale abolition of exchange controls.[2] Indeed, numbers of countries had floated without abolishing exchange controls (for example, the UK in 1972). Given the danger of capital flight in the future, and the problems a major depreciation would pose for the accord with the trade unions in terms of reduced real wages, the decision to abandon controls on all forms of capital outflow was of more long-term significance than the decision to respond to the inflows by floating.

The decision to abolish the controls was explained, some two years later, by the deputy governor of the Reserve Bank:

The Government decided to float the Australian dollar. The decision having been taken, there was not a strong case for retaining exchange controls, which were largely directed to protecting reserve holdings and supporting the managed rate system. They were abolished virtually overnight. (RB *Bulletin*, May 1985, p. 726)

But, of course, the technical abandonment of a fixed rate does not imply a passive acceptance of whatever rate the market chooses to deliver. Acknowledging that the exchange controls then in force could not prevent severe speculative pressure (as the 10% devaluation had shown) did not entail abandoning the controls which would make potential speculative pressure worse. Whether or not such arguments were put, they clearly did not carry the day. It is tempting to believe that part of the reason for the conversion of the Treasury and Reserve Bank to the case for abolition of exchange controls (which both had opposed at the time of their evidence to the Campbell Committee) was the feeling that the greater openness of financial markets would weaken the ability of a Labour Government to behave in an 'irresponsible' way. Whilst the move to a floating rate could certainly be seen as enhancing monetary control (see Harper 1986), abandoning exchange controls would actually *reduce* monetary control under any circumstances in which speculation made substantial intervention necessary (a possibility hardly to be ruled out). As pointed out in the financial Press, however, the freeing of the exchange markets meant that the constraints placed by the financial markets on the government were even tighter:

> The Treasurer argued that by floating the dollar the Government would be forcing the market to determine the value of the dollar on the basis of the strengths and weaknesses of the economy. But inherent in this approach is the acceptance that the Government has an enormous responsibility to keep the economy stable . . . Accordingly the pressure is now on Mr Keating to keep his Budget deficits closely attuned to the stability requirements of the foreign exchange markets. (*AFR*, 16 December 1983)

Section III of this paper analyses how this pressure was exerted and to what effect.

III. MACROECONOMIC OUTCOMES AND POLICIES

The years of Labour government have seen substantially faster growth in Australia than in the OECD as a whole—just over 4% per year from 1982/3 to 1987/8.[3] Exports, and public expenditure in the first half of the period, provided the main impulses for the rapid growth. Since 1983/4, employment growth has been around 3% per year, which has kept consumption growing despite the reduction in real wages secured under the accord.[4] The impact on registered unemployment has been modest (down from 9.3% to 7.8%) because of rapid labour force growth (especially female participation). The current-account deficit expanded from an inherited 4% of GNP to 6% in 1985/6. The deterioration in the terms of trade (costing 3.5% of GNP) and deterioration in the balance of property incomes (costing almost as much), as external debt and interest rates rose, wiped out the impact of growing net export volumes. Subsequently, the slow-down in domestic demand growth and improvement in the terms of trade reversed this trend, so that the Treasurer could forecast a deficit reduced to 3% of GNP for 1988/9. Inflation in the range 8–9% in 1986 and 1987 was far above the average OECD rate, but began to decline after the middle of 1987.

The outstanding weakness of the macroeconomic pattern lay in stagnant business investment. Only in 1984/5, before the turn towards restrictive policies, did business investment rise strongly. By 1987/8 its level was still no higher than in 1981/2, and the growth rate of business capital stock had slipped from around 4% per year to less than 3%, no more than the growth of employment; manufacturing capital stock was virtually static over the whole period. Investment failed to recover strongly, despite the rapid growth and a recovery in the profit rate of about one-third after 1982/3 to a rate similar to that of the late 1970s.

Weakness of investment was reflected in very slow productivity growth—around 1.5% per year after an initial spurt in 1983/4.

The Labour Government faced the real constraints posed by the balance-of-payments weakness, and the necessity to devote substantial real resources to improving it (some 4% of GNP was shifted into net exports in the two years 1985/6 and 1986/7). Under these circumstances, rapid employment growth implied *either* very low productivity growth, so that demand for labour rose rapidly in the market sector, *or* rapid reductions in hours of work (which would have the same effect), *or* big increases in employment in the state sector. Either way, take-home pay had to rise slowly, but with the second or third possibilities real welfare could still grow substantially through increased leisure or improved social services. The Australian pattern corresponds more closely to the first possibility, not at all what the trade union movement had in mind when it negotiated the accord. The OECD 1987/8 survey of Australia (OECD 1988) features a chart showing the closely parallel employment record of Australia and the USA in the 1980s, but does not point out that both economies have shared the same low wage growth/low productivity growth route to high employment (see Glyn 1991).

Thus it is clear that floating the Australian dollar and the abolition of exchange controls did not prevent a growth of employment which is impressive by the standards of EEC countries. The role of the accord is obviously crucial here, but lies outside the scope of this paper (see Archer 1991). But the impact of floating and abolition on the course of the Government's macroeconomic policy, and thus the *form* of this rapid employment growth, remains a central question. I discuss first how policy was influenced by international financial pressures, before looking more broadly at the patterns of fiscal and monetary policy and the course of the exchange rate and capital movements.

III.1. The Pattern of International Financial Pressures

The outgoing Conservative Government had presided over a 4 percentage point rise in Australia's unemployment rate and the first year-on-year fall in GDP since 1952/3, combined with an inflation rate of 13% (about double the OECD average) and a current-account deficit of 4% of GDP. In an effort to cope with this uncomfortable combination, the Conservative Government had reversed its commitment to free-market principles with a wage freeze and introduced an expansionary budget (see Davis 1987). It became apparent soon after Labour was elected that the budget deficit was increasing much faster than anticipated; indeed, the OECD's calculations (*Economic Outlook*, various issues) suggest that in 1983 the general government structural deficit increased by 3% of GDP.

Paradoxically, this allowed Labour both to cut the planned increase in the deficit and still to run an extremely expansionary fiscal policy.

In May 1983 a package of measures, including spending cuts of nearly $A1bn., was seen as having 'rejected the expansionism proposed during the election campaign'; 'the sensitivity of the Government to the reactions of financial markets was apparent' (*AFR*, 20 May 1983). In June, Hawke and Treasurer Keating 'made their first official marketing pitch to the New York financial community . . . with one clear intention—to put to rest any fears of the Mitterrand factor' (*AFR*, 21 June 1983). When the budget deficit of $A8bn. was announced, the Reserve Bank placed on the record in its 1983 *Annual Report* the view it had put to Keating that 'a deficit of that order might conceivably be financed without unmanageable financial pressures' (p. 8). In his Budget speech, Keating said that 'unless the structural deficit were to be reduced, strong recovery in the private sector would ultimately bring about a clash of funds between the two sectors and thus put at risk the recovery'.

Despite these soothing words, the structural deficit increased further in both 1984 and 1985 (by some 0.7% each year, according to the OECD), so the small declines in the actual deficit simply reflected cyclical factors. This was not lost on financial commentators, who greeted Treasurer Keating's 1984 budget with some scepticism:

> A Government which placed enormous store on gathering business confidence to underpin a lengthy period in government has jeopardised the fledgling trust afforded to it by influential sections of that community. By using the funds which flow to the Treasury due to strong economic growth to fund additional expenditure rather than cut the deficit or further reduce taxes the Government has tarred itself as a big spender. Mr Keating's statement that he did not think it wise to have reduced the structural deficit because it would take aggregate activity out of the economy certainly indicated a lack of confidence in the private sector's ability to take further responsibility for recovery from the public sector. (*AFR*, 24 August 1984)

Disquiet about budgetary policy did not coalesce into a serious crisis during 1984, but must have been the explanation for the prime minister's 'trilogy' commitment during the successful election campaign at the end of the year: his government would reduce the ratios (to GDP) of public spending, of taxation, and of the budget deficit.

Difficulties in interpreting monetary aggregates as deregulation of financial markets proceeded caused the Government to abandon its broad money target in January 1985. Nevertheless, the trend in the exchange rate was if anything upward during 1984, and it seemed therefore that the Government's perceived pro-market stance[5] was proving very successful in securing room for government-led expansion without destabilizing the foreign-exchange markets. But the lull proved temporary. The *AFR* reported at the end of the year: 'Traders and analysts are only now coming to contemplate the impact of the manically depressed commodities market on the Australian economy and question whether as a result the Australian dollar is somewhat overvalued' (13 December 1984). 'Somewhat' was soon to prove a dramatic understatement.

Over the next eighteen months the Government was buffeted by a series of violent foreign-exchange crises, concentrated in particular on the periods February–April 1985, November 1985, and May–August 1986. In these three periods the value of the Australian dollar against the TWI fell by 22.4%, 6.2%, and 19.8% respectively. By September 1986 the rate was 41.8% below that of December 1984; allowing for relative inflation rates, the effective depreciation was 34.2%.

The columns of the *AFR* convey the flavour of these periods of crisis and the perceived impact of international financial markets on domestic policy:

[21 February 1985] *Interest Ratchets up as $A slides further*
If the Federal Government had not discovered the real meaning of the floating of the currency, apart from gongs from international financial magazines,[6] the profound shock experienced in the market for the Australian dollar this month must be finally bringing it home . . . that in contrast to the picture widely held 18 months ago of a Government of pragmatic economic managers thought to be running a sound economy, the Government is not prepared to make hard decisions, and despite high nominal interest rates, is running a slack monetary policy . . . A number of factors have been blamed for the currency's decline, including the widening current account deficit, the abandoning of monetary targets, the public service dispute, the Budget deficit and the MX missile crisis.

Public-spending cuts, a substantially reduced budget deficit, and what was regarded as a moderate wage settlement failed to prevent another selling bout in November, and interest rates were hiked up again.

[13 November 1985] *Australia's trade problems worsen . . . Government admits that growth needs to be wound back . . . but world markets keep undermining dollar*
The Hawke Government's much vaunted clean float of the $A is turning into a nightmare as the foreign exchange market's downhill bandwagon was triggered again by its bearish interpretation of last month's balance of payments figures. When the $A was floated nearly two years ago, the Federal Treasurer, Mr Keating, declared that 'the speculators will now be speculating against themselves rather than against the Australian Government.' But while it can be forcefully argued that there was no alternative but to float, the exchange rate now threatens to undermine the Government's Accord-based economic strategy . . .

[6 February 1985] The Aussie dollar is likely to go through similar bouts of apparent recovery and dashed hopes as long as the main support for the currency is unreliable capital inflows attracted by the positive interest rate differential. Behind the tension over monetary policy is the conflict between the finance sector's demands for moderate economic growth in the order of 2–3% and the Hawke Government's need for 4–5% to make inroads into unemployment.

The influential magazine *Euromoney* reported, in its generally positive February 1986 special supplement on Australia (p. 18), the Government's determination not to be 'railroaded into important changes of policy by economic indicators which it considers of transient importance'. It noted, however, that, should the foreign-exchange dealers change their assessments of the Australian dollar for the worse on the basis of such indicators, the Government would be forced to do 'much the same as it did when the 1985 depreciations happened—only more so. Keep monetary policy tight. Keep fiscal policy tight. And—renegotiate the Accord with the unions to keep wage increases tight as well.' This proved prophetic.

In a notorious interview in May, the treasurer said that lack of discipline over wages and economic policy, in the face of depressed commodity prices, would drag Australia down to the status of a 'banana republic'. Selling pressure built up, and in July he was forced into a humiliating retreat over the tax treatment of interest paid overseas, with the *AFR* reporting that the Government was 'struggling to maintain some control over the economy'. A further rise in interest rates, and a cut in the Commonwealth budget deficit to $3.5bn., rapidly followed. The *AFR* summarized the situation as some stability was restored:

> [5 September 1986] The $A crisis of late July/early August forced the Government to undo nearly all its strategy over the first half of 1986 to gradually bring down interest rates, as it tightened fiscal and wages policy. Now, the Government is almost back to where it was when it hiked up interest rates to halt last November's currency crisis.

The financial pressures dramatized in the crises of 1985/6 kept the restrictive trend in policy in place over the next two years. There were further bouts of selling pressure on the foreign exchanges, notably at the time of the July 1987 election campaign[7] and again after the October stock-market crash. But the general trend of the Australian dollar was upwards; by the autumn of 1988 it had reversed two-thirds of its real depreciation of 1985 and 1986.

In order to assess the overall impact of international financial deregulation, we will analyse in turn fiscal policy, monetary policy, the exchange rate, and the pattern of capital movements.

III.2. Fiscal Policy

As already described, the announced cuts in the budget deficit in the early years of the Hawke Government concealed a rise in the structural deficit for the general government sector of some 4.5% of GDP between 1982 and 1985, one of the most expansionary episodes of fiscal policy in any OECD country in the 1980s. Nevertheless, in 1985 the deficit was only some 3% of GDP, below the OECD average. Australia's ratio of gross public debt to GDP was one of the lowest in the OECD, and it ranked in the bottom half of net debt ratios as well. Moreover, according to the OECD's calculations (Chouraqui *et al.* 1986) Australia's mid-1980s level of public-sector deficit would not lead to a long-term rise in the debt ratio. Accordingly the sustained squeeze on government spending, which reduced the general government deficit to zero in 1988 (via a 2.5% of GDP fall in the structural deficit) cannot be justified on the grounds that the deficit was excessive in relation to other comparable countries. Whilst many of the tax measures (capital gains tax, business expenses, more effective monitoring of evasion, etc.—see OECD 1987; 1988) introduced by Labour were of a progressive nature, it is likely that without the pressure of the financial markets they could have been used to fund additional welfare spending rather than retirement of the national debt. In return for extraordinary restraint in bargaining for take-home pay, workers received only modest improvements in the social wage (see Norris 1987), which in turn meant that the public services contributed little to the expansion of jobs and reduction in unemployment.

III.3. Monetary Policy

Soon after monetary targeting was abandoned, the Reserve Bank announced a 'checklist' approach whereby monetary aggregates, interest rates, and exchange rates were all assessed. There seems little doubt that the exchange rate has come to assume major importance in decisions over monetary policy. The strong increases in interest rates when the Australian dollar was under pressure and the downward creep in rates during periods of recovery (early 1986 and 1987) are evidence for this. It is also confirmed by the references to the exchange rate in the Reserve Bank's own explanations of its actions, of which the following is a clear example:

> Monetary policy was tightened sharply on two occasions during 1986/87. In the period leading up to the Budget in August 1986, there was widespread uncertainty and lack of confidence. The exchange rate became the pressure point. A further major fall in the value of the Australian dollar at that time would have been unhelpful both practically and psychologically. The fall in the Australian dollar over the previous 18 months had provided an adequate basis for progressively correcting Australia's external accounts—if other policies were adjusted appropriately and business attitudes responded. Changes in other policy instruments were still to be announced; until they were, options were few. Monetary policy had to be tightened abruptly. The Bank took the unusual step of raising its rediscount rate ahead of the market rate to signal the tightening; market interest rates rose sharply; and large sales of foreign exchange took place out of reserves. (Reserve Bank of Australia, *Annual Report*, 1987: 12)

The impact of interest rates on investment is as controversial in Australia as elsewhere. What cannot be denied is that real interest rates have been very high in Australia, running about the same as the average for the biggest seven OECD countries, with the long-term real rate being about 2 percentage points higher in 1985. Real investment has been the most signal failure of the Government's strategy, with the resultant slow growth in productivity condemning workers to (at best) continuing stagnation of living standards.[8] Moreover, the interest rate and exchange rate uncertainty, which has undoubtedly been exacerbated by the abolition of exchange controls and resulting vulnerability of policy to the vicissitudes of international financial confidence, must have further contributed to the weakness of fixed investment.

III.4. The Exchange Rate

The very fact of interest rate policy being geared towards the exchange rate is itself evidence of the float being 'dirty', as we have already seen. Reserve Bank intervention has also been much more extensive than intended. After the crises of early 1985, the RB stoutly maintained that 'it did not take a view on where the dollar should settle, nor did it seek to support or produce any particular exchange rate outcome. The main object was to keep in touch with the market, to ascertain the nature and strength of the factors at work and to reduce the degree of volatility. This approach still resulted in substantial net sales of foreign exchange by the Bank' (*Annual Report*, 1985: 8). The estimates it gave were of sales of around $US250m. in both February and April. The November 1985 crisis saw intervention of nearly $US400m., again with the object of 'testing the pressures at work and their strength' (RB *Bulletin*, February 1986, p. 10). Intervention was much heavier in the July–August 1986 crisis (some $US1.2bn. net sales over the two months) and more concentrated still in January 1987 ($US1.2bn. in a few days); it was estimated at $2bn. in the days after the stock-market crash.

Whilst it is true that the external environment has been more turbulent than anticipated (notably the gyrations of the US dollar), this heavy management of the exchange rate was obviously a retreat from the extreme free-market optimism evinced by the Campbell Committee and more widely at the time of the float. The notion that the market should be free to determine the exchange rate supposed either that speculation would be stabilizing or that the exchange rate did not matter much. Optimism as to the former proposition was still being expressed early in 1985 by the then deputy governor of the Reserve Bank: 'so far our experience bears out the advice of the Committee of Inquiry that private sector holdings of foreign assets, and foreign holdings of domestic assets could be factors of stability rather than simply a possible source of speculative flows across the exchanges' (RB *Bulletin*, May 1985, p. 726). A couple of years later his successor admitted: 'Our market, like other foreign exchange markets, is a highly strung piece of equipment, prone to react suddenly—sometimes violently—to changes in the news, fundamental or otherwise' (*AFR*, 11 December 1987).

The problem, as Keating admitted in a speech in London in November 1985, was that 'In today's world, decisions taken in the great financial centres like London and New York significantly affect our very open financial market, and, through that, the Australian economy' (*Euromoney* supplement, February 1986, p. 18).

Although the Bank has firmly denied that it has sought to maintain a particular rate, 'by the latter part of 1986 however it was generally believed that the clean float had been dirtied—first by the authorities selling foreign exchange to prevent the $A/$US rate going below 0.60 and later by them buying foreign exchange to prevent it bouncing back above 0.67. That "ceiling" gradually increased into the 70 per cent range in the first half of 1987 (as the US dollar grandually weakened) and further possible increases were prevented by allowing interest rates to fall' (Davis 1987: 35). Discussion about the desirability of abandoning the attempt to cap the dollar (by this time around 0.73) was overtaken by the stock-market crash and the huge Reserve Bank intervention it provoked.

By March 1988, however, the post-crash fall in the dollar had been reversed. By August 1988 a further 18% real revaluation had taken place, and the Australian dollar's real rate had lost practically two-thirds of the increased competitiveness that had resulted from the succession of dollar crises. If the initial fall in the exchange rate was necessary, as many argued, to restore competitiveness to Australia's manufacturing industry, then the subsequent rise during 1988 carried disastrous implications. If the earlier fall was *not* dictated by longer-term considerations, then it has simply had disorganizing and wasteful effects on the pattern of production.

The contrast with Sweden, where the early 1980s devaluations, undertaken deliberately, were succeeded by several years of relative exchange rate stability, is striking. Whilst Swedish exchange controls by no means gave the authorities complete policy autonomy, they certainly contributed to the much less erratic pattern than in Australia.

III.5. Capital Flows

The period since the abolition of exchange controls has seen an enormous increase in capital flows. After showing how substantial these have been (Table 5.1), we indicate their implications for Australia's balance of payments and vulnerability to the vagaries of the financial markets.

TABLE 5.1 Investment inflows and outflows, 1982/3–1986/7

	Australia's investment overseas		Investment in Australia	
	Flows ($Abn.)	Flows as % of 1982 stock	Flows ($Abn.)	Flows as % of 1982 stock
Official	5.7	73	15.9	262
Direct	9.5	162	12.7	47
Portfolio				
Equities	6.9	3,811	4.9	115
Fixed-interest	5.0	725	45.7	326
Trade credit	1.5	128	0.7	40
TOTAL	28.6	212	79.9	144

Source: ABS (1987*a*: tables 2 and 4); preliminary data for June quarter 1987.

Purged of the revaluation effects in the stocks data, the outflows of capital have been substantially greater in relation to initial stocks than have inflows.[9] A little over one-third of the gross inflow has been required to fund the outflow of investment from Australia rather than the current-account deficit. Moreover, this proportion has been rising, and reached one-half in 1986/7. Whilst one-fifth of the outflow has been due to accumulation of additional reserves, the rest represents direct and portfolio investment in both equities and fixed-interest; the portfolio flows in particular have grown explosively since the abolition of controls. As Hogan (1987) emphasizes, the fact that, in the absence of exchange controls, assets overseas cannot be readily mobilized to repay borrowings overseas means that the gross debt is a relevant measure of exposure. This gross debt, and thus Australia's external financial vulnerability, has been substantially increased to finance Australian investment overseas. The implications of this for monetary policy were underlined by the OECD (1988: 33):

> The structure of net capital inflows has been different from that in the 1970s. The bulk of financing has taken the form of borrowing abroad rather than direct investment inflows. The diversification of portfolios after the lifting of most exchange controls in 1983 has accentuated the pattern, as larger outflows have had to be compensated by increased gross borrowing abroad. A major task of monetary policy has been to attract adequate capital inflows and retain the growing share of short-term funds.

Two further effects of this outflow of capital, permitted by the abolition of exchange controls, are worth considering. First, borrowing overseas at fixed interest in order to invest in overseas equities or direct investment will have an immediate deleterious effect on the balance of payments. This is because the interest costs on borrowing are much higher than the dividend yield on the shares (or remitted profits on direct investment). In 1985/6, for example, the total nominal return on Australian portfolio investment overseas was 2.8%, whilst the average interest cost of Australian borrowing overseas was 9.2% (and the marginal cost probably a good deal higher). Thus every billion dollars of Australian portfolio investment, which had to be financed at the aggregate level by overseas borrowing, probably cost the balance of payments over $60m. Including a similar effect for direct investment, the outflows of capital in the five years under consideration must have cost the current account of the balance of payments (as conventionally measured without full accounting for capital gains and losses) at least $1bn. This figure is rising fast, and has made a significant contribution to increasing the burden of net overseas income payments. The outflow has obviously also contributed to pushing the exchange rate lower on average or keeping Australian interest rates higher, as well as exacerbating the recurrent exchange rate crises. To the extent that the government had used monetary policy to try to manage the exchange rate within the band it has thought appropriate, then the capital outflows have exacerbated the effects on domestic interest rates.

Finally, on the liabilities side of the balance sheet, the fact that the greater part of the borrowing necessary to fund the current-account deficit has been undertaken by the private sector has meant that the terms have been dictated by private self-interest. Most of the borrowing has been in overseas currencies, but there has been no co-ordination possible of the portfolio of currencies in which the borrowing took place, or of its maturity composition. The Australian dollar component of this borrowing, especially the marketable element, represents a dangerous 'overhang' which can, and has, put immense pressure on the currency in times of strain. Private borrowing in overseas currencies also creates huge currency risks for the private-sector borrowers, and a rush to cover these risks on the forward market is a further source of potential pressure on the exchange rate. Moreover, the maturity composition of the debt is short—more than 15% of the gross debt being repayable within one year, even leaving out of account the much shorter-term borrowings of the trading banks (Hogan 1987: table 5). This increases financial vulnerability. The social costs of all these financial transactions can therefore deviate enormously from the private costs. Borrowing overseas seems much too sensitive an activity to be dependent on private-market decisions as to how much to invest outside Australia (which affects total borrowing necessary) and as to term structure and currency composition.

IV. CONCLUSIONS

(i) The exchange rate/exchange control system operating when the Hawke Government was elected was not working effectively.

(ii) Whilst some technical changes had to be made to the system of exchange rate fixing then in force, the move to a 'freely' floating rate, was naïve from an economic point of view, and had to be abandoned in favour of heavy intervention.

(iii) Even the decision to float the rate freely did not imply abolishing exchange controls. The result of abandoning controls on outflows, and funding the overseas deficit largely by unregulated private borrowing, has been to increase substantially Australia's vulnerability to exchange rate crises. Whilst the exchange controls in operation in 1983 did not prevent short-term speculative movements, they undoubtedly reduced them, and the case was never made convincingly that the controls could not be tightened up significantly. The subsequent course of the exchange rate has been dominated by capital flows, and the succession of downward lurches, followed by substantial real revaluation, has made economic restructuring much more difficult.

(iv) The decision to float, and more especially to abolish exchange controls, gave the financial markets enormously enhanced power over the Labour Government's policies. The exchange rate crises which repeatedly buffeted the Government had a significant effect on the course of fiscal and monetary policy. Given the balance-of-payments difficulties, the possibilities for sustained fiscal expansion were limited. But the restriction required by the financial markets and implemented by the Labour Government since 1985 was faster, and went further, than would otherwise have been 'necessary', and interest rates have been forced higher. In this sense, progress in reducing unemployment has certainly been limited by international financial integration.

(v) The weak investment growth reflects in part the high level of interest rates, and exchange rate and interest rate uncertainties, for which international financial deregulation (in Australia and more broadly) must take part of the blame. This failure of capital accumulation has meant that rapid employment growth has taken place at the expense of take-home pay, rather than in conjunction with rising productivity and living standards in the broad sense (including improvements to the social wage and reduced hours of work).

Finally, we have not set out to refute the view, widely held amongst Australian observers and officials, that international financial deregulation played a decisive role in fostering the understanding that the Australian economy had to make painful adjustments to meet adverse external circumstances. In this view, the accord between Government and trade unions would never have held without the dramatic impact of foreign-exchange crises, and this fact outweighs their other costs in terms of possibly over-restrictive and panicky policies. Even if the drama of international financial pressure *did* help to hold down real wages, to conclude that this was the best outcome would imply that rapid employment growth could only be achieved at the expense of stagnation in take-home pay and the social wage. Higher investment would render such a conclusion false. The fundamental weakness of the economy under Labour has been the failure of its orthodox financial policies to engineer the expansion of investment, which is universally agreed to be a precondition for a durable restructuring of the Australian economy. Exchange controls are not a sufficient condition for such an expansion; they may well prove to be necessary components of serious industrial policies in countries with a relatively weak manufacturing base.

APPENDIX

Financial Innovations and Exchange Controls

In the unofficial hedge market, transactors ineligible for the official forward market, because their transactions were of a capital nature or because of their failure to request forward cover within seven days, were able to match their risks with private counter-parties. The bank handling the deal could not itself balance the risk through its own foreign-exchange transactions since it could not deal in deposits in foreign currencies. Syntec found that (in 1978) the hedge market may have reduced the official forward market by about 6%, but it was growing very rapidly and, according to the Reserve Bank, by October 1983 the official market was accounting for less than 20% of forward and hedge covering.[10] Reliance on directly matching risks left the hedge market (in 1980) very thin with a 'tendency to become one-sided when expectations of future movements in the $A/$US exchange rate shift firmly in one direction' (Syntec 1982: 73). Syntec noted that 'the same exchange controls which limit the development of the hedge market [i.e. banning of foreign currency deposits] are those which also limit speculative capital movements on the spot exchange market' (p. 73).

Syntec suggested that the banning of non-trade transactions from official forward cover was to some extent vitiated by the hedge market: it allowed trade-related risks which would have gone to the official market to be matched against non-trade risks. This argument is worth considering because it has been argued that this private hedge market had a decisive influence:

> The scope provided by the market to cover capital risks has made the Australian economy more open to destabilising capital flows which exchange controls

could no longer stop. To that extent, the hedge market was perhaps the prime catalyst in the inexorable process of change which culminated in the deregulation of both the forward and spot markets in late 1983. (Lewis and Polasek 1985: 385)

The problem caused by the hedge market was that, when speculative pressure built up, the Reserve Bank was left holding a very one-sided forward exchange book as exporters were tempted by the larger premium (on foreign exchange) ruling in the hedge market to cover their exchange risk there. This drying up of the supply of forward exchange left the RB being obliged to supply importers' needs. The net result was just as though the RB were supplying forward exchange for *non-eligible* risks whilst importers and exporters supplied one another.

The argument seems exaggerated, however. It presumes that all the exporters supplying forward cover to the hedge market would otherwise have covered with the RB. In the situation postulated, of widespread fears of a devaluation of the Australian dollar, the exporters might very well have kept an open position themselves. In effect the hedge market, by offering a higher premium on forward exchange, allowed exporters to turn an uncertain gain from a possible devaluation (if they kept an open position) into a certain, but smaller, gain. Those with a capital risk could insure themselves at a cost. The fundamental reason that the RB was left with such a one-sided 'book' was the one-sided nature of the 'bet', not that all other suppliers of forward exchange were tempted away.

It seems rather inconsistent to stress the importance of leads and lags in generating capital flows (the lags being precisely the actions of exporters to delay their current receipts) and to suppose that the same exporters would, simultaneously, automatically secure forward cover for these receipts. Indeed, the very reference to the market becoming 'thin' suggests just such a shortage of potential for covering capital risks when exchange rate expectations became one-sided. Of course, the hedge market must have attracted some exporters who would otherwise have covered with the RB, thus leaving the RB to cover larger risks; but the extent of this could not be measured by the extent of operations in the hedge market, or even exporters' participation in it. Moreover, there is a difference between the Reserve Bank absorbing a higher level of forward commitments on the one hand, and being forced to supply spot currency on the other (as it would have had to do if banks were able to cover the risk themselves). Of course, *if* the capital flight forced a depreciation, the capital loss to the Reserve Bank (and gain to the hedgers/speculators) would be identical. But the loss of reserves, and thus any immediate pressure to depreciate was postponed, leaving the authorities with the option of taking preventative measures.

Whilst Syntec did not emphasize the private hedge market as a fundamental problem for exchange control, it did point to a parallel problem in the overseas market for the Australian dollar (the 'Euro-$A', in effect). They posited a situation where an overseas bank wanted to provide forward cover for an overseas company with an Australian dollar exposure in Australia. Control on fixed-interest outflows from Australia would prevent the overseas bank from providing cover by borrowing Australian dollars in Australia at the domestic Australian interest rate. Instead, the rate on Euro-$A deposits would rise above the domestic rate, leading (so Syntec argued) to a greater incentive for Australians and others to evade controls. A particular example cited was that overseas banks could in effect adjust their investments in the Australian subsidiaries (though no convincing argument was given as to why this could not be monitored effectively). Syntec said: 'We conclude therefore that the continued development of the offshore market for the Australian dollar will tend to erode the ability of the authorities to maintain control of capital flows into and out of Australia.' But, again, it was not the existence of the overseas market for the Australian dollar which made it worthwhile to evade controls, but the expected depreciation of that dollar; the higher interest rate on Euro-$A simply reflected that expectation. Indeed, as has already been pointed out, covered rates consistently deviated from parity, implying that controls still had an effect despite the temptations posed by the Euro-$A market.

Of course, the multiplication of financial instruments (in this sense the Euro-$A resembles the private hedge market) may have attracted some additional transactors into the market by parcelling up expected gains and risks in more variegated ways. But the conclusion that this or that innovation was inevitably undermining controls presumed that little could be done in response.

NOTES

1. Set up in Jan. 1979 with 5 members, drawn from the financial sector, its final report was published in Sept. 1981.
2. After 8 Dec., the only serious controls which remained were:

   (i) Over foreign direct investment in Australia (and it was noteworthy that 2 weeks after the decision to float it was announced that the Australian Labour Party's policy of increasing the required domestic participation in mining investment from 50% to 51%, and its extension to manufacturing, was dropped).
   (ii) Over holdings of $A by overseas central banks, monetary authorities, and commercial banks, on the grounds that Australia did not want the $A turned into a reserve currency; according to the RB, this latter restriction was aimed at reducing 'short-term flows based on purely "market" considerations' (in which case it was not clear why it applied only to overseas financial institutions).
   (iii) Although the forward market was freed from official intervention, only trade transactions were eligible for cover in the forward market.

   The latter 2 controls were subsequently cancelled.
3. All data in this paragraph are from Commonwealth Government (1988), OECD (1988), ABS (1987*b*).
4. By 1987, average real earnings were some 4% below the 1982 level; the award rates handed down by the Arbitration Commission showed a substantially larger fall.
5. The Government allowed foreign banks authority to operate (16 licences were eventually granted in Feb. 1985), with Keating meeting Labour Party opposition by claiming ingeniously that such institutions had 'led the indus-

trial regeneration of Germany and Japan' (*AFR*, 7 July 1984). This decision provoked much more discussion than abolition of exchange controls (see the interesting analysis by Harper 1986). Whilst it contributed to the integration of the Australian financial system into international markets, its significance, from the point of view of the macroeconomic concerns of this paper, is rather limited. Such integration was permitted by the abolition of existing controls, and would have happened without the direct involvement in Australia of overseas banks.

6. Keating had been named Treasurer of the Year in 1984 by *Euromoney* magazine.
7. On this occasion, as well as intervening heavily, the RB took the 'highly unusual step of publicly reassuring foreign investors that it was supporting the currency' (*AFR*, 9 July 1987). The *AFR* noted that the authorities feared a repeat of the 1983 election flight of capital when 'ironically, investors feared a Labour victory. This year, the money market's bogeymen reside in the Howard [Liberal] camp.' This must have been one of the few instances in the history of social democracy that the speculators were frightened of Conservative victory!
8. It is striking that the proportion of corporate profits paid out as interest and dividends is extremely high in Australia. Over 1983/4 to 1985/6, net interest and dividends paid by private corporate trading enterprises was an extraordinary 73% of net operating surplus. After deducting taxation, this has left undistributed profits making a negative contribution to net investment (in contrast to the positive one in the UK and USA). There are complex problems of inflation accounting involved, and shareholders may have benefited from the high gearing; moreover, negative undistributed income (revealed by the new national accounts which value depreciation at replacement cost) has been a feature of the last 10 years, so cannot be blamed exclusively on recent interest rate policies. Nevertheless, it is hard to imagine that the cash flow implications of this have not been a contributory factor in the weakness of investment (see e.g. the article by John Brunner, chief economist of Broken Hill Proprietary, in *AFR*, 12 Aug. 1986).
9. The data in Table 5.1 add together flow data from different years when different exchange rates were operating; in this sense the data are indicative rather than precise.
10. In 1978 about half the transactions in the hedge market were ineligible for the official market, the other half tempted out by better rates, and (surprisingly) the great majority were apparently linked to trade rather than capital transactions. Unfortunately, there seems to be no comprehensive survey of the hedge market for 1983.

6

Structural Determinants and Economic Effects of Capital Controls in OECD Countries

GERALD A. EPSTEIN AND JULIET B. SCHOR

I. INTRODUCTION

The use of capital controls in the OECD has now reached its lowest point in over fifty years. The European Community is preparing to dismantle remaining controls in 1990. North America and Japan have virtually no controls. Poor countries are being pressured by the international agencies and the USA to give up their controls. The weight of respectable opinion is solidly behind the free movement of capital across national boundaries. Today's situation stands in stark contrast both to the actual practice and to the intellectual climate of forty years ago.

For many years, proponents of controls have held that they create a space for national policy autonomy which would otherwise be eroded by international financial integration. Will decontrol make independent monetary policy impossible for the nations of Europe, as many fear? Will it undermine the possibility for left-wing political action, by facilitating capital flight as a response to anti-business policies? Explaining the recent anti-control ideology is not an easy task. Some governments have almost a half century of what appears to be reasonably good experience with controls. Why are these regulations now being abandoned?

The intellectual case against controls derives largely from two arguments, both of which are firmly rooted in long-standing neoclassical principles. The first is that restrictions on capital are ineffective, because investors anticipating profit opportunities will invariably circumvent them. Governments must always keep one step ahead of clever citizens. The second claim is that controls cause inefficiencies which misdirect investment and limit competition. The ultimate result is a reduction in productivity and output growth. These two arguments now constitute the conventional wisdom on controls.

In the pages which follow, we survey the literature on the effects and effectiveness of controls in order to assess whether the conventional wisdom is actually very wise. We hope to show that the evidence against controls is far from conclusive. Therefore, the mystery of decontrol remains.

The paper begins with a discussion of the Bretton Woods debates over controls and a brief history of controls in the OECD. We then move to a discussion of the literature on controls, in order to determine whether or not they have actually been effective. In the third section we present a simple Keynesian model which shows how controls might affect macroeconomic outcomes. On the basis of this model, we develop a 'political economy of controls'. In Section IV, we test the implications of this political economy by assessing the factors which determine countries' 'propensity to control'. Our findings suggest that the current episode of decontrol may well be politically motivated.

II. CONTROLS IN HISTORICAL PERSPECTIVE

II.1. Controls and the Bretton Woods Institutions

In the planning for a post-war international economic order, the question of controls was at the heart of the alternatives under consideration. Would the new monetary institution permit countries to enact controls on current and capital-account transactions? Answers to this question were predictable. What we may call the 'European' position (as exemplified by Keynes and the original White Plan) was that controls were necessary for national policy and political autonomy. The 'American' view (as exemplified by the State Department and US financiers) was opposed to controls, for reasons of principle, politics, and competition, and in order to deny policy autonomy to expansionist countries.

Keynes's overriding goal was to construct an international monetary system which would permit Britain to pursue full-employment policies.[1] In the 1930s this objective led him to advocate bilateralism and a high level of government planning in international economic transactions. But this course was clearly not acceptable to the Americans, for whom multilateralism and non-discrimination were non-negotiable demands. In the event, Keynes's plan (the International Clearing Union) was consistent with the American objectives, but was also capable of accommodating full employment.[2] The details of the plan are well known. Its novel feature was that the onus of adjustment for disequilibrium in balance of payments was to be shared by deficit and creditor countries, thereby avoiding the deflationary impulses of the gold standard. Keynes was unequivocal on the need for capital controls. In the Clearing Union plan he wrote (Keynes 1980*b*: 52):

> I share the view, that central control of capital movements, both inward and outward, should be a permanent feature of the post-war system—at least so far as we are concerned. If control is to be effective, it probably involves the *machinery* of exchange control for *all* transactions, even though a general open licence is given to all remittances in respect of current trade.

Later, in 1942, in a letter to Roy Harrod (1980*b*: 148–9):

> I disagree most strongly with your view that the control of capital movements may very possibly be unnecessary . . . Surely in the post-war years there is hardly a country in which we ought not to expect keen political discussions affecting the position of the wealthier classes and the treatment of private property. If so, there will be a number of people constantly taking fright because they think the degree of leftism in one country looks for the time being likely to be greater than somewhere else.
>
> [Moreover,] you overlook the most fundamental long-run theoretical reason. Freedom of capital movements is an essential part of the old *laissez-faire* system and assumes that it is right and desirable to have an equalisation of interest rates in all parts of the world . . . In my view the whole management of the domestic economy depends upon being free to have the appropriate rate of interest without reference to the rates prevailing elsewhere in the world. Capital control is a corollary to this.

White's original plan was close to Keynes' on this issue, as he too was concerned about politically motivated capital flight (see Block 1977). However, White's plan was quickly scuttled. It was replaced by a more politically feasible, 'American' document which had no presumption in favour of controls.

US sentiment against controls had been building for a number of years. We may identify two distinct motivations behind the American position. The first concerns intra-capitalist competition and the second stemmed from orthodox economic principles.

In the 1930s, many of the nation's largest corporations had abandoned their traditional protectionist stance. The Democratic Party soon followed (see Ferguson 1984). The State Department had been pushing hard for non-discrimination, free trade, protection of overseas investment, and multilateralism. One rationale behind the American position was clear. Because the USA was the dominant international actor, it stood to gain the most from an unrestricted trading system. The Americans were absolutely determined to dismantle the British system of imperial preference, as well as all other preferential trading arrangements (see Cantor and Schor 1987). An open trading system became especially important after the war once US policy-makers reached a consensus on the need to run an export surplus. A $5–10bn. export surplus (rather than a Keynesian domestic programme) became the policy of choice as the way to avert a return to depression.

An additional argument against controls came from financiers who opposed both the Keynes and the White Plans, and supported the Williams key currency plan. They were looking forward to an era where dollar-based financing would dominate the financial landscape. Free movement of capital was central to their vision.

The weight of the American position was sufficient to reduce the prominence of controls in the final plan for the IMF. The Fund's Articles of Agreement took the view that controls should be removed as soon as possible. In view of the economic difficulties facing member countries, however, they would be permitted to retain controls. After five years, those countries which still had controls on current account would be obliged to consult with the Fund annually on progress toward their removal. Abolition of controls on capital was not expected during this time, although under certain conditions the Fund could demand that they be dismantled.[3] In general, the Articles embodied a presumption against controls, but there was no mechanism to enforce compliance.

Over the years, this basic ambiguity has remained. The Fund, representing the American position, has been committed in principle to an absence of restrictions, and uses its influence at times to further this goal. In practice it has tolerated the existence of controls in deference to individual country preferences. We turn now to an examination of those controls.

II.2. A Brief History of Controls in the OECD, 1950–1986[4]

In most of the countries of what was to become the OECD, exchange and other controls were introduced in the 1930s and 1940s, and remained in force in the early post-war period. Of the sixteen countries considered in this study,[5] only the USA and Canada had no controls during this time. In 1950 the IMF began publishing an annual summary of restrictions. This survey indicated a wide variety of restrictive practices in use. These included:

(i) Exchange control restrictions: restrictions on the use of foreign exchange, including the existence of multiple exchange rates, and the existence of bilateral arrangements;

(ii) Restrictions on current account: licensing requirements for imports and exports, requirements of advance deposits for imports, surrender of export proceeds;

(iii) Restrictions on capital account: restrictions on non-resident accounts, licensing of inward and outward flows of capital in various forms (bank loans, securities, bank deposits, banknotes, real estate), special reserve requirements or other regulations on banks' foreign positions.

Restrictions on current account and the use of foreign exchange were substantially and rapidly reduced after 1952. By the end of 1958 convertibility had been established in Europe. There was less easing of controls on capital. However, Article 3 of the Treaty of Rome committed the EEC to a liberalized environment for capital transactions as well as goods and services. In 1960 and 1962 the EEC passed two directives on capital movements, which mandated the full liberalization of short-term capital movements and conditional liberalization for long-term capital. A marked reduction in restrictions followed. Nearly all countries eased restrictions on non-resident accounts which had been blocked. Curbs on repatriation of income were reduced. In Germany, Switzerland, Belgium, and the Netherlands, capital markets were either totally or virtually freed. Italy, France, Japan, Austria, Denmark, and Finland liberalized to varying degrees. The major exception was the UK, which heightened restrictions on capital outflow beginning in 1961.

By 1964 and 1965 progress toward liberalization had been halted. Facing large capital outflows, the USA introduced the interest equalization tax in September 1964, and added restrictions on overseas investment and lending in 1965. The US outflows also prompted measures by various European countries to limit inflows. At one time or another during this period, Germany, Italy, France, Switzerland, the Netherlands, Sweden, and Japan took action to reduce inflows. The UK continued to increase the severity of its restrictions on outflows. As an indication that the easing was no longer proceeding, we may note that the third EEC directive on capital market liberalization, although introduced in 1967, was not implemented for ten years.

The 1970s brought new strains. The breakdown of the Bretton Woods parities in the early 1970s led many countries to enact capital controls to avert foreign-exchange crises. Many of these regulations were immediately rescinded once relative calm had been restored to foreign-exchange markets following the Smithsonian Agreement. However, the subsequent oil shocks, labour unrest, and world recession led to a tightening of controls in various countries.

By 1979 the pendulum had begun to move against controls again. Most likely this was part of the general move toward deregulation and *laissez-faire* which prevailed in the 1980s. Japan and the UK lifted all restrictions in 1979. Australia completely liberalized in 1985 (see Chapter 5 above). However, controls did not disappear from the landscape, and in the opinion of some observers (Rogoff 1985; Giavazzi and Giovannini 1986) they have been essential to the successful functioning of the European Monetary System.

The most recent development was the dramatic and unexpected announcement in June 1988 that the EC ministers had agreed to a complete removal of capital controls by 1990.[6] This action was taken in conjunction with the more general trade liberalization proposed for 1992.

Whether this is the last word on capital controls in Europe remains to be seen. The Italians have inserted a clause stating that countries which experience precipitous outflows of capital can reinstitute controls for up to six months pending the approval of the other countries. Utilization of this clause will depend on the degree of policy divergence among the member countries. At the present time, the system embodies an inconsistency, which is that it is simultaneously attempting to achieve fixed exchange rates, free capital mobility, free trade, and independent national economic policy. The latest move seems designed to force economic policy convergence and progress toward European monetary union.

II.3. Index of Capital Controls, 1967–1986

In order to answer at least some of the questions posed in the Introduction, it is necessary to have a measure of capital controls. For the most part, the existing literature has taken an indirect approach in that the effectiveness of capital controls has been inferred from estimates of covered-interest differentials (see e.g. Frankel and MacArthur 1987; Ito 1986; Dooley and Isard 1980; or Giavazzi and Pagano 1985). However, other variables, such as political risk or expectations of the future path of controls, can lead to deviations from covered interest parity. Therefore it would be desirable to have independent evidence of the existence of controls.

We have constructed an index of capital controls from the IMF annual reports on exchange arrangements and exchange restrictions. We have calculated the index from 1967 to 1986.[7] This index is composed of restrictions on capital-account transactions and special exchange rates for some or all capital transactions and/or some or all invisibles.

Table 6.1 presents the index for the sixteen countries for twenty years. Each entry represents the number of restrictive practices in each country in that year (maximum = 2). The final row is the total score for each country (maximum = 40) and the final column is the total number of restrictive practices in each year (maximum = 32).

The index shows a wide variation in the use of controls. Some countries (Italy, Norway, France, Finland, and Denmark) have consistently used more than one form of control. Other countries (Sweden) have used controls continuously, but only one type. Some countries switched from widespread controls to free markets (Japan, UK). And finally, a few countries have not used controls at all during this period. (USA, Germany, Switzerland). The index also clearly reveals the less frequent use of current-account restrictions in the OECD in recent years.

We should also note an idiosyncracy of the IMF definition. It does not include some practices which might reasonably be considered capital controls. For Germany and Switzerland, these are the measures against capital inflows which were in force during much of the 1960s and 1970s. For the USA, they are the interest equalization tax and voluntary restraints on overseas investment. Finally, we might also note the restric-

TABLE 6.1. *Capital controls index*

Year	1968	1969	1970	1971	1972	1973	1974	1975	1976	1977	1978	1979	1980	1981	1982	1983	1984	1985	1986	1987	Total
Australia	2	1	1	1	1	1	1	1	1	1	1	1	1	1	1	1	1	0	0	0	18
Austria	1	1	1	1	1	1	1	2	1	1	1	1	1	1	1	1	1	1	1	1	21
Belgium	1	1	1	1	1	1	1	1	1	1	1	1	1	1	1	1	1	1	1	1	20
Canada	0	0	0	0	0	0	0	0	0	0	0	0	0	0	0	0	0	0	0	0	0
Denmark	1	1	1	1	1	1	1	1	1	1	1	1	1	1	1	1	1	1	1	1	20
Finland	1	1	1	1	1	1	1	1	1	1	1	1	1	1	1	1	1	1	1	1	20
France	0	1	2	2	2	2	2	1	1	1	1	1	1	1	1	1	1	1	1	0	23
Germany	0	0	0	0	0	1	0	0	0	0	0	0	0	0	0	0	0	0	0	0	1
Italy	1	1	1	1	1	2	2	1	2	2	2	2	2	2	2	1	0	0	0	0	25
Japan	1	1	1	1	1	1	1	1	1	1	1	1	0	0	0	0	0	0	0	0	12
Netherlands	1	1	1	1	1	2	2	1	0	0	0	0	0	0	0	0	0	0	0	0	10
Norway	1	1	1	1	1	1	1	1	1	1	1	1	1	1	1	1	1	1	1	1	20
Sweden	1	1	1	1	1	1	1	1	1	1	1	1	1	1	1	1	1	1	1	0	19
Switzerland	0	0	0	0	0	0	0	0	0	0	0	0	0	0	0	0	0	0	0	0	0
UK	2	2	2	2	2	2	2	2	2	2	2	2	0	0	0	0	0	0	0	0	24
USA	0	0	0	0	0	0	0	0	0	0	0	0	0	0	0	0	0	0	0	0	0
All countries	13	13	14	14	14	17	16	14	13	13	13	13	10	10	10	9	8	7	7	5	

Source: IMF (1950–87). See text for details.

tions on foreign ownership of Canadian assets which resulted from the Canadian movement for economic nationalism in the 1970s.

Because there is clearly a degree of arbitrariness involved in an index of this kind, we have chosen to use the IMF classifications as they stand. However, we have also created an alternate index which takes account of the restrictions on short-term capital flows in the USA, Germany, and Switzerland. In our econometric estimates we have used both indices.

A second shortcoming of the index is that it does not measure the intensity of control. This problem can be seen in the pattern of the index during the 1970s, which is widely acknowledged as a period of intensification. Countries such as France, Italy, and the UK show little increase in the measure because they already had controls in place. At present, there is no way to avoid this problem.

III. EFFICACY OF CONTROLS

A common theme in the literature on capital controls is that their efficacy is quite limited. The following quote (Walter 1976: 170) has many cousins:

> Due to evasion, capital controls . . . are neither able to stem waves of short-term speculation, nor to lead to the desired long-term results. They merely have a limited effect during a transitional period while market operators are searching for methods of evasion.[8]

A closely related point is that evasion forces governments to continually extend the controls to try to plug the dikes. This proliferation raises the efficiency costs of controls.[9]

There is an existing literature which has attempted to assess the efficacy of capital controls. This literature typically measures efficacy in two ways: by the extent to which controls allow a country's interest rates to differ from international interest rates; and, less commonly (under fixed exchange rates), by the degree to which controls prevent international capital movements from offsetting central-bank credit operations (the so-called offset coefficient).

Standard theory suggests that, if capital controls are effective, they allow governments to maintain a domestic interest rate which diverges from the comparable international rate of interest, holding constant risk and transaction costs. One set of studies has attempted to control for exchange rate risk by analysing onshore and offshore rates denominated in the same currency. These studies find that domestic and offshore nominal interest rates do not equalize for countries which have capital controls. Giavazzi and Giovannini (1986) report significant differentials for Italy and France in the 1980s. Ito (1986) found differentials for Japan during the 1970s. And Dooley and Isard (1980) found these differentials for Germany in the early 1970s. Claassen and Wyplosz (1982), using a measure of the stringency of capital controls in France during 1973–81, find that the more stringent the controls, the larger the differentials.

Where assets have been denominated in different currencies, other studies have held constant exchange rate risk by analysing covered interest parity relations. Early studies of this kind were done by Frenkel and Levich (1975; 1977; 1981), who find that in general covered-interest parity holds. Given that their results are at variance with nearly all the literature, it may be worth discussing them in detail. Frenkel and Levich argue that roughly 85% of the deviations from covered-interest parity between the US dollar and the pound sterling in the 1960s and 1970s can be explained by transactions costs in exchange and securities markets, except for a period of excessive turbulence in the late 1960s when less than 40% were so explained.[10] While a number of problems plague their analysis, the most serious concerns their estimate of transactions costs.

Since no direct measures of transactions costs are available, Frenkel and Levich's innovation was to estimate transactions costs from triangular arbitrage between the dollar and sterling, using either the Deutschmark or the Canadian dollar as the intermediate currency. They took the deviations from triangular arbitrage to be a measure of transactions costs. Yet it is unlikely that these deviations reflect transactions costs in a pure sense. Indeed, they are likely themselves to pick up the effects of risk and exchange controls.

As Frenkel and Levich showed in their 1977 paper, these transaction costs *rose* substantially during the 1960s and early 1970s, despite improvements in technology. It is likely that they reflect risk associated with the greater foreign-exchange instability in the latter period, as well as the increased use of exchange controls in the USA and Great Britain. Hence, the use of these costs overestimates the effects of transactions costs in a pure sense, and underestimates the deviations from covered-interest parity due to capital controls and the like.[11] These results must, therefore, be viewed sceptically.

A second study for the 1960s was done by Fase (1976). He found that countries with capital controls (France, Japan, Italy, and Belgium) had large deviations from covered-interest parity. (The Fase differentials are presented in Table 6.2.)

There is considerably more research using data from the 1970s and 1980s. Kasman and Pigott (1988) find that in both Japan and the UK covered-interest differentials fell sharply after the lifting of controls. In Germany, controls against inflows were also found to be effective.

Giavazzi and Pagano (1985) also calculated covered-interest rate differentials for France, Italy, Germany, and the Netherlands. Their results show large differentials for France and Italy. Germany had small positive

TABLE 6.2. *Covered-interest differentials (absolute values)*

Country	Fase (1961–72)	Frankel and McArthur (Sept.1982–Oct.1985)
Australia	n/a	.79
Austria	n/a	1.80
Belgium	.73	.32
Canada	.04	.13
Denmark	n/a	4.12
Finland	n/a	n/a
France	1.05	2.14
Germany	.43	.50
Italy	.65	.56
Japan	2.69	1.78
Netherlands	.32	.25
Norway	n/a	.65
Sweden	.16	n/a
Switzerland	.46	.06
UK	.20	.02
USA	—	—

Source: Covered-interest differentials calculated from Fase (1976: table 1, col.1) and Frankel (1987: table 5, col.2). In both cases, the reference country is the USA.

differentials, suggesting that capital controls were effective in limiting inflows. For the Netherlands, which had no controls, covered-interest differentials were effectively zero throughout the period. Similar results can be found in Giavazzi and Giovannini (1988). In a similar study, Ito (1986) found that when Japan had capital controls in place (1975–80), covered-interest parity failed to hold, whereas after controls were removed, he could not reject the hypothesis that covered-interest parity held.[12]

Rogoff (1985), using a different method, also tested for the effectiveness of capital controls in France and Italy within the European Monetary System. His paper analysed the extent to which capital controls were important in stabilizing exchange rates within the EMS, despite divergent macroeconomic policies and behaviours. He reasoned that, if capital controls were unimportant and if monetary policy co-ordination were solely responsible for reducing real exchange rate variability within the EMS, one might observe reductions in the variability of real interest rates among EMS members. He found, however, that the (conditional) variance of real interest rates between France and Germany and between Italy and Germany increased in the period of the EMS relative to the period before it. He concluded that capital controls must have played an important role in stabilizing real exchange rates within the EMS.

The studies just described deal exclusively with the OECD. Frankel and MacArthur (1987) present data on covered-interest differentials for twenty countries, including various countries of the South, during 1982–5. Casual inspection suggests that there is a high correlation between countries known to have capital controls and the existence of covered-interest differentials. (Table 6.2 presents these differentials for our sixteen countries.)

Some studies have looked at non-interest rate measures of the efficacy of capital controls. Claassen and Wyplosz (1982) show that, in France, the degree to which capital flows offset monetary policy (the offset coefficient) is smaller the greater the stringency of capital controls. In the case of Latin American debtors, Pastor (1990), using regression equations which explain capital flight, shows that countries with capital controls have significantly less capital flight than countries without controls.

The literature also provides evidence which bears on the issue of long-term evasion and proliferation. If controls were effectively evaded in the long term, one would expect to find that more stringent controls are necessary to maintain a given degree of segmentation. However, the findings by Claassen and Wyplosz suggest that, as more stringent controls were put in place in France, they had increased effects on interest differentials.[13] Our control index also provides evidence against the view that controls proliferate, as it records a marked downward trend in the use of controls. Within individual countries, periods of intensified control are followed by periods of less control. If anything, controls follow a cyclical pattern.

In this section we have tried to provide an answer to the question, 'Are controls effective?' It must be acknowledged that the literature on the OECD strongly supports an affirmative answer, if we mean by effectiveness an ability to maintain, for considerable periods of time, a domestic interest rate which diverges from rates prevailing outside the country. How can we reconcile this finding with the widespread perception that controls are ineffective?[14] First, we must distinguish between effectiveness, in the sense we have defined it, and evasion. The evidence surveyed here suggests, not that individuals do not evade controls (surely they do), but only that evasion is not sufficiently widespread to equalize interest rates. The perceptions of policy-makers that controls are 'ineffective' may be an expression of their judgement that levels of evasion have been unacceptable.

A second finding is that controls can impart some autonomy to domestic monetary policy under fixed-exchange rate systems, as measured by the offset coefficient, and capital flight.[15] Finally, our research suggests that the burden of proof surely lies on those who claim that proliferation and long-term ineffectiveness are inevitable results of controls.

IV. HOW DO CONTROLS WORK? A KEYNESIAN VIEW

Most of the discussion of the effects of capital controls has been based on neoclassical general-equilibrium models, according to which market interference can improve world welfare only in the event of market failure (Caves 1976; Claassen and Wyplosz 1982).[16] In the presence of imperfections which generate divergences between private and social rates of return, such as international tax differentials, second-best arguments for capital controls can be devised. However, as with all second-best arguments, the first-best response is to correct the distortion directly.

Macroeconomic reasoning tends to be more auspicious for controls. Mainstream Keynesian arguments favouring controls still operate within the general-equilibrium tradition, but allow for rigidities of wage and price setting (Basevi 1985; Dornbusch 1986*b*; 1986*c*). However, real rigidities and sluggish adjustment imply that changes in nominal exchange rates have real effects, at least in the short run.[17] Thus, within the asset market approach to exchange rate determination there may be large misalignments in exchange rates for significant periods of time, which can reduce domestic output and distort production between traded and non-traded sectors. In these Keynesian models, exchange rate variability may increase uncertainty or reduce support for free trade and, through economic or political processes, reduce trade and the gains from international specialization (De Grauwe 1988).

The likelihood of such wild swings in exchange rates is increased when more distinctly Keynesian characteristics are introduced into financial markets. In the *General Theory*, Keynes makes the distinction between enterprise and speculation as determinants of asset prices: enterprise determines asset prices based on long-term fundamental values; speculation, on the other hand, determines asset prices on the basis of the market's short-term expectations of what everyone else expects (Keynes 1936: ch.13). Keynes says that, when asset markets are freely accessible, speculation is likely to dominate enterprise, and the job of resource allocation is unlikely to be well done.

In the context of foreign exchange markets, there is increasing evidence that such speculation can drive rates away from 'fundamentals' for long periods of time. (This evidence is summarized in Dornbusch and Frankel 1987.) Here, capital mobility is likely to lead to distortions, lost output, and pressures for protectionism (Dornbusch 1986*a*; 1986*b*; for empirical evidence, see De Grauwe 1988).

Thus the mainstream Keynesian argument for capital controls rests on the argument that, either under fixed or under flexible exchange rates, capital mobility will undermine the ability of countries to pursue expansionary policy faster than the financial markets, driven by greed, fear, and irrationality, will allow (see Glyn 1987). While most Keynesians acknowledge that controls might have resource misallocation effects, they contend that these are outweighed by the macroeconomic benefits.[18]

The so-called Left or Cambridge Keynesians have additional reasons for supporting the use of capital controls. In their models, the presence of capital controls facilitates high growth. One channel is through investment, which may be encouraged by low interest rates, or by an increased supply of funds. A second channel is that financial controls may retard imports, thereby raising aggregate demand. We turn now to a characteristic Cambridge Keynesian macroeconomic model, with a neo-Marxian flavour, to study the effects of controls.

IV.1. The Analytics of Capital Controls

We begin with a simple Keynesian macroeconomic model (see Marglin and Bhaduri 1990; for a neo-Marxian version, see Bowles and Boyer 1990). Following Marglin and Bhaduri, investment depends on the expected profit rate, which in turn depends on capacity utilization and the profit share.

$$g^d = i/K = i(r^e(\pi, z), \sigma) \quad i_{re} > 0, \; i_\sigma < 0 \tag{1}$$

where

g^d = desired rate of investment (normalized by the capital stock)
i = investment
K = capital stock
r^e = expected rate of profit
π = profit share
z = capacity utilization
σ = real interest rate

Equation (1) says that the rate of investment depends positively on the expected profit rate and negatively on the real interest rate.[19] Expected profits in turn depend positively on the profit share and capacity utilization.

Next we analyse savings behaviour.

$$g^s = s\pi z a^{-1} + (t - g) + cad(\pi, z, \tau) \quad cad_z > 0; cad_\pi < 0; cad_\tau > 0 \tag{2}$$

where g^s = savings rate (normalized by the capital stock); s = marginal propensity to save of profit-earners;[20] a = capital/output ratio at full capacity utilization; $(t - g)$ = government budget surplus; cad = current-account deficit; τ = terms of trade.

Since increases in the profit share reduce consumption, the current-account deficit will fall when the profit share increases.[21] When capacity utilization increases, consumption will increase, causing the current-

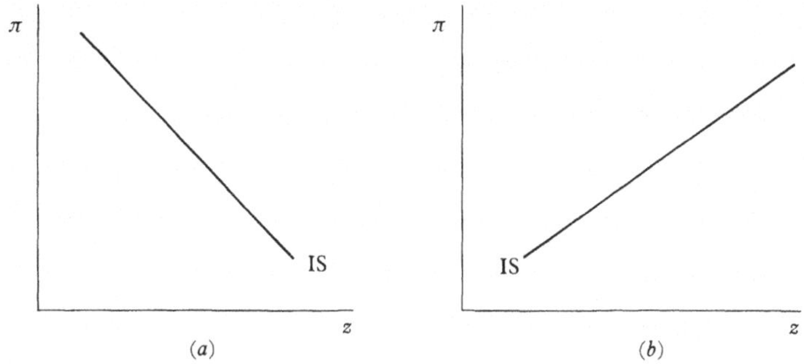

FIG. 6.1. The Investment–Savings Balance. (*a*) Stagnationist. (*b*) Exhilarationist.

account deficit to increase. An improvement in the terms of trade is assumed to worsen the current-account deficit.[22] In equilibrium, savings will equal desired investment.

$$i(r^e(\pi, z), \sigma) = s\pi z a^{-1} + (t - g) + cad(\pi, z, \tau) \quad (3)$$

Equation (3) is an IS curve, which, for a given real interest rate, capital/output ratio, and budget surplus, can be represented in πz space. The slope of the IS curve is indeterminate, however. It depends on the responsiveness of consumption to capacity utilization relative to the responsiveness of investment to profitability.[23] The stagnationist argument (Rowthorn 1982; Taylor 1985) is based on the IS curve sloping downward (Fig. 6.1 (*a*)); however, it could slope upward in an 'exhilarationist' mode (Fig. 6.1 (*b*)), where a rise in the profit share increases investment more than it decreases consumption, resulting in an increase in capacity utilization. (Marglin and Bhaduri 1990)

Whatever the slope of the IS curve, it cannot determine equilibrium by itself. One must add a producers' equilibrium condition. Here we

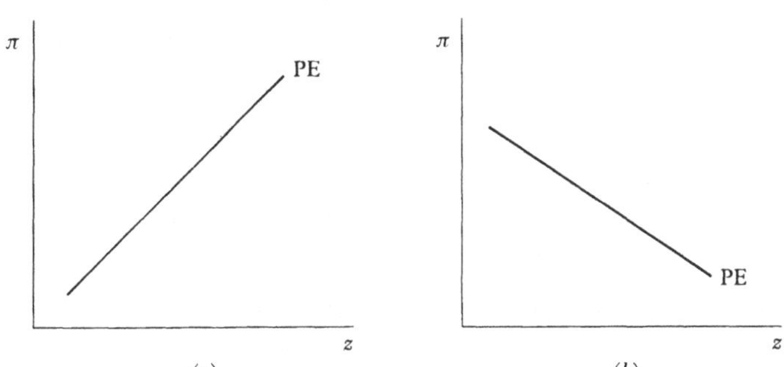

FIG. 6.2. Producers' Equilibrium. (*a*) Upward-sloping PE. (*b*) Downward-sloping PE.

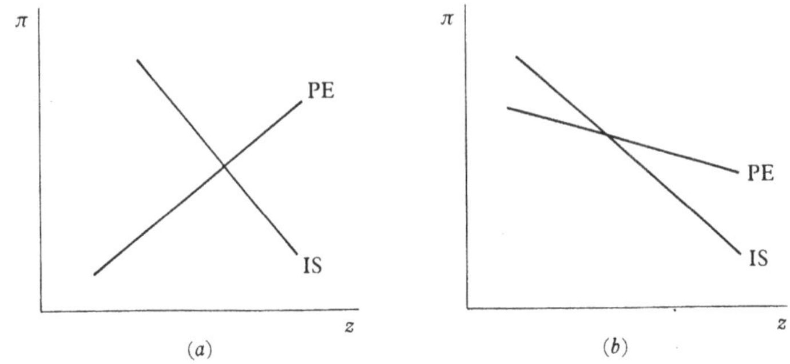

FIG. 6.3. Equilibrium. (*a*) Upward-sloping PE. (*b*) Downward-sloping PE.

follow Marglin and Bhaduri and use an extremely simple Kaleckian variable-mark-up model of producers' equilibrium.

$$\pi = \pi_0 + b(z) \quad (4)$$

where $b(z)$ represents the sensitivity of the mark-up to capacity utilization. Again, several cases are possible. If $b'(z) > 0$, then the producers' equilibrium (PE) is upward sloping. This might result from the producers' ability to increase the mark-up as demand increases and shortages develop (Fig. 6.2(*a*)).

On the other hand, it is possible that for some range $b'(z) < 0$. Increases in capacity utilization and the reduction in unemployment increase the bargaining position of workers, allowing them to shift the distribution of income away from capital. (Bowles and Boyer 1990; Boddy and Crotty 1975; Glyn and Sutcliffe 1972). This is more likely to happen with increasing international competition under fixed exchange rates, which prevents firms from increasing their prices in response to higher wage costs (Epstein 1989*a*; Fig. 6.2(*b*)).

Fig. 6.3 shows the determination of equilibrium as the intersection of the producers' equilibrium and the savings–investment balance schedules.[24]

To analyse the effects of capital controls, it is necessary to close the model by discussing the factors that determine the real interest rate (σ). If international financial markets were 'perfect' in the Walrasian sense, then the interest parity theorem should hold.[25] This implies Equation (5).

$$R = R^* + (E^e - E)/E \quad (5)$$

where R = domestic nominal interest rate; R^* = foreign nominal interest rate; E^e = expected exchange rate (domestic/foreign currency); E = current spot exchange rate.

Adding expected domestic inflation, subtracting expected foreign inflation from both sides, and defining the real rate of interest (σ) as the nominal interest rate minus the expected rate of inflation, yields a relationship between domestic and foreign real interest rates and expected real exchange rate changes.

$$\sigma = \sigma^* + (q^e - q)/q = \sigma^* + \varepsilon \qquad (6)$$

where σ^* = foreign real interest rate; q^e = expected real exchange rate; q = actual real exchange rate; ε = expected percentage change in the real exchange rate.

With perfect capital mobility and neutral money, as assumed in most neoclassical models, monetary policy affects neither σ nor ε. Changes in monetary policy are fully offset by changes in expected inflation, and changes in expected inflation are fully offset by changes in nominal exchange rates, resulting in no change in real exchange rates.

Neoclassical models with sticky prices allow for short-run links between monetary policy and real interest rates, but with perfect capital mobility, the short-run effects are on the real exchange rate. For example, a loose monetary policy, which in the short run reduces the domestic real interest rate, will cause a real depreciation of the exchange rate (see Eq. (6)). Indeed, sticky-price models suggest that the depreciated currency will 'overshoot' its equilibrium, resulting in real exchange rate instability. Countries wishing to avoid such effects will have to forgo expansionary monetary policy.

In the absence of capital controls, an expansionary monetary policy may result in a short-run depreciation in the nominal exchange rate. The effects on the IS curve will depend on the effects on the trade balance and the real interest rate. If prices are very responsive to depreciation, then the real exchange rate will not change; nor will real interest rates. If, however, there is a real depreciation in the exchange rate, then domestic real interest rates will rise (see Eq. (6)). This will reduce investment. Exports may be increased; but in the short run (with the J curve effect) an *increase* in the current account deficit is more likely. Thus, in the presence of perfect short-term capital mobility, expansionary monetary policy can shift the IS curve inward and actually be stagflationary.

A country trying to maintain a fixed exchange rate in the face of looser monetary policy will find itself losing international reserves, as capitalists try to buy foreign assets which are now yielding a higher rate of return (the left-hand side of (6) is less than the right-hand side).

Capital controls work by interfering with international capital markets, and therefore break the links between domestic real returns and foreign real returns. Thus, σ need not equal σ^*, although, in the absence of perfect controls, there will be some links. We represent this relationship in the following way:

$$\sigma = \sigma(\sigma^*, \varepsilon(R), R; C) \quad \sigma_{\sigma*} > 0; \sigma_\varepsilon > 0; \sigma_{\varepsilon c} < 0; \sigma_R > 0; \varepsilon_R < 0; \varepsilon_{RC} < 0 \qquad (7)$$

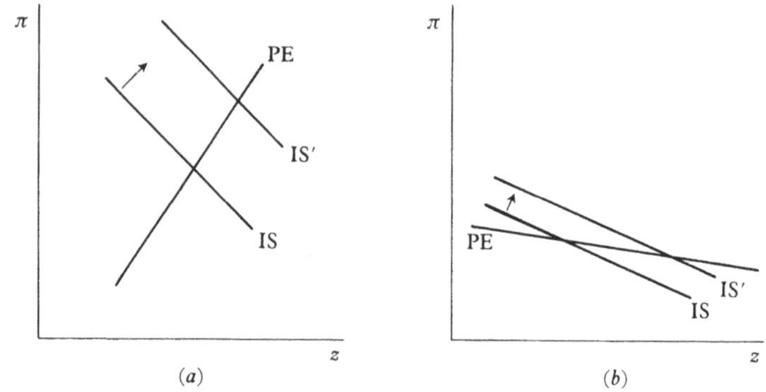

FIG. 6.4 Expansionary monetary policy with capital controls. (*a*) Upward-sloping PE. (*b*) Downward-sloping PE.

where *C* refers to capital controls. Equation (7) states that the relationship of σ to σ^*, and the degree to which σ affects $\varepsilon(R)$, depend on the nature of capital controls, *C*. Similarly, the rate of gain (or loss) of foreign exchange (δF) in response to differential rates of return will depend on the degree of capital controls, *C*.

$$\delta F = F(\sigma - \sigma^* - \varepsilon;\ C)\ F_{1c} < 0 \tag{8}$$

Thus, in the presence of effective capital controls, an expansionary monetary policy can reduce domestic real interest rates without real exchange rate changes or reserve losses as would occur in their absence. An expansionary monetary policy, by reducing the real cost of borrowing, will shift the IS curve outward. Similarly, an expansionary fiscal policy, though it might increase real interest rates at home, will not appreciate real exchange rates as much as in a flexible-rate world, and therefore will not reduce exports. The IS curve will shift out as a result of expansionary fiscal policy. Similarly, with controls, an increase in σ^*, or changes in $\varepsilon(R)$ resulting from foreign policies, will have less effect on σ, and, by implication, on domestic investment.

Putting the pieces of the model together, Fig. 6.4(*a*) and 6.4(*b*) show the effects of an expansionary monetary policy in the presence of capital controls. The IS curve shifts out. Whether the PE curve is upward- or downward-sloping, expansionary policy will increase capacity utilization. The shape of the PE curve will crucially affect the distributional effects of the policy, however. It is to that issue that we now turn.

V. THE POLITICAL ECONOMY OF CONTROLS

Expansionary policy has different effects on the profit share depending on whether the PE curve slopes upward or downward. If capitalists care about the rate of profit, and workers care about the wage bill, we need to know how the rate of profit varies with the profit share and capacity utilization.

$$r = \pi z a^{-1} \qquad (9)$$

From (9) we can derive iso-profit lines which will be rectangular hyperbolas in πz space (see Fig. 6.5). Now it is possible to analyse the political economy of controls. If, as in Fig. 6.6(*a*), the PE curve slopes upward, then an expansionary monetary policy allowed by controls will result in increased rates of profit. Capitalists (as well as workers) will gain from controls.[26] In this case, opposition to controls would come from financial investors, whose real rates of return fall relative to those abroad.[27]

If, however, the PE curve in the relevant range is sufficiently downward-sloping, then an expansionary monetary (or fiscal) policy made possible by controls would be opposed by capitalists concerned about their profit rates[28] (Fig. 6.6(*b*)). Workers, on the other hand, would support controls, since their wage bill is increasing. Financial investors (rentiers) would be joined by industrial capitalists, in their opposition to controls.[29] This analysis is summarized in Table 6.3.

IV.2. Estimating the 'Propensity to Control'

This political economy of controls suggests a few hypotheses about the propensity of governments to use controls, which we can test cross-nationally using our capital controls index. The first hypothesis is that countries in which labour is stronger are more likely to use controls. In our earlier work, we found that the best proxy for the strength of labour is the percentage of the electorate voting for left-wing political parties (Left-wing vote gain, LWVG).

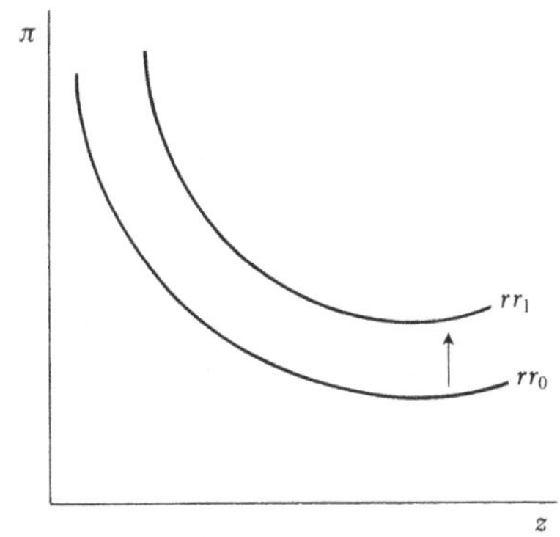

FIG. 6.5. Iso-profit rate curves.

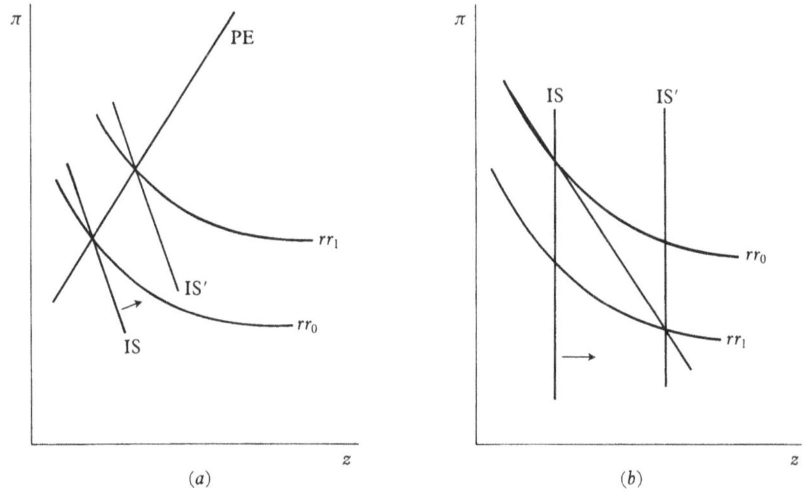

FIG. 6.6. Expansionary policy and the rate of profit. (*a*) Expansionary monetary policy increases profit rate (stagnationist mode). (*b*) Expansionary monetary policy reduces profit rate (stagnationist mode).

The second hypothesis is that countries in which financial capital is stronger are less likely to use controls. In our previous work (Epstein and Schor 1986; 1988; 1989; 1990*a*; 1990*b*), we have argued that powerful and independent financial sectors tend to be represented by independent central banks. As a measure of the power and independence (from industry) of the financial sector, we use our measure of central-bank independence, and expect that the more independent the central bank the less will be the propensity to control.[30] There is one caveat to this test. We must differentiate between controls on inflows and outflows, given that independent central banks have tended to support the freedom to block inflows. We can differentiate between these two motivations of policy by comparing our two capital control indices.

For the case of industrial capital, attitudes towards controls depend on the shape of the PE curve. Because we have no independent evidence on that issue, we do not have a clear test.

There is one final hypothesis, which involves the link between expansionary macropolicy and controls. Following the earlier discussion, we test whether countries which want to use expansionary macroeconomic policy will have a greater propensity to employ controls. In theory, we would like to include both fiscal and monetary policy. However, since capital controls have their most direct effect on interest rates, we have confined ourselves to a measure of fiscal policy—the average structural budget deficit.

TABLE 6.3. *The political economy of controls*

Slope of prducers' equilibrium schedule	Benefit from controls	
	Yes	No
Upward	Industry Labour	Finance
Downward	Labour	Finance Industry

TABLE 6.4. *Data*

Country	Capital controls index[a]	Adjusted capital controls index[b]	Left-wing vote[c]	Central-bank independence[d]	Budget surplus (+) or deficit (−)[e]
Australia	18.0	18.0	44.7	0.0	0.4
Austria	21.0	21.0	46.7	1.0	−0.4
Belgium	20.0	20.0	32.9	1.5	−5.2
Canada	0.0	0.0	15.2	1.0	−1.0
Denmark	20.0	20.0	31.6	2.0	−0.1
Finland	20.0	20.0	43.2	3.0	3.4
France	23.0	23.0	40.6	1.0	0.0
Germany	1.0	9.0	40.5	3.0	−0.9
Italy	25.0	25.0	39.5	1.25	−8.9
Japan	12.0	12.0	31.4	1.0	−1.7
Netherlands	10.0	10.0	31.3	1.5	−1.0
Norway	20.0	20.0	47.4	1.0	4.1
Sweden	19.0	19.0	50.5	1.0	1.3
Switzerland	0.0	7.0	29.0	3.0	n/a
UK	24.0	24.0	42.9	1.5	−0.7
USA	0.0	7.0	0.0	2.0	0.3

Notes: For full definitions, see Data Appendix.

[a] Sum of restrictions 1968–87 (from Table 6.1).

[b] Adjusted to include restrictions on inflows.

[c] % of electorate voting for left-wing parties 1960–80.

[d] Epstein–Schor index of central-bank independence.

[e] Structural surplus (+) or deficit (−) as percentage of potential output.

Table 6.4 contains the independent variables we have been discussing. Table 6.5 presents the cross-section regression results. All equations were originally estimated with a constant, which was insignificant in all cases. The regressions are Ordinary Least Squares, and involve sixteen countries, except for BUDG, which omits Switzerland for reasons of data availability.

These equations provide support for our model of controls. Both LWVG and INDEP are statistically significant, with expected signs. Together, these two variables explain 50% of the variation in controls across countries (Eq. (2)). The structural budget deficit, on the other hand, does not appear to have an impact.

TABLE 6.5. *Estimates of the 'propensity to control'*

Equation No.	Dependent variable	LWVG	INDEP	BUDG	$\bar{R}^2$
1	CCI	.481	−1.480	−.576	.500
		(6.73)	(−.89)	(1.09)	
2	CCI	.513	−2.478		.522
		(7.21)	(−1.63)		
3	CCADJ	.454	−.281		.456
		(7.58)	(−.22)		

Variable definitions:
CCI Capital control index.
CCADJ Capital control index adjusted to include inflows and US controls.
LWVG Left-wing vote gain.
INDEP Independence of central bank.
BUDG Budget surplus (+) or deficit (−) as % of GNP.
Nos. in parantheses are *t* statistics. All equations are OLS.

In Equation (3) we use our alternative capital control index (CCADJ) to test the hypothesis that INDEP provides less explanatory power when restrictions on inflows are included. Central banks are apparently less averse to controls when they can be used to reduce the supply of capital in the economy, as the reduction of the coefficient of INDEP suggests.

In addition to the equations shown in Table 6.5, we added interaction terms among the independent variables (none significant) and tested other independent variables (such as population and a measure of integration between industry and finance, neither of which was significant). We also tested an alternative variable for the strength of labour (average unionization rate), but LWVG was a superior performer.

Fig. 6.7 presents the residuals from Equation (1). The countries are arranged in alphabetical order. Australia, Japan, and the UK are nearly perfectly predicted. The largest prediction errors are for Denmark, Italy, and Germany. In the case of Germany, the equation apparently cannot capture the strong bias toward 'liberalism' in economic policy which was a legacy of hyperinflation and of the American influence on the shape of post-war Germany. In the case of Denmark, the high degree of inde-

Residual	Actual	Fitted	Country
−4.92591	18.0000	22.9259	Australia
−0.47411	21.0000	21.4741	Austria
6.84248	20.0000	13.1575	Belgium
−5.31826	0.0000	5.3183	Canada
8.74801	20.0000	11.2520	Denmark
5.27613	20.0000	14.7239	Finland
4.65449	23.0000	18.3455	France
−12.33910	1.0000	13.3391	Germany
7.83805	25.0000	17.1619	Italy
−1.62698	12.0000	13.6270	Japan
−2.33691	10.0000	12.3369	Netherlands
−1.83313	20.0000	21.8331	Norway
−4.42307	19.0000	23.4231	Sweden
−7.44092	0.0000	7.4409	Switzerland
5.71364	24.0000	18.2864	UK
4.95514	0.0000	−4.9551	USA

FIG. 6.7. Residuals for Capital Controls Prediction Equation (1).

pendence and a relatively low LWVG reduced the fitted value. For Italy, the size of LWVG may underestimate the effect of the Left, given that it is Communist rather than Socialist.

VI. CONCLUSION

There is increasing evidence that financial openness has created serious difficulties for national economic management, particularly for expansionary and redistributive economic policy. Some countries have been able to mitigate the worst effects of this financial openness by placing controls on international capital mobility. These controls have allowed some countries, for example, France and Italy, to pursue relative exchange rate stability. Despite the apparent effectiveness of controls, governments within the EC are in the process of dismantling them. Australia and Japan have recently liberalized. Nor are right-wing governments the only ones following this path, as the cases of Australia and France illustrate.

Our results suggest that, over the post-war period, controls have been associated positively with the political power of the Left and negatively with the power of the financial sector. Thus, the current decontrol may plausibly be related to changes in the political power or economic situations of these groups. For example, there has been a marked decline in the power of the Left in Italy and France. Likewise, as Pringle (Chapter 4) argues, financial interests have been on the ascent in the 1980s. Whatever the particulars, the analysis presented here suggests that explanations of decontrol which are primarily technical, or narrowly 'economic', are missing an important aspect of the shift.

The dismantling of controls raises several important issues for left-wing governments. Are they simply responding to a new reality which our analysis fails to capture? Or are they perhaps responding to an old ideology and a new assault by conservative and business forces? There is little in the way of compelling evidence that international financial markets have changed so dramatically that left-oriented policy requires the dismantling of controls. If anything, the opposite is the case. However, the ideology and political power of the Right is undoubtedly an increasingly powerful force. We need much more theoretical and empirical research on the implications of capital mobility and controls for the prospects for Left-oriented policy to help us and others distinguish between fact and their fancy.

DATA APPENDIX

Variable Definitions and Sources

BUDG: structural budget stance.
surplus (+) or deficit (−) as a share of potential output, averaged over 1970–84.
Source: Price and Muller, 1984.

CCINDX: capital control index.
Calculated as total number of restrictions each year, 1967–86.
Source: IMF, 1950–87.

CCADJ: Same as CCINDX, except that restrictions on inflows in Germany and Switzerland are included, as is interest equalization tax and measures against capital inflow in the USA.

INDEP: degree of independence of central bank (index from 0–3, with 0 least independent).
Source: Epstein and Schor, 1986; Bade and Parkin, 1980.
The following modifications have been made:
Netherlands, UK and Belgium: Bade and Parkin classify these countries as 1, but the institutional evidence suggests more independence. We have given them 1.5.
Austria, Finland, Norway, and Denmark are not in the Bade and Parkin index. Based on papers by Uusitalo (1984), Kurzer (1987), and Martin (1986), we have given these countries the following scores, respectively: 1, 3, 1, 2.

Canada is no longer independent after 1967. Our capital control index begins at this time, so Canada receives a value of 1.
Italy becomes formally independent in 1981, and *de facto* independence occurs in 1983. Italy's score is a weighted average, which equals 1.25.

LWVG: left-wing vote gain.
Source: Lange and Garrett, 1985.
This is the average electoral vote gained by left-wing parties from 1960 to 1980. Switzerland from Mackie and Rose, 1982.

NOTES

1. For an excellent discussion of Keynes's view on controls, see Crotty (1983).
2. We do not presume to venture an opinion on the issue of whether Keynes would have been converted to multilateralism in the absence of American pressure.
3. The distinction between controls on current and capital accounts was not surprising. While the USA was in principle opposed to all controls, the former were of more immediate importance, given the desire to export. There was little fear that Europe would turn down capital exports from the USA.
4. This section relies on a series of case studies of capital controls which we have undertaken for the large countries in our sample. They are available from the authors.
5. Australia, Austria, Belgium, Canada, Denmark, Finland, France, Germany, Italy, Japan, Netherlands, Norway, Sweden, Switzerland, UK, USA.
6. Exemptions have been granted for a number of the less developed countries until 1992.
7. Before 1967 the Fund did not make a designation about whether a restrictive practice was in place, so that construction of the index would be arbitrary.
8. This idea has been developed in a formal model by Gros (1988), who shows that, if evasion has costs associated with transferring capital, the effectiveness of capital controls, measured by yield differentials or control over domestic credit, will diminish over time. His results do not hold for controls on outstanding stocks of assets, however.
9. See e.g. the remarks by A. Szasz, of the Central Bank of the Netherlands, in Swoboda (1976: 173): 'This tendency [to proliferate] is, I believe, to a large extent unavoidable and constitutes one of the most disturbing aspects of [controls] . . .'.
10. They argue that the other 15% does not represent unexploited profits since, because of lags, traders using a simple trading rule could not profit from the differentials. Their data are weekly, however, and trades do not take a week. This argument is, therefore, not convincing.
11. Other criticisms of their estimates include the fact that they assume costs are proportional to transactions when they are likely to be declining. Also, as they pointed out in a footnote, Deardorff argued that their estimates of

costs assume that investors always carry out the complete covered-interest transaction, rather than using the proceeds to invest in another currency. This would also lead to an overestimate of costs (Frenkel and Levich 1977: 1211, n. 2).

12. Ito and Giavazzi and Pagano tried to control for transactions costs by taking into account bid–offer spreads, and in the case of Ito, the offshore covered-interest differential between the yen and the US dollar. Even when these costs are included, covered-interest parity failed during the controls period, sometimes quite substantially.
13. They also distinguish between controls on banks and non-banks, and find that to a large extent they are substitutes rather than complements. This constitutes evidence against the argument that controls tend to proliferate.
14. See e.g. the discussion in Ch. 4 of policy-makers' and financiers' attitudes toward controls.
15. These findings provide some evidence against the increasingly popular view that central banks have no control over conditions in money and credit markets, because private agents can create money or money substitutes on their own.
16. These models consider a variety of capital controls: quantitative restrictions, taxes, and dual exchange rates. There is a general equivalence among types of control on any particular transaction category. See Adams and Greenwood (1985) on some equivalence theorems; Dornbusch (1986*a*) on multiple exchange rates; and Greenwood and Kimbrough (1985) for more equivalence results.
17. These short-run effects can even become long-run effects if one adds so-called 'hysteresis' or path-dependent effects to these models.
18. Dornbusch (1986*c*) argues, however, that the argument for resource misallocation is mistaken when applied to interest rate controls, on the grounds that it confuses the marginal productivity of capital with a financial interest rate, which in general will not be closely related. Moreover, our preliminary econometric work does *not* support the critics' arguments. In both cross-sectional and pooled cross-sectional time series regressions, we found that controls, as measured by our capital controls index, are not associated with inefficiency as measured by productivity growth. Moreover, we found that controls are positively associated with the rate of growth of fixed capital (in our time series cross-sectional analysis) and negatively associated with GNP gaps in both our cross-sectional and our cross-sectional time series regressions. Thus controls *do* seem to be associated with better macroeconomic performance.
19. The direct effects of real interest rates on investment are the subject of substantial controversy. If real interest rates do not affect investment through the cost of capital, they can do so by altering expectations of future levels of output and therefore expected profit rates.
20. We assume that the marginal propensity to save of wage-earners is zero.
21. The partial derivatives of the current-account deficit may differ from the signs assumed here. See Bhaduri and Marglin (1987) for a discussion.
22. Although, as we see below, in the short run, through the J curve, a depreciation of the real exchange rate could worsen the current account.

23. This can be seen by totally differentiating (3) and solving for $d\pi/dz$, which gives the slope of the IS curve.

$$d\pi/dz = (s\pi a^{-1} + cad_z - i_z)/(sza^{-1} + cad_\pi - i_\pi)$$

The sign of $d\pi/dz$ is indeterminate.
24. We will only present graphs of selected cases in the remainder of the paper to avoid tedium and confusion. A sufficient condition for stability of the model is that the IS curve be steeper (in absolute value) than the PE curve.
25. The interest parity theorem states that rates of return across assets, including expected changes in the exchange rate, should equalize.
26. This assumes workers are concerned about the wage bill.
27. These may be foreign as well as domestic investors. To analyse fully the conflicts between financial and industrial capitalists, it is necessary to incorporate the effects of interest rates on the distribution of income, and to include assumptions about the relative propensities to spend of financial and industrial capitalists and workers (see Epstein 1989*b*). The implicit assumptions in the analysis here are that financial and industrial capitalists have the same propensities to save, and that changes in real interest rates alter the distribution of income between industrial and financial capitalists (rather than between financial capitalists and workers, as it would if changes in interest rates affected the mark-up).
28. Whether or not expansionary policy will reduce the profit rate when the PE curve is downward-sloping will depend on the elasticity of the PE curve and the iso-profit line.
29. For these results we have assumed that the downward-sloping PE curve is steeper than the iso-profit lines, and that the downward-sloping IS curve is steeper than the iso-profit line. Similarly, the upward-sloping IS curve is assumed to be steeper than the PE line.
30. For this study we have had to expand our index of independence to include all 16 countries. The original index was based on statutory characteristics of central bank/government relations, derived largely from Bade and Parkin (1980). Information on these characteristics was not readily available for all the additional countries, so we have had to rely on the institutional literature to include Switzerland, Austria, Denmark, Norway, and Finland. Under the circumstances, we also took the opportunity to modify the original index to correct those cases which were anomalous from the point of view of the institutional literature. These were the Netherlands, Belgium, Japan, and the UK. The major sources we relied on were Uusitalo (1984), Kurzer (1987), and Martin (1986). We are aware that these modifications are more subjective than the original characteristics, but we are convinced that the institutional literature is more accurate. Finally, we should note that Italy's score was updated to include the change in the status of the Banca d'Italia. See Epstein and Schor (1989*a*).

Part III

LOOKING AHEAD: POLICY BEHAVIOUR IN AN OPEN WORLD

Introduction to Part III

TARIQ BANURI

The aim of the papers in this part is to examine the consequences in terms of opportunities and constraints for nation states in a world where financial markets have become far more open, and thus unpredictable. A second theme is the examination of different types of policy response to the changed environment.

In Chapter 7, Epstein and Gintis present an asset balance model of international capital market equilibrium which can be used to frame these questions. The model is consistent with the stylized facts of increased capital mobility on the one hand and the approximate equality of domestic savings and investment on the other hand. The central prediction of the model is that each country has a target net external position (debtor or creditor) which is stable over considerable periods of time (years or decades), short-run deviations from which induce portfolio adjustments sufficient to restore equilibrium over the medium run. They show that this target position is unresponsive to short-term changes in prices, interest or exchange rates, or cyclical macroeconomic conditions, and responds only to such major international dislocations as the two world wars, the Great Depression, the demise of Bretton Woods, and the two oil crises.

The model suggests that, while the structural nature of various countries' debtor or creditor status implies a certain degree of implicit international co-ordination, and hence a somewhat greater scope for macroeconomic policy, it also creates a significant degree of constraint on national policy-making, in that macroeconomic policies, domestic financial institutions, and the political stance of individual countries will need to be oriented towards maintaining their target asset position instead of other economic or political objectives.

Chapter 8, by Jaime Ros, can then be interpreted in this framework as making the following points. First, the increase in oil prices in the 1970s (together with low real interest rates on international loans) led to an upward revision of oil-exporting Mexico's target debtor position; and this led to a rapid increase in foreign borrowing to finance higher consumption as well as investment spending. Second, this revision in the asset stance was not reversed despite the subsequent fall in oil prices and increase in interest rates. As Ros points out, the main reason for this was that for a long time the adverse movement of prices was viewed as temporary. Third, the inability to revise the target position imposed excess welfare costs on the economy. Some welfare costs have been discussed in the literature (see Eaton *et al.* 1986) as resulting from a transfer problem, or a revenue constraint on the borrowing government. Ros introduces yet another type of cost associated with a government's inability to influence macroeconomic conditions because of the constraints imposed by asymmetric capital mobility. Fourth, this means that, even though the target asset position may subsequently have been revised downwards, the new target has become unattainable through standard macroeconomic means. Therefore, some form of debt relief is necessary for economies like Mexico to get out of the bind, and to be able again to maintain their revised target asset position.

Similarly, Tariq Banuri's paper (Chapter 9) can be seen as a generalization of the Epstein–Gintis problem in yet another direction. Here, the problem is created, not by external borrowing (which influences a country's status as a net creditor or debtor) but rather by discretionary unrequited flows, namely, worker remittances. These flows also influence a country's long-term expectations of resource inflows, and thus induce revisions in target asset positions. However, as Chapter 9 suggests, just as macroeconomic policy and financial institutions in a country can become hostage to the need to maintain the level of resource inflows, they can also become centred around the need to maintain the expected level of remittances. In practice, this has led to growing policy impotence in most remittance-receiving countries, such as Pakistan, Turkey, Egypt, and Yugoslavia. The only exception is India, which did not revise its target asset position despite the emergence of large but volatile remittance inflows, and thus for a long time did not become dependent on these flows. As a result, India succeeded in maintaining a level of policy effectiveness greater than other countries in the sample.

The operative part of the discussion is that international capital mobility, whether in the form of borrowing or of remittance flows, imposes unanticipated costs on both the debtor and creditor countries. The former suffer from political and economic vulnerability and policy ineffectiveness, and the latter from the need to invest in enforcement regimes. Policy-makers, at both national and global levels, need to take account of these invisible costs in formulating current policies as well as in the examination of alternative possibilities of institutional reform. This is the key challenge of the 1990s.

7

International Capital Markets and the Limits of National Economic Policy

GERALD A. EPSTEIN AND HERBERT GINTIS

I. INTRODUCTION

Students of international economics have noted a dramatic increase in international capital mobility in recent decades. This development has contributed to a conceptual revolution in macroeconomic theory: a nation's supply of investment credit, long considered dependent upon domestic savings, is increasingly held to be determined by international supply and demand, domestic economies being compelled by competition to adjust more or less rapidly to a uniform world interest rate.[1]

This open-economy perspective challenges several tenets of traditional economic policy. Most prominent is the notion that market-clearing requires the equality of domestic savings and investment. This linchpin of Keynesian economics is rejected by open-economy macroeconomics, which argues that a change in domestic savings affects domestic investment only via its impact on the international interest rate, while a shift in domestic investment affects the current account rather than the rate of interest.

In consequence, open-economy macroeconomics suggests that economic policies that alter domestic saving cannot alter the cost of capital, the real rate of interest, or the supply of domestic credit. Government deficits, in particular, do not crowd out private investment, and hence alter the time profile of national consumption rather than lowering the rate of economic growth. By the same token, however, policies promising more rapid growth through the encouragement of private saving (so-called 'supply-side' policies) are without merit.

In technical terms, the shift from closed- to open-economy macroeconomic models replaces one policy constraint—balancing the current account—by another—equalizing domestic and international rates of return. More pointedly, in an open economy, the power of workers to raise their wages or working conditions above world levels, or the ability of governments to impose environmental and occupational safety regulations upon industry, or the power of the monetary authority to run a more expansionary monetary policy than those abroad, are all compromised by the threat of capital flight.

The evidence in favour of this new perspective is ambiguous. Proponents cite the decline in capital controls, the growth of Euro-currency markets, reduced communication and transportation costs, the maturation of international financial intermediaries, and the rapid growth of financial transactions across national boundaries. Also, Euro-currency and other inter-country asset markets increasingly constrain the returns to offshore financial instruments to follow quite closely those of comparable assets issued domestically (Obstfeld 1985; Cumby and Obstfeld 1984; Frankel 1985).

The major prediction of the open-economy model, however, that increased international capital mobility has broken the traditional savings–investment linkage, is repeatedly and decisively rejected in econometric studies. Rather, studies tend to support the traditional notion that, while current-account 'imbalance' allows significant independent movement in savings and investment in the short run, over the medium run the equality of savings and investment tends to reassert itself in most national economies.[2]

TABLE 7.1(*a*). *Net foreign assets relative to tangible capital*[a] *(%)*

	1880	1914	1940	1950	1960	1973	1977
Australia			- 10.3	- 5.7	- 5.0	- 3.6	- 2.9
Belgium	9.7	18.0	17.7	5.6	7.6	13.5	11.0
Canada				- 13.3	- 14.0	- 8.9	- 7.8
Denmark	8.8	- 10.8	- 5.2	- 3.6	- 2.2	- 4.6	- 5.3
France	15.5	22.5				- 1.7	- 0.9
Germany			1.7	- 5.0	3.0	1.2	2.5
GB	63.0	67.4	40.3		5.9	1.6	- 2.5
India	- 15.1	- 20.2	- 18.4	5.1	- 3.8	- 6.5	- 3.1
Italy	- 7.4	- 2.4			0.7	2.1	0.5
Japan	- 8.9	- 7.0	1.1	1.8	- 0.5	1.4	1.6
USA	- 5.9	- 2.0	7.3	4.3	3.3	1.1	1.0

[a] Actual dates: Australia: 1947, 1956, 1965, 1973, 1977. Belgium: 1895, 1913, 1939, 1948, 1965, 1973, 1976. Canada: 1955, 1965, 1973, 1978. Denmark: 1880, 1913, 1938, 1948, 1965, 1973, 1978. France: 1880, 1913, 1972, 1976. Germany: 1895, 1913, 1938, 1950, 1960, 1972, 1977. GB: 1895, 1913, 1937, 1957, 1965, 1973, 1977. India: 1895, 1913, 1939, 1950, 1960, 1970, 1975. Italy: 1895, 1914, 1938, 1951, 1963, 1973, 1977. Japan: 1885, 1913, 1940, 1955, 1965, 1970, 1977. USA: 1880, 1910, 1939, 1950, 1965, 1973, 1978.

Source: 1880–1977; Goldsmith (1985).

This result suggests that international capital markets deviate considerably from perfect competition. There is additional evidence. The Capital Assets Pricing Model (Sharpe 1964; Lintner 1965) predicts an extremely high elasticity of substitution among international securities of similar risk profiles (e.g. Elton and Gruber 1984: ch. 10) in the absence of market impediments. Yet Lessard (1986: 28) has estimated that, were capital markets perfect in the CAPM sense, the equity in most countries would be overwhelmingly foreign-owned: foreign investors would hold 95% of Swiss, 90% of British, 80% of Japanese, and 50% of US assets. Such predictions are, of course, at least an order of magnitude too large.

TABLE 7.1(*b*). *Net foreign assets relative to GNP*[a] *(%)*

	1880	1914	1940	1950	1960	1973	1977	1985
Australia			-27.5	-19.3	-20.0	-11.5	-11.4	
Belgium	53.2	81.4	71.6	17.8	24.3	40.6	40.8	
Canada				-37.5	-39.5	-24.0	-24.9	-35.6
Denmark	17.9	-32.9	-16.2	-12.2	-6.7	-12.3	-19.3	
France	69.5		97.1			-4.8	-2.9	-1.8
Germany			6.1	-13.8	5.0	4.0	8.1	7.8
GB	141.4	153.3	93.0		8.2	5.3	-12.6	20.6
India	-27.9	-32.6	-43.4	11.4	-11.4	-19.7	-12.1	
Italy	-23.9	-7.8			2.3	6.4	1.7	-6.7
Japan	-30.1	-21.8	29.9	24.8	-0.9	2.4	3.7	8.1
USA	-14.6	-5.3	21.8	11.5	8.6	3.1	3.1	-3.1

[a] Actual dates: Australia: 1947, 1956, 1965, 1973, 1977. Belgium: 1895, 1913, 1939, 1948, 1965, 1973, 1976. Canada: 1955, 1965, 1973, 1978, 1985. Denmark: 1880, 1913, 1938, 1948, 1965, 1973, 1978. France: 1880, 1913, 1972, 1976, 1985. Germany: 1895, 1913, 1938, 1950, 1960, 1972, 1977, 1985. GB: 1895, 1913, 1937, 1957, 1965, 1973, 1977, 1985. India: 1895, 1913, 1939, 1950, 1960, 1970, 1975. Italy: 1895, 1914, 1938, 1951, 1963, 1973, 1977, 1985. Japan: 1885, 1913, 1940, 1955, 1965, 1970, 1977, 1985. USA: 1880, 1912, 1939, 1950, 1965, 1973, 1978, 1985.

Source: 1880–1977, Goldsmith (1985), 1985, IMF (1988*b*).

These considerations do not, however, warrant a return to the older, closed-economy model. Tables 7.1 (*a*) and (*b*) chart the net asset position of selected countries over selected periods in relation to their capital stock and GNP. It is clear from these data that national economies do not balance their current accounts, but rather have a tendency to hold a net debtor or creditor position over extended periods. The size of the asset position of various countries appears too large to support the traditional closed-economy model, yet too small (especially in the period after the Second World War) to support the open-economy alternative.

This paper presents an asset balance model of international capital market equilibrium which is compatible both with the 'stylized facts' of increased capital mobility on the one hand and with the (approximate) equality of domestic savings and investment on the other. This model holds that each country has a target net external-asset position (debtor or creditor) in relation to its capital stock, short-run deviations from which induce portfolio adjustments sufficient to restore equilibrium over the medium run.[3] These adjustments, which normally occur through a combination of spontaneous market behaviour and economic policy, entail a high correlation in the secular movement of savings and investment.

A central prediction of the asset balance model is that a country's target asset position is stable over considerable periods (years or decades), and is unresponsive to short-term changes in prices, interest and exchange rates, or cyclical macroeconomic conditions. Creditor and debtor countries thus occupy structural positions in the international economy for extended periods, changes in their target asset positions being precipitated by such major international dislocations as the two world wars, the Great Depression, the demise of Bretton Woods, and the two oil crises of the 1970s.

Our model is consistent with those critics of the open-economy model who stress that, while gross capital flows may have increased significantly in recent decades, capital mobility, as reflected in the size of countries' net asset positions appears, if anything, to have declined from 1880 to 1980. On the other hand, heightened gross mobility, coupled with reduced net mobility, engenders an increased exposure of national economies to the vicissitudes of capital movements, a point all but ignored in 'insular' Keynesian economy and supply-side models.[4]

The policy implications of the asset balance model reduce neither to those of the open nor to those of the insular models. First, our approach suggests that capital mobility is potentially less constraining than is implied by the open-economy model. Since credit-rationing prevents the international equalization of profit rates, economic policies which lower the domestic return to investment, for example, may be effective to a greater degree than suggested by the open-economy model. Second, since short-term capital is highly mobile in the asset balance model, the need to maintain a target asset position may circumscribe policy to a greater extent than implied by the insular model. For example, the interest rate chosen by the central bank, which is unconstrained by international forces in the insular model, must equilibrate short-term financial markets in the asset balance approach. Third, the asset balance model suggests that the domestic financial system of a debtor country, being obliged to meet certain long-run structural conditions of creditworthiness in order to satisfy its international creditors, may be significantly constrained in its domestic stabilization and growth policies. Conversely, the requirement that creditor countries maintain the power to ensure the collection of their debts may constrain domestic policy (for example, creditors might need to maintain open markets and/or a strong military).

Section II below discusses the central deviation of international capital markets from the axioms of Walrasian general equilibrium, and in particular from those of the international version of the Capital Assets Pricing Model: the absence of third-party enforcement financial contracts. Section III presents a simple asset balance model of international capital market equilibrium, implying the existence of a target net external-asset position. We test this model directly in Section IV. The asset balance model implies that the true coefficient of savings in a properly specified regression of savings against investment depends upon the observed country's target asset position, but will generally be near unity, as found in most empirical studies. The model also predicts that an Ordinary Least Squares regression for single countries is mis-specified, but that cross-sectional and pooled time series cross-sectional regressions are considerably less subject to specification bias. We close, in Section V, with a discussion of the general policy implications of the asset balance approach.

II. INTERNATIONAL CREDIT MARKETS AND THE PROBLEM OF ENFORCEMENT

In this section we will argue that, while transactions costs in international financial markets may have decreased, enforcement costs probably have not; both the level and the mix of international asset exchanges remain conditioned by the absence of third-party enforcement costlessly available to partners to exchange.[5] The Walrasian model of market-clearing is therefore inoperative, the 'law of once price' is routinely violated, and capital-rationing is the rule, whatever the volume of international financial transactions and its sensitivity to market conditions.[6]

Under conditions of endogenous enforcement, we suggest, a debtor's asset position is constrained by the fact that, as debt rises, the ability to repay becomes fragile and the incentive to default increases. Credit is rationed because a prospective lender, faced with an over-extended debtor, recognizes that no interest rate is sufficient to compensate for the increased risk of default, since an increase in the interest rate merely renders default more probable. Prudent debtors, recognizing the possibility of being rationed out of the market in unfavourable states of the world, are reluctant to borrow beyond a certain limit, however auspicious the domestic investment prospects. A country's target net debt position is a result of this interaction between reluctant borrowers and reluctant lenders.

Endogenous enforcement also imposes fairly strict limits on the ability of a country to export capital. Indeed, our model suggests that capital-exporters must possess the wealth, international political influence, and military power to impose credible sanctions against possible defaulters.

Such creditors are likely to be few in number, and their target asset positions are determined by the limits of their enforcement resources.

Let us now turn to a more formal analysis of the problem. Consider an exchange between two economic actors, A and B. Models of market equilibrium typically assume that any agreement between A and B can be costlessly and exogenously enforced, usually by the judicial system of the transacting agents. Yet in many important exchanges, contract fulfilment depends on the strategic behaviour of the transacting parties themselves. Exogenous enforcement will be inadequate when important terms of the exchange can be measured only at considerable cost, when the relevant evidence is not admissible in a court of law, when there is no possible means of redress, when uncertainty concerning future states of the world relevant to the exchange preclude a fully specified contract or, most pertinent to the theory of international finance, when there is no third-party enforcer, as when A and/or B are sovereign states.

We refer to such a situation as one of 'contested exchange' (Bowles and Gintis 1988*a* and *b*), since in such cases the *ex post* terms of exchange are determined by the monitoring, sanctioning, and incentive mechanisms instituted by agents to induce acceptable behaviour in their contractual relations.[7]

Financial markets involve contested exchange, since lender or stockholder A transfers funds to an enterprise, receiving *ex ante* neither a determinate return nor even a specific probability distribution of returns, but rather a contractually unenforceable *promise* of future returns. Thus a stockholder receives a specified share of a random variable (profits) whose expected return and risk are both contractually unspecifiable and not directly observable. Similarly, a bank receives a fixed return on its loans, but cannot fix the probability of repayment: the conditions of borrower insolvency remain outside contractual specification and enforcement.

In this situation, A must employ an enforcement strategy to induce B to hold the probability of default within tolerable limits. A can be expected to choose least-cost strategies for achieving any given level of loan security, and to choose a level of enforcement expenditure which, on the margin, balances the costs of default reduction against its benefits in the form of the present value of the loan. The strategies available to A include: gain-sharing, retaliation, contingent renewal, reliance on reputation, joint control, and collateralizing. We shall begin by discussing these strategies in the context of two private agents to exchange, A and B, subject to the same political jurisdiction. We will then extend the analysis to the international case.

Profit-sharing involves A offering B a portion of the benefits deriving from B's activity. For instance, A may be a firm's stockholders, who offer manager B stock options to induce B to maximize profits. Profit-sharing is particularly effective when A's gain is large compared to the payment to B.[8]

Reputation effects operate by several agents A pooling information concerning the behaviour of B, thereby inducing B to perform adequately in order to retain transacting partners (Okun 1981; Rogerson 1983). Reputation effects are of limited effectiveness in financial markets, since borrower performance tends to have an 'all or nothing' character: bankruptcy involves the dissolution of the enterprise or a regime change, while changing economic conditions may quickly render obsolete information concerning the borrower's historical performance.

Retaliation involves A imposing extra-contractual costs on B, such as physical violence, harassment, and boycott, in the event of non-performance. The effectiveness of retaliation as a means of contract enforcement is limited by two conditions. First, where A and B are subject to the same political jurisdiction, retaliator A may be vulnerable to civil redress and criminal penalties. Second, after B defaults, A may have no *ex post* incentive to impose the threatened penalties, since the loan is likely to be irrecoverable. The threat of retaliation will not be a credible deterrent, therefore, unless imposing the penalties on B induces A's other debtors not to default.

Contingent renewal is an endogenous enforcement mechanism in which A elicits performance from B by promising to renew the contract in future periods if satisfied, and to terminate the contract if not. For instance, firm A may promise employee B continual employment contingent upon satisfactory performance; or lender A may offer borrower B a short-term loan, with the promise of rolling over the loan if B is found to behave prudently.

Non-renewal of contract is a threat, of course, only if the expected value of B's gain from access to A's credit exceeds the expected value of seeking alternative funding. Thus A must offer B an enforcement rent, the size of which determines the effectiveness of the contingent renewal strategy. The cost of contingent renewal as a lender strategy includes both this enforcement rent and the cost of monitoring B's behaviour.

Contingent renewal is a cost-effective enforcement mechanism when borrowers are collateral-poor but have access to investment opportunities with high expected rates of return. Its effectiveness in financial markets is limited by the lender's general difficulty of access to information relevant to renewal, and the borrower's hesitancy to accept short-term financing of long-term projects, given that lenders have the *ex post* option of withdrawing credit on the basis of bad information, or correct information unrelated to the borrower's investment behaviour (e.g. economic conditions pertinent to the expected success of the project).

Joint control occurs when B agrees to allow A, or agents of A, to influence directly the decisions which determine B's behaviour. For example, bank A may require firm B to include A's agents on B's board of directors, or may retain veto power over certain of B's decisions.

Finally, collateralizing takes the form of A requiring that B expose an asset to loss or confiscation in case B's performance is unsatisfactory. In financial markets, collateralizing involves lender A requiring borrower B to commit a certain amount of equity to a project. The prospect of asset loss may induce B to avoid behaviour risking bankruptcy, thus benefiting A even should the collateral turn out to be unattachable by the lender in case of default.

Endogenous enforcement in the savings–investment market is, on balance, likely to involve some combination of contingent renewal and collateralizing. Both, it should be clear, entail credit-rationing even in market equilibrium: borrowers are quantity-constrained in that willingness to pay the equilibrium interest rate is not sufficient to attract a supply of funds. Collateralizing as an enforcement mechanism implies that collateral-poor firms are excluded from the credit market, and firms are refused credit when their debt/equity ratio becomes sufficiently large. Credit-rationing in contingent-renewal credit markets takes a more extreme form: one borrower may have access to credit while another potential borrower, identical in all respects, is excluded (Gintis, 1988).[9]

The analysis of contested exchange in financial markets is considerably altered in the international context, when the contracting parties are not governed by the same political authority. We will consider only the most important case: that between a private lender and a sovereign borrower. In this situation, the total absence of third-party enforcement[10] implies that insolvency is no longer a necessary condition of default: the borrowing government can choose not to honour its debts for any reason whatever—or for none at all (Eaton and Gersovitz 1981; Eaton *et al.* 1986).

As a result, collateralizing, a most potent endogenous enforcement strategy domestically, is ineffective in the international context, since default does not jeopardize the real resources of the delinquent government or its subjects. The creditor's home-country and international courts may be able to seize a debtor's exposed assets, such as exported goods and working capital in foreign banks. But, save in exceptional cases, such creditor initiatives are unlikely to have a serious deterrent effect, since a government's exposed assets are rarely extensive, and attaching the exposed property of the debtor country's nationals, besides being highly irregular, invites retaliation by the debtor.

Profit-sharing and joint control, like collateralizing, depend upon a degree of third-party enforcement. This takes the form of contracts with enforceable provisions concerning the division of the proceeds from an investment, and the rights of lenders to participate in decision-making. Even this degree of third-party enforcement is absent in the international context, since borrowers have the power to change the rules at will. Hence such mechanisms are ineffective in relations between agents within distinct political jurisdictions.

Reputation is also of limited value in an international context, since reputation concerns the systematic behaviour of particular agents, while governments change frequently, and the game-theoretic conditions which govern their behaviour lack more than short-term stability.[11] Thus, state decision-makers cannot expect their current actions to have more than short-term effects upon the future availability of credit to their economic system, except in so far as their decisions affect the underlying variables used by the international financial community to assess the integrity of their loans.[12]

Contingent renewal may remain an effective enforcement mechanism in the international context. It is certainly conceivable that a lender should offer a loan package sufficiently more attractive than the expected value of the borrower's alternatives that the prospect of losing this preferred line of credit deter default. However, given the oligopolistic character of international lending and the co-ordination of international banking by the International Monetary Fund and related organizations, the international lender has less reason to take the borrower's alternatives as given. Indeed, collusion among lenders can ensure that default by a sovereign debtor effectively freezes the debtor from further loans for a considerable period of time. This strategy, of course, is retaliatory, in that it is aimed, not at securing repayment, but rather at deterring defaults by other borrowers in the future.

Retaliation, then, is likely to be the endogenous enforcement mechanism of choice in the international arena. Nor is the threat of retaliation limited to denial of future credit. Creditors may be capable of disrupting the debtor's trade relations by withdrawing the debtor's access to short-term commercial banking services. In addition, creditors may be sufficiently influential to induce their governments to impose embargoes and tariffs upon, or to withdraw most-favoured nation status from, the offending debtor. Military retaliation is also conceivable—if not in the 'gunboat diplomacy' characteristic of classical imperialism (Lipson 1985), then in such more limited forms as threatening the withdrawal of military support for the debtor country or its governing regime, and cutting off access to military equipment and spare parts.

The costs of applying sanctions remain high—indeed, higher than in the domestic case, since the debtor now has an array of military responses at its disposal. But the threat of retaliation against a sovereign debtor now becomes credible, since the debtor is not necessarily insolvent and hence may be quite able, however unwilling, to pay.[13]

Since the major forms of retaliation involve military sanctions, trade embargoes, and interference with the sovereign defaulter's ability to obtain future loans, it follows that lenders are likely to be militarily powerful, as well as holding a prominent position in international trade and finance. Borrowers are, by contrast, likely to be militarily weak, and incapable of marshalling sufficient international support to protect themselves against their irate creditors.

The military solution, while in the past apparently considerably effective, is currently out of fashion. The USA, for example, exercised direct politico-military control at one time or another in the period before the First World War over Puerto Rico, Cuba, the Dominican Republic, Haiti, Nicaragua, Honduras, and Panama, and American troops intervened twice in Mexico (Frieden, forthcoming). Rising costs of intervention, however, have rendered this strategy virtually unused in recent decades.[14]

Non-military retaliation is difficult to render effective when there are more than a few creditors involved. Denial of future credit requires careful co-ordination among lenders. It is certainly in the self-interest of any single bank or government to strike a deal with a potential defaulter, accepting immediate partial repayment while other creditors remain waiting in the aisles for a chance to negotiate. In this situation a skilful debtor, by playing creditors off against one another, can render the threat of retaliation virtually powerless.[15]

Contemporary international financial institutions do, nevertheless, allow considerable latitude for collusion among lenders, since a handful of international banks control the bulk of credit activity, and such international intermediaries as the IMF co-ordinate their activities and attend to their collective needs.

One indication of the power of threat of retaliation is how infrequently such threats have been actually carried out. In a careful historical and statistical study, Lindert and Morton (1987) indicate that, while international lenders over the past century have earned sizeable risk premiums, defaulting borrowers have seldom been punished, either with direct sanctions or with access to future credit. Defaulters are especially likely to escape retaliation during global crises. The 1910s brought wholesale defaults in the Mexican and Russian revolutions and the fall of the Ottoman empire. The greatest wave, however, came in the early 1930s (Eichengreen and Portes, 1986), when all of Latin America, most of Eastern Europe, Turkey, and China defaulted. For additional historical perspectives, see Bittermann 1973, Kindleberger 1978, Fishlow 1985, Kaletsky 1985, and the papers in Eichengreen and Lindert 1989.

III. THE ASSET BALANCE MODEL

The asset balance model, while incompatible with a Walrasian conception of markets, does emerge in a straightforward manner from a simple microeconomic model of financial-market equilibrium. This model exploits the notion that, where contingent renewal is employed as an enforcement device, markets do not clear in equilibrium, adjustment to equilibrium involves quantity as well as price adjustment, and the structure of decision-making on the 'short side' of the market substantively affects the equilibrium configuration even under perfectly competitive conditions (Bowles and Gintis 1988*a* and *b*).

The asset balance model predicts that national economies will be subject to credit-rationing, the net asset position of a country being the effect, not of the interest rate and time preferences, but rather of the 'creditworthiness' of borrowers (i.e. their ability to pay and vulnerability to sanctions in case of default) and of the 'carrying capacity' of lenders (i.e. their ability to protect their net international creditor position through the application of sanctions). Our target asset position is the result of these complex considerations, and the adjustment to equilibrium, represented by a simple autoregressive process, involves reluctant lending, reluctant borrowing, policy reaction functions, the fragility of financial confidence, and various other exotica which inevitably enter into economic equilibration when prices fail to adjust to ensure market-clearing.[16]

The implications of our analysis are best presented by developing a general model of national-income determination, of which the closed, open, and asset balance models are special cases. We begin with some national-income accounting identities:

$$y = i + c + x + rd \tag{1}$$

$$e = x + rd \tag{2}$$

$$s = y - c \tag{3}$$

$$y = ak + rd \tag{4}$$

$$\dot{d} = e \tag{5}$$

$$\dot{k} = i \tag{6}$$

$$s/y = b + \varepsilon \tag{7}$$

$$i/k = \alpha + \mu \tag{8}$$

$$d(0) = d_0;\ \ k(0) = k_0 \tag{9}$$

where

y = income
e = current account
x = trade balance
r = interest rate
k = capital stock
b = propensity to save

α = *rate of growth*
a = output/capital ratio
k_0 = initial capital stock
i = investment
c = consumption
d = net creditor position
s = saving
a = income/capital ratio
ε = random error in s/y
μ = random error in i/y
d_0 = initial debt ratio

Equations (1)–(9) are standard and require little comment (note that we now interpret d as a net credit as opposed to a debit position). The open-economy model can be interpreted as (1)–(9) with the added assumption:

$$\varepsilon \text{ and } \mu \text{ are uncorrelated.} \tag{10a}$$

For in this case $e/y = sy/y - i/y = (b - \alpha) + \varepsilon - \mu$, so the current account is perfectly negatively correlated with investment, while saving is uncorrelated with investment. The closed-economy model consists of (1)–(9) with the assumption:

$$i/y = s/y + \nu \tag{10b}$$

where ν is a random error uncorrelated with μ and ε.

We propose to replace (10a) and (10b) with the following two equations:

$$l = d/y \tag{10}$$

$$\dot{l} = -\beta(l - l^*) + \nu \tag{11}$$

where l is the net asset position and ν is a random error term. In other words, we assume that a national economy has a target debt income position l^*, which may be either positive or negative, deviations from which engender corrective forces of one form or another.[17]

It is easy to verify that if the long-term equilibrium of (1)–(11) is to satisfy

$$d/y = l^* \qquad i/y = \alpha \qquad s/y = b \tag{12}$$

then the long-run debt/capital ratio l_k^* must satisfy

$$l_k^* = al^*/(1 - rl^*) \tag{13}$$

and we then have[18]

$$b = \alpha(1 + l_k^*) \tag{14}$$

The error terms ε, ν, and μ can then be seen to satisfy

$$\nu = (1 - rl)\varepsilon + \beta(l - l^*) - (1 + l_k^*)\mu \tag{15}$$

It is clear from (15) that an OLS regression of savings on investment will generally produce a biased estimate of the equilibrium effect of a shift in saving on the level of investment. When (12) holds, we can derive the equation

$$\frac{i}{y} = \frac{1}{1 + l_k^*}\frac{s}{y} \tag{16}$$

(note that this reduces to the closed-economy model when $l_k^* = 0$, as it should). However using (15) and assuming rl (the share of interest in national income) is small, and $(l - l^*)$ is uncorrelated with the other error terms, we find

$$\gamma_2 = \frac{1}{1 + l_k^*} \frac{1 + \dfrac{\sigma_{\mu\nu}}{\sigma_\mu^2}}{1 + 2\dfrac{\sigma_{\mu\nu}}{\sigma_\mu^2} + \dfrac{\sigma_\nu^2}{\sigma_\mu^2}} \tag{17}$$

Several special cases of (17) are of particular interest. First, if $\nu = 0$, so that the asset adjustment equation holds perfectly, then the closed-economy model appears to be supported: the OLS estimate of γ_2 will be unbiased, but will not equal unity unless the country's target net asset position is zero. Second, if σ_μ is small, then γ_2 will be biased towards 0, tending to support the open-economy model. Third, if $\varepsilon = 0$, then ν and μ are perfectly negatively correlated and $\gamma_2 = 0$, again supporting the open-economy model. This result should not be surprising: when the savings rate is considerably more stable than investment (a normal case), the open-economy model will appear valid whatever the long-run behaviour of the economy.

We will validate the asset balance model by showing that econometric estimation of Equation (11) yields significant and meaningful values for the target asset position l^* and the adjustment coefficient β. This justifies treating l^* as a critical indicator of a country's position in the international financial system, and considering the world pattern of l^* as a basic indicator of the structure of economic power and the nature of international financial intermediation.

The ultimate test of the asset balance model, however, involves developing a persuasive political economy of the credit positioning of national economies, revealing the economic and political forces which determine the sign and magnitude of the target asset position l^* of national economies. The political economy of credit positioning must also enquire into the factors causing the repositioning of particular national economies within the international financial system.

The system of international financial intermediation, moreover, exhibits substantial periods of stability punctuated by brief periods of restructuring. If credit positioning has the efficacy suggested in this paper, such restructuring would be expected to engender a rapid and relatively synchronized repositioning of l^* in many national economies. The political economy of credit positioning should be capable of identifying and interpreting these periods of punctuated restructuring, both on the level of international financial politics and in the behaviour of the asset balance equation (11).

Unfortunately, we merely brush the surface of these more complex issues in the present paper.

IV. TESTING THE ASSET BALANCE MODEL

The heart of the asset balance model of international financial-market equilibrium is Equation (11), which implies (i) that countries have a target net asset position, deviations from which engender non-price restorative forces; and (ii) that this target asset position is relatively impervious to short- and medium-run fluctuations in prices, interest rates, macroeconomic conditions, savings propensities, and investment behaviour.

One type of evidence in favour of this model is the long series of studies which have attempted to account for the net asset position of national economies in terms of the equalization of supply and demand through the adjustment of the interest rate. The existence of such a process is clearly predicted by both capital-assets pricing and portfolio balance models of financial equilibrium. Yet evidence in favour of its operation has not been forthcoming.[19]

Thus it is reasonable to subject our model to the direct test, as expressed in Equation (11), that economies adjust to maintain a target net foreign-asset position l^*. If the asset balance model is correct, then estimates of β should be between 0 and 1, and estimates of l^* should reasonably reflect a country's qualitative position in the international monetary order.

From (10), we have

$$\dot{l} = \frac{\dot{d}}{k} - \frac{\dot{k}}{k}\frac{d}{k} = \frac{e}{k} - \frac{\dot{k}}{k}\frac{d}{k}$$

where e is the current account. Since d/k is generally small, we shall use the approximation $l = e/k$. We thus rewrite (11) as

$$(e/y)_t = \beta(l^* - l_{t-l}) + \varepsilon_t \tag{18}$$

or

$$(e/y)_t = \beta l^* - \beta l_{t-l} + \varepsilon_t \tag{19}$$

where CA = current-account surplus[20] and Y = gross national product.[21] From the estimate of the constant term $\beta_0 = \beta l^*$ and the regression coefficient $\beta_1 = \beta$, we may derive the estimate β_0/β_1 of l^*.

An important characteristic of (11) and (19) is that l^* is not likely to be constant over time. Significant changes in political and economic factors at the domestic and/or international level can produce changes in a country's target net-asset position. These changes can also produce changes in the speed of adjustment to l^*. These structural changes can be represented by intercept dummy variables which reflect changes in

$l^*(D_i)$ and slope dummy variables $(d_i l_{t-1})$ which reflect changes in the speed of adjustment to l^*. Thus we have[22]

$$(e/y)_t = \beta l^* + D_1 - \beta l_{t-1} - D_1 l_{t-1} + e_t \qquad (20)$$

Table 7.2 presents estimates of Equation (20) for several countries over varying periods for which data are easily available.[23] Here l^* and l are measured as net-asset position relative to GNP. (Table 7.4 presents estimates for l^* and l defined relative to capital stocks.) Where correction for serial correlation was necessary, the value of the serial correlation coefficient ($\dot{\rho}$) is presented. The numbers in parentheses are t statistics.

For all countries in the sample, the adjustment coefficient on l_{t-i} has the appropriate negative value, giving a statistically significant value for β between 0 and 1, as the theory suggests. The lag on 1 is two periods for all countries except for the USA, which has a lag of one period. The estimates for about half the countries required correction for serial correlation.

TABLE 7.2. *The adjustment of net-asset positions as a percentage of GNP (dependent variable: current-account/GNP)*

	C	D1	D2	l_{t-i}	$\bar{R}^2$	DW	ρ
Canada	−.09	.02		−.17	.54	1.7	
	(6.14)	(5.80)		(−4.70)			
Finland	−.02	−.04		−.10	.57	2.1	
	(−3.19)	(−5.21)		(−1.70)			
France	−.01			−.19	.15	1.3	
	(−2.30)			(−2.20)			
Germany	.02	−.01		−.46	.49	1.7	.4
	(3.50)	(−3.40)		(−2.90)			
Japan	.02			−.50	.29	1.8	.6
	(2.20)			(−2.00)			
Norway	−.06	−.09		−.30	.71	1.8	
	(−4.80)	(−6.90)		(−5.40)			
Sweden	.00	−.04		−.13	.38	1.7	
	(.98)	(−3.90)		(−3.00)			
UK	.01	.02		−.20	.54	1.7	.5
	(1.00)	(2.84)		(−2.80)			
USA	.03	−.01	−.02	−.24	.23	1.8	.2
	(3.10)	(−2.40)	(−3.30)	(−2.70)			

T statistics are in parentheses, l_{t-i} is net-asset position/GNP, and D1, D2 are dummy variables; for dates see below. All current-account data from OECD (1976). All other data from IMF, *International Financial Statistics*, unless otherwise stated.

Canada: 1958–86 D1 = 0. 1958–66; D1 = 1, 1967–86. Net foreign assets, 1947–74, from *Historical Statistics Canada*, 2nd edn. (1983). 1978 from Goldsmith

(1985); 1980–6 from IMF (1988*b*); all other interpolated using current-account balances.
Finland: 1963–84. D1 = 0, 1963–73, 1977–84; D1 = 1, 1974–6. Net foreign assets, 1963–79, from Central Bank of Finland; 1980–4 derived by accumulating current-account balances.
France: 1963–86. Net foreign-asset position, 1972, 1976, from Goldsmith, (1985); 1982–6 from IMF (1988*b*); 1960–71 extrapolated from 1972 using current-account balances. GNP data from OECD (1988*a*).
Germany: 1960–84. D1 = 0, 1960–78; D1 = 1, 1979–84. Net foreign-asset position, Deutsche Bundesbank.
Japan: 1965–82. Net foreign assets, 1971–82, from Bank of Japan, *Balance of Payments Monthly*; 1965–70 derived from accumulating current-account balances.
Norway: 1963–85. D1 = 0, 1963–74, 1981–5; D1 = 1, 1975–9. Net foreign assets, 1970–85, from Norwegian Central Bank.
Sweden: 1965–85. D1 = 0, 1965–78; D1 = 1, 1979–85. Net foreign assets, 1977–85, Swedish Central Bank, 1965–76, derived from current-account balances.
UK: 1965–86. D1 = 0, 1965–79; D1 = 1, 1980–6. Net foreign-asset position from CSO (annual).
USA: 1951–82. D1 = 0, 1951–66, 1972–82; D1 = 1, 1967–71; D2 = 0, 1951–71; D2 = 1, 1972–82. Net foreign-asset position from *Survey of Current Business*.

From Table 7.2, we can calculate the estimated values of l^* and β. These are presented in Table 7.3. Most of the l^* estimates seem reasonable. For most countries (France and Japan excepted), l^* changed over the estimation period.[24] But in most cases the value of β does not change, as measured by the t statistics on the interactive dummy coefficients (not shown).[25] The adjustment coefficients range from 10% to 50%, but most are concentrated in the middle teens. For most countries, then, the rate of adjustment to the net-asset target takes more than five years.

These estimates reveal a wide range of net-asset targets, from very large negative targets for Canada in the late 1950s and early 1960s to moderately high positive targets for the USA in the 1950s and 1960s. Yet the range is much smaller than those implied by the data for the nineteenth century (Table 7.1 (*a*)). The estimates also reveal that most countries' net-asset targets shifted in the 1970s, with the fall of the 'Golden Age' as many countries in our sample repositioned themselves in the face of domestic and international adversity.[26] There seems to be a new repositioning occurrring in the 1980s, but it is too early to obtain reliable estimates of the new l^* for some countries, notably the USA and Japan.

In general, the estimates are consistent with the idea that most countries choose, or have thrust upon them, net foreign-asset targets to which they adjust, but that these targets change over time with significant domestic and international events. The Vietnam War and the decline of US dominance in the 1970s, for example, led the USA to adopt lower net-asset positions, while the rise to power of Thatcher in Great Britain in the late 1970s led the UK to pursue greater net-asset positions.

TABLE 7.3. *Net foreign-asset targets* (l^*)[a] *and adjustment rates* (β) (%)

	l^*	β
Canada		
1958–66	– 53.0	17
	(– 16.2)	
1972–86	– 37.0	
	[– 6.0]	
Finland		
1963–73	– 23.0	10
	(– 3.1)	
1974–6	– 66.0	
	[1.6]	
1977–84	– 23.0	
France		
1963–86	– 4.4	19
	(– 6.8)	
Germany		
1960–78	9.8	50
	(10.0)	
1979–84	5.6	
	[2.9]	
Japan		
1965–82	3.8	50
	(2.8)	
Norway		
1963–74	– 21.0	30
	(– 9.7)	
1975–80	– 52.1	
	[5.4]	
1981–5	– 21.0	
Sweden		
1965–78	2.9	13
	(1.1)	
1979–85	– 24.8	
	[5.5]	
UK		
1965–79	– 26.5	20
	(– 1.0)	
1980–6	16.2	
	[– 3.0]	
USA		
1951–66	11.3	24
	(13.5)	
1967–71	8.2	
	[2.8]	
1972–82	3.4	
	[3.7]	

The t statistics testing the null hypothesis that l^* is equal to 0 are in parentheses. The t statistics testing the null hypothesis that a country's l^* is different from the previous l^* are in square brackets.

[a] Here l^* is net foreign-asset position divided by GNP. Calculated from Table 7.2; l^* is the constant from Table 7.2 plus appropriate dummy coefficients divided by the negative of the coefficient on l_{t-i}. β is the negative of the coefficient on l_{t-i}. The coefficients in Table 7.3 might differ from those calculated from Table 7.2 because of rounding.

TABLE 7.4. *The adjustment of net-asset positions as a percentage of capital (dependent variable: current account/capital stock)*

	C	D1	D2	l_{t-i}	$\bar{R}^2$	DW	ρ
Canada	−.03	.01		−.10	.25	2.1	.3
	(−2.40)	(1.80)		(−1.90)			
Finland	−.01	−.01		−.15	.55	2.0	
	(−3.50)	(−4.90)		(−2.20)			
France	−.01			−.14	.09	1.3	
	(−2.00)			(−1.80)			
Germany	.02	−.01		−.46	.51	1.7	.4
	(3.50)	(−3.40)		(−2.40)			
Norway	−.02	−.02		−.32	.70	1.7	
	(−4.40)	(−6.20)		(−1.65)			
UK	.002	−.01		−.17	.47	1.5	.5
	(.90)	(−2.20)		(−1.80)			
USA	.01	−.003	−.01	−.24	.34	1.8	.3
	(3.00)	(−2.30)	(−2.3)	(−2.60)			

T statistics in parentheses.

All current-account data from OECD (1976) unless otherwise stated. All capital-stock data are net capital from OECD, (1987*a*) unless otherwise stated. For net-asset data, see Table 7.2.

Canada: 1963–85. D1 = 0, 1963–6; D1 = 1, 1967–86.

Finland: 1963–85. D1 = 0, 1963–73, 1977–85; D1 = 1, 1974–6.

France: 1963–84.

Germany: 1963–84. D1 = 0, 1963–78; D1 = 1, 1979–84.

Norway: 1965–85. D1 = 0, 1965–74, 1981–5; D1 = 1, 1975–80.

UK: 1965–86. D1 = 0, 1965–79; D1 = 1, 1980–6.

USA: 1950–82. D1 = 0, 1950–66, 1972–82; D1 = 1, 1967–71; D2 = 0, 1951–71; D2 = 1, 1972–82. Net capital-stock data are net reproducible tangible wealth, excluding consumer durables, *Survey of Current Business*, Nov. 1987.

TABLE 7.5. Net foreign-asset targets (l^*) [a] and adjustment rates (β) (%)

	l^*	β
Canada		
1963–6	– 31.0	10
	(– 5.4)	
1967–85	– 22.0	
	[– 2.1]	
Finland		
1963–73	– 6.5	15
	(– 4.7)	
1974–6	– 15.0	
	[2.0]	
1977–85	– 6.5	
France		
1963–84	– 4.3	14
Germany		
1963–78	2.0	46
	(10.1)	
1979–84	2.0	
	[3.4]	
Norway		
1965–74	– 5.8	17
	(– 9.2)	
1974–9	– 12.3	
	[4.7]	
1980–5	– 5.5	
UK		
1965–79	1.5	17
	(1.3)	
1980–6	5.5	
	(3.2)	
	[– 1.9]	
USA		
1951–66	5.0	24
	(13.4)	
1967–71	3.8	
	[2.6]	
1972–82	1.6	
	[4.3]	

The t statistics testing the null hypothesis that l^* is equal to 0 are in parentheses. The t statistics testing the null hypothesis that a country's l^* is different from the previous l^* are in square brackets.

[a] l^* is net foreign-asset position divided by net capital stock. Calculated from Table 7.2; l^* is the constant

from Table 7.2 plus appropriate dummy coefficients divided by the negative of the coefficient on l_{t-i}. β is the negative of the coefficient on l_{t-i}. The coefficients in Table 7.5 might differ from those calculated from Table 7.4 because of rounding.

Tables 7.4 and 7.5 present estimates of l^* and adjustment rates β where l and l^* are defined relative to the country's stock of fixed capital. The sample here excludes Japan and Sweden, which lack capital-stock data. In general, the results are consistent with those of Tables 7.2 and 7.3. Table 7.5 presents the estimates of l^* and β for different periods, and the results are similar to those in Table 7.3, the adjustment coefficients being mostly in the high teens and low twenties, and target asset positions changing for most countries over time.

V. POLICY IMPLICATIONS

Our model of international capital market equilibration conforms neither to neoclassical price adjustment nor to Keynesian quantity adjustment. An analysis of the implications of the asset balance model for economic policy is thus complex, and cannot be addressed with any degree of precision without a more explicit model of the domestic economy than we can feasibly provide in this paper. Hence in this section we will explore policy implications only to the extent that they are amenable to general treatment.

Macroeconomic models fall naturally into two categories: those that treat the domestic economy as only loosely connected to the rest of the world through international trade and finance (so-called insular models), and those that view domestic economy as inextricably linked to its position in an international system of market relations (so-called global models). The asset balance model falls clearly in the global camp, along with the textbook open-economy model, which views prices of all traded goods and financial instruments as set on international markets. By contrast, classical Keynesian and supply-side models, both permitting a strong degree of independence of domestic profit and interest rates from international levels, and both predicting a strong association between domestic investment and savings, fall clearly in the insular camp.

In this section we compare policy implications of the asset balance model with those of the open-economy model and the two insular models. In addition, we will analyse the asset balance model under two distinct assumptions: first, that a country's target asset position is exogenously determined, in which case the economy's external constraint is the requirement that its current account adjust to restore asset balance for a given l^*; and second, that the long-term asset position l^* is endogenously determined, and its maintenance constrains a country's policy choices.

Our results may be summarized as follows. In terms of short-run stabilization (see Table 7.6), the asset balance model is in significant agreement with the open-economy model, except that under fixed exchanges the open-economy model holds that monetary policy can affect only the level of reserves, and so is ineffective for internal balance, while the asset balance allows an effective monetary policy. Most important, however, is that, when the impact of capital flight[27] on an economy's long-run asset position is taken into account (the variable l^* case), the asset balance model predicts a more constrained range of policy alternatives than the other models.

In terms of long-run policy (see Table 7.7), by contrast, the asset balance model conforms to the predictions of the insular models in the fixed l^* case. However, the policy implications are much less conventional when it is recognized that sustaining a long-term asset position imposes serious constraints. Creditor countries must be economically and militarily powerful; debtor countries must be vulnerable. These

TABLE 7.6. *A comparison of alternative paradigms: short-run stabilization policy*

	Insular		Global		
	Keynesian	Supply side	Open economy	Asset balance fixed l^*	Asset balance variable l^*
Constrained by threat of capital flight	Yes	No	No	No	Yes
Fiscal policy is effective for internal balance	Yes	No	Yes	Yes	Yes
Fiscal policy is effective for external balance	Yes	No	Yes	Yes	Yes
Monetary policy is effective for internal balance					
Fixed exchange	No	Yes	No	Yes	Yes
Flexible exchange	No	Yes	Yes	Yes	Yes
Monetary policy is effective for external balance					
Fixed exchange	No	Yes	Yes	Yes	Yes
Flexible exchange	No	Yes	Yes	Yes	Yes

imperatives of long-term lending and borrowing, ignored in other models of international capital flows, are the central policy implications of the asset balance model. In particular, the asset balance model implies that international credit relations impose more serious constraints than suggested by the insular model.

In the final section, we describe the relation between the asset balance model and the global liberal model (Bowles and Gintis 1986; Wachtel 1987). Here we argue that the asset balance model operates much like a global liberal model with non-Walrasian foundations. As in the global liberal model, national autonomy, and in particular, the extension of democratic rights in the state and economy, might be severely compromised in countries that are fully integrated into international credit markets.

TABLE 7.7. *A comparison of policy paradigms: the long run*

	Insular		Global	
	Keynesian	Supply side	Open-economy	Asset balance
Savings–investment linkage	Autonomous investment	Savings-driven	None	Savings-limited
The profit rate as a policy variable	Yes	Self-defeating	No	Yes
Effectiveness of taxing wealth	Yes	No	Yes	Yes
The foundations of global liberalism	n/a	n/a	Perfect markets	Endogenous enforcement

V.1. Insular and Global Models

Modern open-economy policy analysis has been concerned with one overriding question: can macroeconomic tools achieve domestic goals (internal balance) when a country must satisfy external constraints (external balance)? The models used to answer this question, and indeed the question itself, have evolved over time. Early post-war discussion centred on short-run stabilization policy and balance-of-payments equilibrium. More recently, concern has shifted to long-run growth and international borrowing and lending implying current-account equilibrium as the external constraint (Kenen 1984).

Policy issues in this context have been framed by two models. The first, the insular model, posits an extensive role for macroeconomic policy in achieving domestic goals subject to external constraints (McKinnon 1981), since according to this view, economies are international price-makers. Exchange rate policy can alter a country's terms of trade; monetary policy can alter a country's relative interest rate; and the domestic profit rate can be altered through fiscal, trade union, or tax policy.[28]

Open-economy models, while often in agreement with insular models on the efficacy of short-run stabilization policy, assume that national economies are price-takers in internationally integrated markets. Traded goods prices, interest rates, and profit rates, equalized internationally by goods, financial, and capital arbitrage, are unaffected by macroeconomic policy.[29] Hence the latitude for short-run policy is more limited than in the insular case.

The policy implications of these models are starkly different, both in the short and in the long term. For short-term stabilization policy, the insular model implies that internal goals, such as full employment, need not be sacrificed to external constraints (Meade 1951; Mundell 1968). In the long run, the implications of the two models are also significantly different. The insular models operating at full employment are constrained by domestic savings, whereas open economies are not.[30] This means that, under full employment, expansionary fiscal policy will crowd out domestic investment as in the supply-side model of Feldstein and Horioka. In neo-Keynesian insular models, domestic economic growth is likewise domestically constrained, either by saving or by investment (Marglin 1984).

By contrast, in the open-economy model, current government deficits do not crowd out investment at full employment. Over time, the price-taking country engages in 'inter-temporal trade', increasing current consumption and investment, at the expense of future consumption (Frenkel and Razin 1987). While the open-economy model implies that a country can engage in inter-temporal trade at the going profit rate, it has no power to cause the profit rate to deviate from its international level. A government wishing to redistribute income from capital to labour, or tax capital for distributional purposes, will find its economy shrinking. The insular economy, on the other hand, is not constrained by the international profit rate. Domestic, not international, factors thus determine the extent to which governments can achieve their goals by altering the distribution of income (Marglin 1984). In short, the insular economy can and must manage its own destiny; the open economy has greater access to world resources, but its ability to manage them is limited by an externally imposed system of interest and profit rates.

V.2. The Asset Balance Model in the Short Run

The asset balance model differs from the open-economy and insular models in its stress upon the possibility that monetary and fiscal policy may be constrained by adverse short-term international financial flows.

For instance, in the standard Mundell–Fleming model, full employment can be attained while international financial-market equilibrium is maintained, through proper settings of monetary, fiscal, and exchange rate policy.

On the other hand, if short-term financial flows are sufficiently disruptive—as in the case of destabilizing exchange rate speculation, or where policy measures weaken the expectation of creditors as to the country's ability to maintain its current long-term asset position—then the asset balance model implies that domestic governments will be unable to achieve domestic goals in the face of their asset target constraint. In this case, the short-run policy implications of the asset balance model are much more pessimistic than that of the insular model. Countries will be forced to maintain their external balance targets without the macroeconomic tools to maintain full employment. Here domestic goals would have to be sacrificed to external balance, as contemporary post-Keynesian and some Keynesian critics are suggesting (Minsky 1982).[31]

Capital flight illustrates the potential gravity of this phenomenon. In the insular model with imperfect capital mobility, capital flight is a manageable problem. An increase in domestic interest rates, or a decline in the exchange rate, are sufficient to stem and even reverse capital flight. In the open-economy model, capital flight is even less problematic. Since financial flows are highly elastic with respect to rates of return, the interest rate and exchange rate changes (see Krugman 1979) required to inhibit capital flight are relatively small.

In the asset balance model, by contrast, where debtor countries are faced with credit-rationing, capital flight can be a serious problem. Capital flight typically involves the loss of foreign exchange. If foreign assets held abroad and the income from them are attachable by the debtor country, then, the asset balance model suggests, capital flight is of no significance since capital flight will simply involve the exchange of one foreign asset (e.g. reserves held by the central bank) for another (e.g. real estate in Miami). However, if these assets are not attachable by the domestic government, then capital flight involves an increase in the debtor countries' debt position, equal to the loss in foreign exchange as a share of the country's capital stock.

Given the country's l^* such a loss could then entail significant difficulties. The loss of foreign income would worsen the country's current account, requiring further adjustment to reach the country's l^*. More significantly, if the country must maintain its given l^*, then its loss of foreign-exchange reserves would reduce its asset position (l) below its target (l^*); as a result, the country would be forced to implement an even greater reduction in current-account position. Changes in domestic interest rates or profit rates, in the face of credit-rationing, are unlikely to be sufficient to stem or reverse such capital flight.

V.3. The Asset Balance Model in the Long Run

If we assume the long-run asset position of a national economy is fixed, then the long-run asset balance model operates as a modified long-run insular model (Marglin 1984)—modified because, unlike the insular model, countries do borrow and lend over the long run, and thus a country's growth rate can be augmented by foreign savings. It agrees with the insular model, however, in that, by contrast with the open-economy model, when the country's asset position is in equilibrium, additional fiscal stimulus crowds out investment, since foreign borrowing cannot be increased. Thus, given its l^*, domestic growth is ultimately savings-limited if the economy is at full employment, or investment-limited, if it faces chronic underemployment.

Furthermore, like the insular model and unlike the open-economy model, domestic profit rates need not equal foreign profit rates. For the movement of capital in the face of profit rate differentials is counterbalanced by the tendency of financial markets to maintain an economy's actual debt position in line with its target l^*; i.e. there are significant barriers to the international flow of capital. By the same token, since countries are not price-takers at the going rate of profit, capital funds will not massively leave a country in response to profit rate differentials. Hence there is considerable latitude to use the profit rate as an instrument of long-run policy.

V.4. The International Credit Regime

Until now we have assumed that a country's long-term asset position l^* is exogenously given. In this case, the model implies possibly significant policy constraints in the short run, but in the long run it operates much like the insular model.

However, the long-run policy implications of the asset balance model are, in fact, far-reaching once one recognizes that a country's l^* is endogenous. This means that a country must undertake particular behaviours and, more importantly, implement particular policy structures to sustain its asset target. It is these behaviours and structures which entail significant constraints of international credit relations. And because they affect prerogatives of power and the distribution of wealth, these structures represent objects of intense domestic and international political struggle.

More concretely, creditor countries must possess the political and military power, and international trading and financial structures, to credibly threaten recalcitrant debtors. Debtors, on the other hand, must possess the economic and political structures to credibly commit themselves to servicing their debt. Adjustments of interest rates, fiscal policies, or even profit rates will not suffice.

We call the set of creditor and debtor structures which sustain a particular world configuration of l^* an international credit regime. An international credit regime includes an enforcement structure and a repayment structure.[32] The enforcement structure consists of those institutions, both domestic and international, which major creditor countries have developed to provide rewards and to impose sanctions on debtors. In the post-war period these institutions included the International Monetary Fund and the World Bank (Payer, 1974), the US Government's commitment to free trade (Block 1977), the US Marines, and the Central Intelligence Agency (Kolko 1988).

The repayment structure consists of the institutions and behaviours of debtor countries which support their target asset positions. These institutions convince lenders that the debtors will repay, and thus determine their creditworthiness. They include an outward-oriented trade policy which makes a debtor vulnerable to trade sanctions, and a debtor government's dependence on US military aid which makes a government vulnerable to military sanctions. The repayment structure interacts with the enforcement structure effectively to impose costs and benefits. This interaction of the enforcement structure and the repayment structure sustains the global configuration of target asset positions.

The international credit regime is likely to be the object of political struggles at the international and domestic levels. Domestically-oriented business in a creditor country, for example, may oppose a government commitment to open import markets, while organized labour may oppose governmental support of outward foreign investment. Similarly, groups in debtor countries who lose from IMF austerity programmes, and national capitalists in debtor countries who are harmed by export-oriented growth, may oppose the government's commitment to maintaining a debtor's creditworthiness.

History is filled with examples of such conflicts. The series of political battles in the USA, and between the USA and Great Britain, over the establishment of the Bretton Woods System in the post-war period, provides a classic example of the confluence of political and economic forces giving rise to an international credit regime (Block 1977). The erosion of the USA's commitment to free trade and the rise of Japanese power represent historical forces which undermine such a regime.[33]

It is important to note that an international credit regime accounts for a configuration of *target* asset positions, not the actual asset positions at any particular time. A country's asset position at any particular time is determined by an array of factors, from random fluctuations in exchange rates to bouts of optimism, pessimism, or loan-pushing. But whatever these fluctuations, it is the structures embodied in the international credit regime which determine whether these shocks are ratified by a country's long-term target, or evaporate with the next wave or fashion.

There are many important historical examples of swings in creditor positions which proved ephemeral. During the First World War, for example, the USA became a net international creditor for the first time. Banks in the New York financial markets actively floated bonds for European and Latin American borrowers, as the USA's credit position accumulated (Fishlow 1985; Darrity and Horn 1988). Yet the USA's enforcement structure was not sufficient to sustain its creditor position in the face of domestic opposition, foreign competition, and, of course, the Great Depression (Frieden, forthcoming; Lipson 1985). Only the Second World War, and the reconstruction of domestic and international relations which followed, were sufficient to create an international credit regime capable of sustaining the USA's massive creditor position.

The asset balance model thus differs fundamentally in its policy implications from the insular and open-economy models, which, while differing in important respects, share a lack of concern for the structural implications of international financial relations. There is no important place for such structural issues in open and insular models, since they assume that international financial relations are governed by Walrasian adjustment.

By contrast, the asset balance model stresses such structural implications. Where movements in market rates of return are unable to achieve international financial equilibrium, such structural factors as the nature of a country's trading patterns, the potential for exercising national military and political power, and the political alliances of national governments play an essential role in the equilibration of international financial markets.

In short, while the insular and open-economy models view international financial equilibration purely in terms of adjustments in quantity and prices, the asset balance model recognizes that international financial equilibration implies the maintenance and transformation of particular financial, trading, and political regimes. The asset balance model thus replaces the zero current-account constraint of the insular model, and the equal-profit rate constraint of the open model, by the structural imperatives of sustaining a country's position in international credit markets. From this perspective, the asset balance model suggests that international credit markets allow countries to overcome temporal budget constraints, but only by following specific inter-temporal 'rules of the game'. As in other areas of political economy, these rules involve serious constraints for all, while providing benefits to some and costs to others.

VI. GLOBAL LIBERALISM REVISITED

We end with the basic question addressed by this volume: how much autonomy do nations have in the contemporary global economy? The global liberal model (Bowles and Gintis 1986; Wachtel 1987) says very little:

> In this (the global liberal) form of accommodation, the democratic structure of the state is rendered vacuous. . . . Unless the economy in question has special advantages that make it more attractive to capital, it must do what it can to match the profit-enhancing strategies enacted by competing states. When economies are so thoroughly integrated in the world economic system that the supply of investment in any given economy is highly responsive to small differences in the expected profit rate, the effective range of choices may be reduced to a single set of policies, a global equivalent to Henry Ford's 'you can have any color car you want, as long as it is black'. (Bowles and Gintis 1986: 191.)

The asset balance model poses a distinct, yet no less demanding, set of constraints on national policy. While profit rate equalization is not a binding constraint on national governments in the asset balance model, maintenance of creditworthiness for debtors, and the capacity to collect for creditors, becomes a key factor in policy-making.

The need for the endogenous enforcement of debtor–creditor relations implies that the Walrasian capital-adjustment mechanism underlying the global liberal approach is generally inoperative. National economies are not forced by the market to play particular roles in international credit markets; the configuration of their domestic political forces and their position in the international economy can determine their relationship to international credit markets along a spectrum of roles—within, however, the rules of the international credit regime governing the global distribution of target asset positions.

Thus, to attract foreign investment, or, conversely, to become large creditors, nations do mortgage their economic and political autonomy. For debtor countries, effective repayment structures may conflict with the broad extension of democratic rights within the economy and state. For large creditors, enforcement structures preclude policies to reduce military forces and political intervention.

In short, according to the asset balance model, global credit relations do not force nations to conform to some internationally determined rate of profits, but what they do impose—political and economic vulnerability for debtors, and military and political intervention among creditors—is no less challenging to our political will and imagination.

NOTES

1. See Dornbusch (1980) and Frenkel and Razin (1987). For early contributions, see Fleming (1962) and Mundell (1963).
2. Feldstein and Horioka (1980) was the first in what is now an extensive literature to stress this phenomenon. See Gordon (1988) for additional theoretical and empirical criticisms of the open-economy model.

3. We do not use the term 'optimal' or even 'chosen' in connection with net foreign asset position. For the target may not be optimal with respect to society as a whole nor, in the case of credit-rationed countries, voluntarily chosen.
4. We shall refer to these models as 'insular' rather than 'closed' since, rather than ignoring international trade and finance altogether, they treat the foreign sector as affecting domestic prices and quantities.
5. Indeed, enforcement costs may well have increased: the relative military and political power which creditors could bring to bear on debtors in the 19th c. may have been greater than today. The replacement of colonialism with more market-integrated forms of 'neo-colonial' relations, may simply not be as effective in enforcement. See Lipson (1985).
6. On the general implications of endogenous enforcement for general equilibrium theory, see Bowles and Gintis (1988*a*; 1988*b*; 1990). On the failure of market-clearing in labour, capital, and other markets involving 'moral hazard', see Stiglitz (1987). For models of domestic credit-rationing, see Stiglitz and Weiss (1981), and Gintis (1988). On international credit-rationing, see Eaton and Gersovitz (1981), Eaton *et al.* (1986), and Kharas (1984).
7. The problem of enforcement is treated as problematic in several modern approaches to the theory of exchange, including property rights (Alchian and Demsetz 1972), transactions cost (Williamson 1985), and principal-agent (Laffont and Maskin 1982) theories.
8. Profit-sharing is also more effective the closer B is to being risk-neutral. Indeed, when B is risk-neutral, an externally enforceable contract can sometimes be implemented by transferring residual-claimant status to B (Shavell 1979; Holmström 1979).
9. The excluded agent is willing in this case to offer the lender a supra-market interest rate, but the lender will not accept, since the higher interest rate induces the borrower to assume more risk, thus lowering the lender's expected return.
10. While a lender might theoretically have recourse to the sovereign borrower's courts, it is rare that a judicial system enforces the transfer of assets to foreigners against the will of the regime in power. A judgement against the sovereign borrower may be obtainable in the lender's own courts, but the lender's government cannot be counted upon to mobilize the coercive instruments needed to enforce such a judgement (Lipson 1985; Frieden, forthcoming).
11. Lindert and Morton (1987) present convincing evidence that investors pay little attention to the past repayment record of the borrowing governments. While it is possible to identify some problem areas (Latin America, Eastern Europe, Africa) and some generally prompt repayers (Western Europe, the Arab nations, Asia east of the Persian Gulf), *ex ante* differences in interest rates offered to borrowing countries were not good predictors of *ex post* returns—apparently due to the difficulty in obtaining accurate predictions.
12. See our discussion of 'repayment structures' below.
13. Lindert and Morton (1987: 13) relate the story of Khedive Ismail, monarch of Egypt, who in 1879 partially defaulted on his outstanding bonds. The

British and French Governments prevailed upon the Ottoman sultan to depose Ismail, and British and French officials assumed control of Egyptian finances. Egypt fully repaid at a high interest rate.

14. This change in policy on the part of the USA and Great Britain is carefully charted and analysed in Lipson (1985). It is unclear the extent to which this shift is due to economic changes (e.g. the shift in foreign investment in LDCs away from primary production for export and towards industrial production for the local market) as opposed to military changes (especially the costs of intervention and occupation). The superpowers' relative lack of success in conventional warfare against LDCs in recent years leads us to favour the military explanation.
15. In domestic financial markets this sort of behaviour is generally illegal. In the USA, for instance, an insolvent debtor must declare bankruptcy and allow the courts to adjudicate among creditors.
16. Our model, therefore, does incorporate willingness to pay as a central determinant of lending behaviour.
17. Eq. (16) is a typical stock-adjustment equation in a model of credit market equilibrium based upon rationing and endogenous enforcement. Eq. (16) also serves as a formalization of the policy reaction interpretation of the Feldstein–Horioka results noted by Fieleke (1982), Caprio and Howard (1984), and others.
18. It may be noticed that Eqs. (1)–(10) give rise to a long-run equilibrium debt/capital ratio given by $l^o = (ab - \alpha)/(\alpha - rb)$, which need not, and in general will not, coincide with the target asset ratio l^*. We have shown elsewhere (Epstein and Gintis 1988) that the period of adjustment to l^o is very large compared to the period of adjustment to l^*, and in general the influence of l^o on the dynamics of the model is insignificant. We shall ignore this effect here.
19. See Frankel (1982*a*; 1982*b*; 1989); Dooley and Isard (1979); Boothe *et al.* (1985). The last contains an excellent review of this now extensive literature.
20. Valuation effects, caused by differential changes in asset prices and exchange rates, also produce changes in a country's net-asset position. However, a country has less control over asset price changes than over its current-account balance as a way of reaching l^*. Exchange rate changes are unlikely to be an effective way of achieving target net-asset positions, especially for large creditors or debtors, because of retaliation effects from other countries. For now we will think of a country as primarily adjusting its current account to reach l^*.
21. We have estimated (18) with capital stock in the denominator, with little change in the conclusions.
22. Dummies were chosen to conform to expected structural breaks resulting from such major international changes as the Vietnam War, breakdown of the Bretton Woods system, or oil price shocks. Dummies which were not significant were dropped from the reported equations. In addition, there are several possible econometric problems in estimating Eq. (20). One is possible simultaneity bias resulting from the fact that l is an endogenous variable, depending as its does on the current-account balance. This is mitigated,

however, by using lagged values of l which do not depend on the contemporaneous current-account balance. A second is serial correlation, for which we have corrected when appropriate.

23. The periods for each country are given in the notes to Table 7.2 and can be more easily gleaned from Table 7.3.
24. The exception was Canada, which in some regressions had a significant shift dummy around the time of the Vietnam War. The size of this shift seemed too large and may be due to data problems. The Canadian case requires further study.
25. The t statistics, testing the significance of the l^*s, were calculated using a linear approximation for the standard error of $(-\beta_0/\beta)$—see Marglin (1984: 445). Wald tests were performed, and decisively rejected in all cases the hypotheses that the coefficients are jointly zero.
26. See esp. Glyn, Lipietz, Hughes and Singh, and Epstein and Schor, in Marglin and Schor (1990).
27. By 'capital flight' we mean the outflow of finance in response to expected changes in future real rates of return. Capital flight occurs in the asset balance model when financial investors expect a change in the creditworthiness of assets denominated in a particular currency or held by a particular national economy—i.e. when some change in l^* is expected.
28. There are different versions of the insular model: models oriented primarily toward short-run analysis (Meade 1951; Mundell 1968; for a survey see Kenen 1985); long-run supply-side models (Feldstein and Horioka 1980) which assume full employment; and long-run non-neoclassical models along neo-Keynesian and neo-Marxian lines (Marglin 1984).
29. For a survey see Dornbusch (1980) and Frenkel and Razin (1987). Non-neoclassical models, such as Bowles and Gintis's global liberal model, share some of the characteristics of the open-economy model, but will be discussed under a separate heading below.
30. Of course, these savings can include foreign-exchange reserves earned by accumulated trade surpluses, though the spirit of the insular model is that, in the medium term, trade surpluses and deficits will balance out. The point is, however, that countries cannot borrow large amounts in advance of such savings. Moreover, government-negotiated loans can also supplement domestic resources.
31. These views have much in common with Nurkse's classic analysis (1944) of the inter-war monetary system and Keynes's analysis in 'National Self-Sufficiency' (1933), which argued that countries must reduce their international financial interactions (Crotty 1983).
32. Our discussion of international credit regimes has benefitted from Lipson (1985), who, however, is unconcerned with the political economy of domestic enforcement and repayment structures or their microfoundations.
33. Davis and Huttenback (1986) discuss the political economy of the enforcement regime in 19th-c. Britain.

8

Capital Mobility and Policy Effectiveness under a Credit Run: The Mexican Economy in the 1980s

JAIME ROS

I. INTRODUCTION

The international debt crisis of the 1980s has been extensively analysed in recent years. The conceptual and theoretical aspects of the breakdown of international lending have been the object of many important contributions, and related issues of solvency, liquidity, and enforcement in the context of sovereign debt have been thoroughly re-examined.[1] Similarly, the consequences of the debt crisis, in terms of the reverse transfer of resources from affected developing countries, a reinforced conditionality on domestic policy by international financial institutions, and economic and social performance at the national level, have also been widely discussed.

Other writers have looked at the impact of solvency issues on fiscal policy from the framework of optimal debt accumulation. For instance, Sachs (1984) models debt repayment as a constraint on the government budget, to argue that if the revenue constraint is binding in the repayment period the government should borrow less than the amount indicated by pure market considerations. As Eaton *et al.* (1986) point out, however, this argument works both ways: if the government were constrained in the initial, rather than in the repayment period, then optimality conditions would suggest a borrowing level higher than one which equates the world interest rate to the domestic marginal product of capital.

This paper goes beyond this debate to suggest that the undesirable consequences of over-indebtedness extend not only to repayment difficulties but also to the very effectiveness of macroeconomic policies. These are a related but different and largely unexplored set of issues, dealing with the consequences of the debt crisis on domestic policy management through the sharp reduction in the ability of governments to attract foreign capital and retain domestic savings within the country. The paper argues that the breakdown of lending—from both foreign and domestic lenders—by drastically altering the pattern of capital inflows and outflows has caused a considerable worsening of the trade-offs between the different macroeconomic objectives, with a corresponding loss of effectiveness in governments' macroeconomic policies. Throughout the paper the Mexican experience will be examined and used to exemplify the main points. In our view, this experience illustrates in a particularly radical way the abrupt changes brought about by the debt crisis, and the interactions between the foreign credit run, the Government's policy difficulties, and private capital flight.[2]

The paper is organized as follows. Section II briefly discusses the international and national conditions which determined the large expansion of foreign public debt in Mexico and many other developing countries during the 1970s, as well as the role of foreign debt in the operation and effectiveness of macroeconomic policies over that period. The remaining sections concentrate on the conditions prevailing after the debt crisis. Section III introduces the notion of a credit run into a standard macroeconomic model, through the assumption of credit-rationing in the market for government debt, and Section IV discusses the loss of effectiveness of macroeconomic policies resulting from a worsening of trade-offs between internal and external balance under a fixed exchange rate regime as well as between external and 'distributive balance' in a regime of flexible exchange rates. An appendix provides a formal analysis of the main conclusions.

II. ASSET MARKETS AND CAPITAL MOBILITY BEFORE AND AFTER THE DEBT CRISIS

The large expansion of international bank loans to Latin American and other developing countries is a well-documented feature of the evolution of the world economy during the 1970s (Banuri 1991; Sachs 1984). In the Mexican experience, its dimensions took a rather extreme form. Foreign debt, of the order of $8bn. (or about 20% of GDP) in the early 1970s, had increased already to over $20bn. by the mid-1970s (see Table 8.1). Following a short-lived financial crisis and economic recession in 1976–7, the oil bonanza from 1978 to 1981 turned Mexico into a preferred customer of international banks, and foreign lending was conceded in amounts and conditions which were notably more favourable than for the other developing countries. Thus, while international bank loans to developing countries as a whole increased by 76% from 1978 to 1981, in the case of Mexico—already a very large debtor by 1978—they rose by 146% (Frieden 1984). While the bulk of these loans was channelled to the public sector—which absorbed around 80% of total foreign lending—the domestic private sector also benefited from the easier availability of credit.[3] By the end of 1981, public foreign debt had risen to $64.8bn. and private debt to $14.9bn. (reaching a peak of $20.6bn. in 1983).

TABLE 8.1. *The Mexican economy: basic indicators, 1970–1987*

	1970–5	1976–7	1978–81	1982–7
Annual growth rates (%)				
GDP	6.5	3.8	8.4	- 0.2
Average real wages	4.6	3.1	3.5	- 7.8
Inflation (consumer prices)	12.2	23.3	21.1	80.8
Foreign debt (end of period, $bn.)				
Public	15.4	25.9	64.8	94.1
Private	5.0	5.4	14.9	13.5
Total	20.4	31.3	79.7	107.6

Sources: Banco de México (1987); SPP 1970–8, 1979–81, 1981–3, 1984; Economia Aplicada (1989).

The surge in foreign borrowing followed from a combination of international and national circumstances. Externally, the recycling of OPEC funds into the international banking system, together with economic recession in industrial countries, created conditions of excess liquidity which awakened the interest of international banks in lending to fast-growing developing economies. Internally, many of these countries faced, to varying degrees and for widely different reasons, structural trade imbalances and weak public finances.[4] Their correction through domestic reforms involved no easy options, while their importance could be minimized, given the large room for manœuvre enjoyed by macroeconomic policies under the virtually unconstrained availability of credit prevailing in external financial markets.

Thus, in the international conditions of the 1970s, foreign debt played a critical role in making possible an international and domestic macroeconomic framework within which the major objectives of macroeconomic policy could be broadly and simultaneously achieved. The absence of foreign credit constraints implied, just as in the standard model of perfect capital mobility, that there was always a mix of monetary and fiscal policies which was able to reconcile a high level of domestic economic activity with equilibrium in the overall balance of payments. Moreover, the broad access to foreign borrowing gave fiscal and exchange rate policies the necessary room for manœuvre simultaneously to maintain domestic social conflicts and the price level within manageable limits. The results were a prolonged period of fast economic growth, rising real wages and incomes, overall external balance, and a rate of inflation which, by present standards, remained at relatively low and stable levels (see Table 8.1).

The operation of macroeconomic policies over this period can be illustrated by an analysis of the flow of funds between the public, private, and external sectors. These are shown in Table 8.2, which corrects the public and private financial surpluses (or deficits) for the effects of inflation on nominal flows.[5] Before 1981, flow of funds showed typically the following pattern: the public-sector deficit (of the order of 4–6% of GDP) had as its counterpart a current-account deficit in the balance of payments, equal to about two-thirds of the public-sector deficit, and a private-sector financial surplus, corresponding to the remainder of the public-sector deficit. The private-sector surplus comprised in turn a financial deficit with the external sector (due mainly to borrowing by private firms from foreign banks) and a financial surplus with the public sector which more than compensated for the former, and which financed between half and two-thirds of the public-sector financial deficit. The remaining part was then obtained through the Government's borrowing abroad, in amounts sufficient simultaneously to finance the current-account deficit in the balance of payments and the desired increase in international reserves.

In this period, monetary management was effective in altering the domestic–foreign-asset composition of the private-sector financial surplus, as well as changing the amount of public debt sold to the foreign sector. As a result, fiscal policy enjoyed a sufficiently large degree of freedom to achieve internal and external balance simultaneously without threatening exchange rate stability. In sum, the policy-making process operated effectively with three objectives—internal, external, and distributive balance—and three main policy instruments—fiscal policy, monetary/exchange rate policy, and foreign-debt management.

The process led, however, to growing financial fragility, and became unsustainable when previously favourable external conditions began to change in 1981–2. Foreign real interest rates, which had been rising since 1980, reached a peak of around 9% in 1981–2, while oil prices started falling at a time when oil export revenues represented around 70% of total merchandise exports. In 1981, the expansion of the public-sector financial deficit was accompanied by a larger current-account deficit and a significant increase in the private-sector financial surplus. But now, rapidly deteriorating exchange rate expectations stimulated a massive capital flight, of the order of $20bn. from the beginning of 1981 to mid-1982, and the net acquisition of foreign assets by the private sector turned from negative to a large positive figure (see Table 8.2). Temporarily, the Government compensated for the effects of capital flight on the balance of payments through a massive increase in external borrowing, but very rapidly foreign loans became increasingly rationed. After two exchange rate crises and dramatic devaluations of the Mexican peso in February and August 1982, the Mexican Government suspended payments on its foreign debt, signalling the beginning of the international debt crisis.[6]

TABLE 8.2. *Mexico: flow-of-funds identity, 1978–1987 (% of GDP)*

	1978	1979	1980	1981	1982	1983	1984	1985	1986	1987
1. Public-sector financial deficit	4.3	5.2	6.1	9.8	6.0	1.8	0.1	1.2	3.5	−1.9
2. Current-account deficit	2.9	3.6	3.9	6.4	2.1	−3.6	−2.2	−0.9	0.8	−2.7
3. Private-sector financial surplus	1.9	1.9	−0.2	3.6	4.4	4.8	1.2	0.0	0.3	−3.9
3.1 Net acquisition of public debt[a]	2.5	3.3	2.1	2.2	0.6	−0.9	−0.9	−3.0	0.2	−6.3
3.2 Net acquisition of foreign assets	−0.6	−1.4	−2.3	1.4	3.8	5.7	2.1	3.0	0.1	2.4
4. Public-sector borrowing abroad[b]	2.3	2.2	1.6	7.8	5.9	2.1	−0.2	2.1	0.9	−0.3
5. Statistical discrepancy[c]	−0.5	−0.3	2.4	−0.2	−0.5	0.6	1.1	2.1	2.4	4.7

[a] Residual: (3) – (3.2).
[b] Net of change in international reserves.
[c] Residual: (1) – (2) – (3).

Source: Banco de México (1987).

After the 1982 debt crisis, foreign lending to the Mexican public sector shrank to negligible proportions (mainly explained by involuntary bank lending under IMF stabilization and adjustment programmes). At the same time, the proportion of the private-sector financial surplus invested abroad, in contrast to the period before 1981, remained high, and actually increased during the post-1983 recession, notwithstanding the large real devaluations which substantially reduced the dollar value of financial outflows. In fact, from 1983 onwards, the change in the real value of the private-sector holding of Mexican public debt has actually been negative, and thus the whole of the private sector's net real savings has been invested abroad. This flight away from government debt by both the domestic and the foreign private sector has eliminated the previous room for manœuvre of fiscal policy, and has led to a drastic change in the Government's fiscal stance. The present surplus in the public-sector financial accounts is to a large extent the counterpart of the fiscal and external constraints imposed by the debt crisis as well as by a major alteration in the asset composition of the private sector's net financial savings.

III. CAPITAL MOBILITY UNDER A CREDIT RUN

The changes after the 1982 debt crisis can be interpreted and analysed in terms of a sharp modification in the nature and extent of international capital mobility.

We consider a Mundell–Fleming economy, i.e. one with perfect international capital mobility—with one addition: that the substitutability between domestic and foreign financial assets depends upon the level of indebtedness of the country.[7] The key assumptions are summarized in Fig. 8.1, which gives the relation between the stock of government debt (internal as well as external) and the interest rate on government bonds, given the level of foreign interest rates, private wealth, and GNP. The interest rate i_1 is the minimum interest rate at which government bonds will be held by the private sector. As in conventional analyses, this is the interest rate on government bonds at which foreign assets and public debt become perfect substitutes. Thus, in the absence of capital controls, i_1 must be equal to the foreign interest rate (corrected for expected exchange rate devaluation) plus a 'normal' risk premium.

The modification of the model pertains to levels of debt above D_1, which is the maximum amount of government debt that can be sold at the minimum interest rate. Below D_1, the Mundell–Fleming assumption of perfect, and perfectly symmetric, capital mobility holds: foreign and domestic financial assets are perfect substitutes, and the Government faces a perfectly elastic demand for its debt.

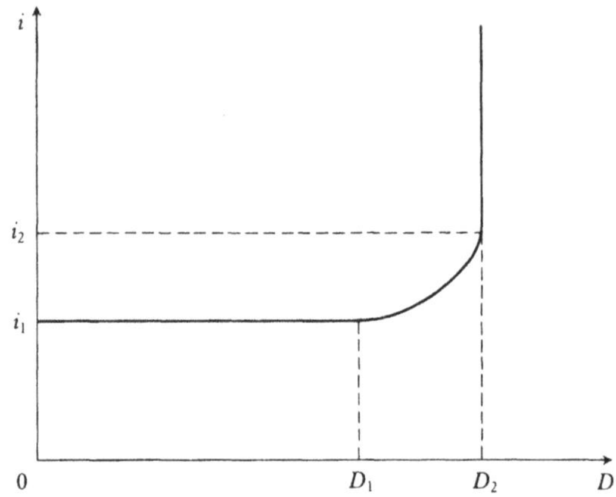

FIG. 8.1. Macroeconomic equilibrium with default risk and imperfect information.

Beyond D_1, the model is amended to account for country risk considerations. We model this very simply, by assuming that additional sales of government debt can only be effected at the cost of an increasing risk premium.[8] This is equivalent to the assumption that the demand for government bonds becomes increasingly inelastic with increases in debt levels. The risk premium or spread (s) is then determined via the condition:

$$(1 - \rho(D, i))(1 + i + s) = (1 + i);\ 0 \leqslant \rho < 1$$

where i is the safe, base rate and ρ the probability of default or of total loss of present value (Eaton *et al.* 1986). Following the literature on bank runs and credit rationing, the probability ρ of default as perceived by any single bank can be seen as a function of the volume of lending by other banks, due to the presence of informational externalities, as well as of the level of the interest rate (i) itself, which affects the creditor's ability to pay or its willingness to do so.[9] Since ρ increases with i, there will generally be a level of i at which $\rho \rightarrow 1$ and $s\ \{= \rho/(1 - \rho)(1 + i)\} \rightarrow \infty$, and at which no credit is available no matter how large the spread.[10]

There is, thus, a maximum limit to the process of increasing risk premium and bond sales. When the stock of government debt has reached a level which, in the perception of lenders, endangers the Government's ability or willingness to pay, higher interest rates would only add to the deterioration of lenders' expectations. This 'fiscal trap' is represented in Fig. 8.1 by the maximum level of government debt D_2 and the interest rate i_2 at which the demand for government bonds becomes perfectly inelastic.[11] This is the Mundell–Fleming assumption

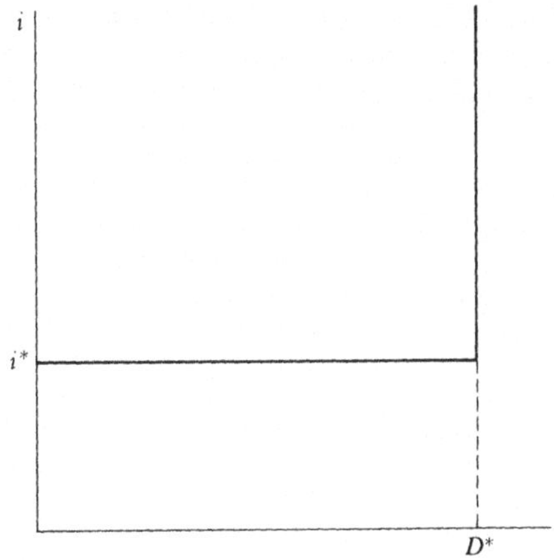

FIG. 8.2. Macroeconomic equilibrium with asymetric capital mobility.

turned on its head: there is no interest rate at which the Government can sell additional amounts of its debt, and capital inflows are perfectly inelastic to increases in domestic interest rates.

The margin between i_2 and the minimum interest rate i_1 is thus the maximum risk premium (over and above normal) which lenders are willing to accept for holding public debt instead of foreign assets, and is determined by the lenders' state of confidence, in turn affected by the level of foreign interest rates. If confidence is eroded owing, for example, to an increase in the foreign interest rate, the maximum risk premium shrinks and eventually disappears. The relation between the stock of government debt and domestic interest rates takes, then, the form of a kinked curve, as in Fig. 8.2, with the kink corresponding to the minimum interest rate and the stock of government bonds demanded at that rate.

A kinked demand curve for government debt carries with it the implication of asymmetric capital mobility in the market for foreign financial assets. For domestic interest rates higher than i^*, capital inflows are fully inelastic, since the stock of debt D^* is the maximum amount of public debt that the foreign and domestic private sectors are willing to hold at any rate of interest. However, D^* is not a minimum: at interest rates equal to or lower than i^*, the 'liquidity trap' phenomenon still holds and capital outflows become fully elastic, since the perceived return on foreign assets is greater than the return on holding public debt.

The analysis of the Mexican experience in the first section of the paper can now be rephrased within the present framework. In the early 1970s, starting from relatively low levels of external debt, the Mexican economy operated well below its 'indebtedness potential' (D_2 in Fig. 8.1, and even below D_1). In the mid-1970s, the discovery of abundant oil reserves and the subsequent massive inflow of oil export revenues enlarged still more the access of the Mexican public sector to international credit. The financial markets for public debt and foreign assets operated over this period in conditions which approached the assumption of perfect international mobility. The accumulation of foreign debt became eventually unsustainable as a result of two abrupt changes. First, the increase in foreign interest rates imposed an additional burden on debt service, the balance of payments, and already weak public finances, and reduced the 'maximum risk premium' that lenders were willing to accept for holding government debt.[12] Second, the state of confidence was also rudely shaken by the sharp reversal in the expected long-term trend of real oil prices from 1981 onwards. The result of these two changes was the 1982 debt crisis and the complete reversal of the conditions that had prevailed in international capital markets. Over this period, depending on the state of public-sector accounts and devaluation expectations, the narrow limits between the two 'traps' have even been reversed at times, giving rise to an exchange rate crisis followed by a period of normalization of exchange rate expectations. An episode featuring this phenomenon took place in mid-1985, when the domestic private sector increased its stock of foreign assets by depleting its holdings of government debt (see Table 8.2).

IV. CAPITAL MOBILITY AND POLICY EFFECTIVENESS

In a world of perfect capital mobility and fixed exchange rates, the policy conclusions of the Mundell–Fleming model apply. Fiscal policy is fully effective in the achievement of internal balance, while monetary policy is a powerful instrument for influencing the balance of payments. The relative effectiveness of the two instruments is reversed in a regime of flexible exchange rates, but in both cases there is always a mix of fiscal and monetary policy which can simultaneously achieve internal and external balance.[13]

Asymmetric capital mobility has several consequences for the operation of macroeconomic policies. First, it tightens the constraints on fiscal policy. A fiscal expansion financed through an increase in government bonds, sold either to the domestic or the foreign private sector, is not an available policy option, given the presence of credit-rationing in the market for government debt. Even if the government relaxes these constraints through the regulation of local banks, the effectiveness of a fiscal expansion financed by increased sales of government bonds to the domestic banking sector stands in sharp contrast to the operation of fiscal policy under conditions of perfect capital mobility. In the latter, under a fixed exchange rate regime, fiscal expansion leaves the domestic interest rate unchanged while, at the same time, improving both the level of economic activity and the overall balance of payments (through increased capital inflows). In the present case (as shown formally in the appendix below), the inelasticity of external capital inflows implies that there are no capital movements to keep in check the upward pressure on domestic interest rates exerted by the expanding stock of domestic government bonds. As a consequence, the former positive effects of fiscal expansion on the balance of international reserves are not warranted, while at the same time its effects on aggregate output are now offset by rising interest rates and its negative consequences on private expenditures. Fiscal policy thus becomes largely ineffective.

Monetary policy under a fixed exchange rate is also largely ineffective in terms of its effects on economic activity. Just as in the model of perfect capital mobility, the main consequences of a monetary expansion are capital outflows and a deterioration of the balance of international reserves. The high interest elasticity of capital outflows dampens the effects of monetary expansion on domestic interest rates and, thus, on private expenditures and economic activity. The main difference with respect to the standard model of perfect capital mobility is that the present case introduces an asymmetry into the operation of monetary policy itself. The effectiveness of a restrictive monetary policy in improving the overall balance of payments is largely lost. Indeed, the inelasticity of capital in-flows in response to increases in domestic interest rates implies that an improvement in the balance of external reserves can at best be achieved only at the cost of increases in domestic interest rates and reductions in the level of economic activity.

In sum, credit-rationing in the market for government debt and asymmetric capital mobility exacerbate the role of fiscal and balance-of-payments constraints as a result of the increased inelasticity of capital inflows and the demand for government debt in response to increases in domestic interest rates. The resulting erosion of the effectiveness of monetary policy in the achievement of external balance, and that of fiscal policy with respect to internal balance, implies that there will hardly be any mix of monetary and fiscal policy which, under a regime of fixed exchange rates, is able to achieve both objectives simultaneously. A policy mix which is effective in raising the level of aggregate demand and output, such as a combined monetary and fiscal expansion, will do so only at the cost of sacrificing external balance, and vice versa.

Before we go on to discuss flexible exchange rates, it is important to point out that, because of the reasons given above, asymmetric capital mobility renders the use of fixed exchange rates untenable. The slightest changes in economic conditions or in the Government's policy stance leads to capital flight and severe payments crises. As happened in Mexico, the inevitable result is a shift towards some type of floating rate. This, however, creates a different set of problems.

IV.1. External and Distributive Balance under Flexible Exchange Rates

The loss of policy effectiveness, which in the context of a fixed exchange rate regime takes the form of a worsening of the trade-off between internal and external balance, expresses itself differently in a regime of flexible exchange rates. While the ability of monetary policy to reconcile external and internal balance is restored, as in the standard model, by the mere fact that exchange rate flexibility affects both of them in the same direction, a new problem emerges. This pertains to the distributional consequences of exchange rate movements, in particular the altering of real wages in relation to labour productivity, which in turn will lead to changes in the domestic inflation rate, under realistic assumptions on price and wage formation. Thus, while monetary policy operating through a devaluation can affect the internal and external performance of the economy, it will do so at the cost of exacerbating internal 'distributive unbalances' whose most apparent expression is a deteriorating inflation performance.[14]

This trade-off is obscured, or, more precisely, absent, in the Mundell–Fleming analysis of macroeconomic policy because this is a model with two rather than three policy objectives, where the absence of distributional constraints implicitly assumes that exchange rate movements have no costs. Yet it remains true that, under perfect capital mobility and flexible exchange rates, there is always a mix of fiscal and monetary policy which is able to achieve internal and external balance at any exchange rate and, thus, to overcome distributional constraints. But this degree of freedom no longer exists when capital inflows are inelastic with respect to increases in domestic interest rates, since there is no way then to avoid the consequences of an expansion in domestic output for the balance of payments, under fixed exchange rates, or for the exchange rate, under a regime of flexible exchange rates. The counterpart of policy ineffectiveness that was examined in the case of a fixed exchange rate is thus a worsening of the trade-off between internal and external balance on one side and 'distributive balance' on the other.

In the recent experience of the Mexican economy, this trade-off is expressed in Fig. 8.3 as one between the non-oil trade balance and the rate of inflation, and in Fig. 8.4 as one between the real exchange rate and real wages. Since 1982, Mexico's balance of payments has been subject to successive shocks, chiefly the rise in foreign interest rates and the drying up of new international loans in 1981–2, and the oil price collapse of early 1986, when oil prices fell from above $US20 per barrel to around $US11 per barrel, which drastically cut foreign-exchange earnings and fiscal revenues obtained from the government's oil corporation. The loss of oil revenues over 1986 was of the order of $US7bn., or about 6–7% of GDP, at 1986 prices.

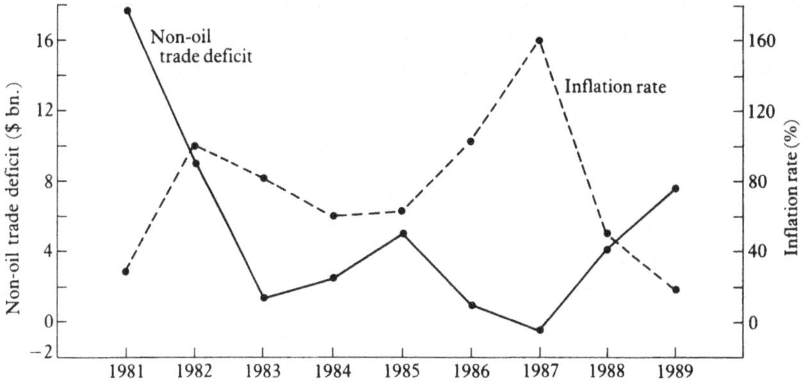

FIG. 8.3. Mexico: trends in inflation rate and non-oil trade deficit.

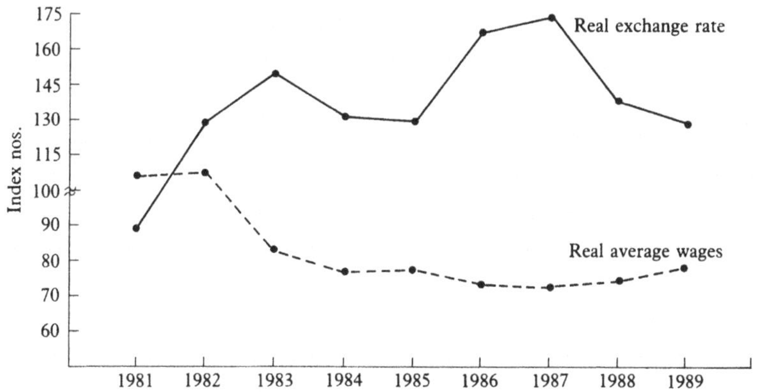

FIG. 8.4. Mexico: trends in real wage rate and real exchange rate.
Sources: Economía Aplicada (1989; 1990); based on Banco de México, *Indicadores Económicos,* and SPP, *Sistema de Cuentas Nacionales*

In the absence of compensatory capital inflows, restoring external balance involved in both cases a major adjustment in the non-oil trade balance, which was in turn achieved through drastic devaluations and fiscal contraction. More precisely, the short-term policy response to the 1982 debt crisis and the 1986 oil price collapse included three main policy measures: (i) major fiscal adjustments, which came about from sharp reductions in public investment and in the real wages and salaries of public-sector employees, as well as from an upward adjustment of public-sector relative prices and indirect taxes (net of subsidies); (ii) massive devaluations of the peso–dollar exchange rate, of the order (in real terms) of 70% in 1982–3 and 30% in 1986–7 (with a moderate real appreciation in the interim years); and (iii) a very restrictive 'wage policy stance' which, especially over 1983, involved a sharp alteration of wage indexation rules by setting minimum wage adjustments well below the rate of past inflation.

Fiscal contraction and devaluation succeeded in sharply reducing the non-oil trade deficit and restoring external balance, but at the cost of severely disruptive effects on the internal distribution of income and inflation. Real average wages fell by almost 30% over 1982–4 and by an additional 6% in 1986–7. By 1987 they were over 30% below their 1981–2 level, while inflation had accelerated sharply from a 28% annual rate in 1980–1 to almost 160% in 1987.

The same policy dilemmas were faced over 1988, when a different approach to counter-inflation policy was followed. In late 1987 an agreement was reached between the Government, labour unions, and business confederations on a comprehensive attack on inflation, involving a de-indexation programme—the central element of which was a freeze of the exchange rate, wages, and prices—together with a tight fiscal and monetary policy, as well as an accelerated pace of import liberalization measures. The programme has been successful in reducing inflation—to around 50% in 1988 and 20% in 1989—but at the cost of a very rapid deterioration of the trade balance, with the non-oil trade balance in 1989 recording a deficit of the order of $7–8bn. The real exchange rate appreciation which contributed to the reduction of the inflation rate, together with the massive import liberalization, are at the roots of the import boom which led to the sharp deterioration of the balance of payments.

V. CONCLUSIONS

From the perspective adopted in this paper, present troubles in domestic policy management appear to be determined as much by the abrupt end of voluntary lending from international banks as by the increased propensity to save abroad on the part of the domestic private sector; more precisely, by what both of these phenomena reflect, a credit run or a flight away from government debt.

Both the origins and consequences of the debt crisis need to be looked at from this perspective. Our analysis suggested, for example, that present problems originated not only in the excessive lending and borrowing up to 1981–2 but also in the impact of rising international interest rates on the state of confidence (or the maximum risk premium which lenders were willing to accept for holding government debt). This influence is additional to the consequences of high interest rates on the debt-service burden and on balance-of-payments constraints. It suggests that debt relief, through a reduction in either interest rates or principal, would contribute to the resolution of the crisis not only by reducing debt service—which, although important, would not by itself restore the effectiveness of macroeconomic policies—but also by relaxing the credit-rationing conditions prevailing at present in the market for government debt.

A second aspect of the current situation is that, as long as present conditions in financial markets continue, there is little scope for overcoming the crisis through macroeconomic policies. The policy problem, as suggested by our analysis, is one of too few policy instruments, and its solution may depend on the effectiveness of other, less conventional, economic policies (industrial, trade, or financial). However, policy reforms which can moderate the trade-offs between the different macroeconomic objectives and enlarge the room for manœuvre of government policies are not necessarily perceived as such by international and domestic lenders, in which case they can lead simultaneously to a further deterioration of the state of confidence. In fact, as argued elsewhere (Ros, 1987), while some aspects of present policy conditionality imposed by international financial institutions (i.e. the conditions established by creditors on debtors in exchange for restoring confidence) may temporarily improve access to international capital markets, these policies can lead to a worsening of the trade-offs between different macroeconomic objectives. It is this paradox which makes present policy dilemmas particularly intractable, and which may explain why the resolution of the debt crisis has been such a long and painful process.

APPENDIX

The Effectiveness of Fiscal and Monetary Policies under Alternative Assumptions on Capital Mobility

In this appendix we introduce the assumption of asymmetric capital mobility into a standard macroeconomic model, examine its implications for the effectiveness of fiscal and monetary policies, and compare them with the conventional policy conclusions in the case of perfect capital mobility. We consider a small open economy for which the foreign levels of income, prices, and interest rates may be taken as exogenously given, and distinguish five institutional sectors: the private sector, the Government, the central bank, commercial banks, and the foreign sector. No price changes are considered, and thus there is no need to distinguish between nominal and real magnitudes. For simplicity, we also leave aside interest payments on all financial liabilities. We shall limit our analysis to the case of the fixed exchange rate regime, and thus to the trade-offs between internal and external balance.

In a simple form, the model contains the following structural equations and budget constraints:

$$Y = PE + G + NX \quad (1)$$

$$PE = a_0 + a_1 (Y - T) - a_2 i \quad (2)$$

$$T = t Y \quad (3)$$

$$NX = m_0 + m_1 . Y + m_2 e \quad (4)$$

$$D = d_0 + d_1 (Y - T) \quad (5)$$

$$H = hD \quad (6)$$

$$FA = f_0 + f_1 i_f - f_2 i \quad (7)$$

Budget Constraints

Private sector: $Y - T = PE + D + FA - L$ (8)

Government: $G - T = B_c + B_b + B_f$ (9)

Commercial banks: $D = H + B_b + L$ (10)

Central bank: $H = R + B_c$ (11)

Foreign sector: $R = NX + B_f - FA$ (12)

where:

Y = national income
PE = private expenditures
G = government expenditures (exogenous)
T = tax revenues
NX = trade balance
i = domestic interest rate (on government bonds and bank loans)
i_f = foreign interest rate (exogenous)
e = exchange rate (exogenous)
D = change in bank deposits
FA = change in foreign financial assets
L = change in domestic bank loans
H = change in monetary base (banks' cash reserves)
B_c = change in central bank credit to the government (exogenous)
B_b = sales of government bonds to the local commercial banks
B_f = sales of government bonds to the foreign sector
R = change in international reserves

So far, the model comprises twelve unknowns (Y, PE, NX, T, D, FA, L, H, i, B_b, B_f and R) and eleven independent equations, since only four of the five budget constraints are independent from the national-income identity Eq. (1). Depending on the assumptions on capital mobility, the model can be closed in two alternative ways. Under perfect capital mobility, the model is completed by the additional condition:

$$f_2 \rightarrow \infty, \text{ which implies } i = i_f \tag{13a}$$

The perfect elasticity of capital inflows and outflows implies the equality between domestic and foreign interest rates, since then domestic and foreign liabilities are regarded as perfect substitutes.

Under asymmetric capital mobility, the model is completed as follows:

$$i > i_f, \quad \text{with } f_2 \rightarrow \infty \quad \text{when } i < i^* \tag{13b}$$

$$\text{and } f_2 \rightarrow 0 \quad \text{when } i > i^*; \text{ and}$$

$$\hat{B}_f = B_f \tag{14}$$

where $\hat{B}_f < B_f^*$, the desired level of foreign borrowing. This means that the volume of foreign-resource inflows cannot be decided by macroeconomic policy.

Condition (13b) expresses asymmetric capital mobility in the form discussed in Section IV of the paper, and differs from the analysis in Section III. Here the perfect inelasticity of capital inflows in response to increases in domestic interest rates does not imply a perfect inelasticity of the demand for government bonds. The government is able to expand its sales of public debt to the domestic banking sector, although with no consequences on the capital account of the balance of payments.

Fiscal Policy

The analysis of fiscal policy under perfect capital mobility replicates the properties of the Mundell–Fleming model. Fiscal policy is fully effective (see Table 8.3). Consider, for example, the effects of an increase in government expenditures at given levels of central-bank credit and government bond sales to the foreign sector. The fiscal expansion has a positive effect on the level of economic activity given by the open-economy multiplier. Interest rates, determined by foreign interest rates, remain unchanged, and thus, far from being crowded out by government expenditures, private expenditures are stimulated by the expansion of income. The trade balance deteriorates as a result of overall economic expansion, but the overall balance of payments improves as a consequence of capital inflows, which more than compensate for the deterioration of the trade balance.

The full process can be described as follows. The increase in government expenditures is only partially financed through increased tax receipts resulting from the higher level of income; given the assumptions on central-bank credit and government borrowing abroad, the rest of the increased government deficit is financed through bond sales to the domestic banking sector. The supply of bank loans to the corporate sector is thereby reduced, which, together with the increased investment expenditures, puts an upward pressure on the loan rate. The latter is arrested, however, by a substitution of domestic loans by foreign loans (or by a reduction in private holdings of foreign assets) which, given the assumption of a perfectly elastic supply of foreign loans, allows the increased demand for loans to be met at an unchanged interest rate. The process may also be seen from the perspective of the central-bank balance sheet: in the new equilibrium, the higher level of income determines an increased demand for 'high-powered' money which, at unchanged levels of domestic interest rates and central-bank credit, requires an improved balance of international reserves.[15]

TABLE 8.3. *Multiplier effects of fiscal expansion (d/dG) under perfect and asymmetric capital mobility*

Variable	Perfect capital mobility	Asymmetric capital mobility
Y	$1/A_1$	0
PE	a_1/A_1	-1
i	0	$1/a_2$
NX	m_1/A_1	0
FA	$(m_1 - s.h)/A_1$	0
R	$s.h/A_1$	0

Note:
$A_1 = 1 - a_1(1 - t) - m_1$
$s = (1 - a_1)(1 - t)$

Consider now an expansion of government expenditures accompanied by increased sales of government bonds to the domestic banking sector in the case of asymmetric capital mobility (see Table 8.4). Given the interest inelasticity of capital inflows, there are no capital movements now to keep in check the upward pressure on domestic interest rates exerted by the expanding stock of domestic government bonds. Large increases in domestic interest rates are now unable to attract capital inflows, implying that the former positive effects of fiscal expansion on the balance of international reserves are not warranted. At the same time, the effects on aggregate output are now hindered by the increasing interest rates and its negative consequences on the level of private investments. Fiscal policy thus becomes largely ineffective.

Monetary Policy

Both under perfect and under asymmetric capital mobility, monetary expansion is fully ineffective in its consequences on private expenditures and economic activity (see Table 8.4, where we assume, in the case of asymmetric capital mobility, that the economy is operating initially at the kink of the demand curve for foreign assets). Consider an expansion of central-bank credit in the form of an acquisition of government bonds. The immediate result is an increase in cash reserves in the commercial banking system, which expands the supply of bank loans and exerts a downward pressure on the loan rate. The latter is kept in check, however, by an increased acquisition of foreign assets and an expansion of the demand for domestic loans. The end result is a deterioration of the capital account in the balance of payments, and of the balance of international reserves, which offsets the original expansion of the monetary base and compensates for the effects on domestic interest rates of the original acquisition of government bonds by the central bank. Since the latter is unable to affect interest rates (and thus the level of investment and income), the process continues until the re-establishment of the stock of high-powered money at its original level, implying that the deterioration in the balance of international reserves is exactly equal to the original increase in central-bank credit (see Table 8.5). Thus, monetary expansion has no effect on the level of output, investment, or the trade balance.

Its consequences are limited to a deterioration of the overall balance of payments through a capital outflow (or a reduction of capital inflows). In the end, all that happens is a substitution of government bonds for foreign exchange in the portfolio of the central bank.

TABLE 8.4. *Multiplier effects of monetary expansion* (d/dB_c) *and contraction* ($d/d-B_c$) *under perfect and asymmetric capital mobility*

Variable	Monetary expansion[a]	Monetary contraction+	
		Perfect mobility	Asymmetric mobility
Y	0	0	$-1/(A_1 - A_2)$
PE	0	0	$-(A_1 + a_1)/(A_1 - A_2)$
i	0	0	$A_1/a_2.(A_1 - A_2)$
NX	0	0	$-m_1/(A_1 - A_2)$
FA	1	-1	0
R	-1	1	$-m_1/(A_1 - A_2)$

Notes:
$A_1 = 1 - a_1(1 - t) - m_1$
$A_2 = (1 - h)s + t - a_1$
[a] Perfect and asymmetric capital mobility.

In the case of perfect capital mobility, the ineffectiveness of monetary policy is, however, only relative to the level of domestic economic activity, or to the objective of internal balance. Monetary policy remains crucial in this model for the achievement of external balance, or an appropriate level of international reserves. Its effectiveness in this respect is best seen when we consider a restrictive monetary policy: then, following a reasoning analogous to the one presented above, monetary contraction leads to an improvement of the overall balance of payments without any costs in terms of investment and domestic output. Given the properties of fiscal policy, these features imply that in a regime of fixed exchange rates and perfect capital mobility, there is always a mix of fiscal and monetary policy which is able to achieve both internal and external balance. Even if the model is unrealistic in several aspects (e.g. in leaving aside inflation and its emphasis on the overall balance of payments rather than its composition), it makes the point that a perfect and perfectly symmetric capital mobility considerably relaxes the constraints on macroeconomic policies.

In contrast, asymmetric capital mobility introduces an asymmetry into the operation of monetary policy itself. The effectiveness of a restrictive monetary policy in improving the overall balance of payments has now been largely lost, given that, as a result of the inelasticity of capital inflows in response to increases in domestic interest rates, monetary contraction has no consequences on the capital account. Any improvement in the balance of international reserves can only be achieved through changes in the trade balance, and thus at the cost of reductions in the level of economic activity determined by the rise in domestic interest rates. In sum, under a regime of fixed exchange rates, asymmetric capital mobility erodes the effectiveness of monetary policy in the achievement of external-balance objectives and that of fiscal policy with respect to internal balance, implying that there will hardly be any mix of monetary and fiscal policy which is able to achieve both objectives simultaneously.

NOTES

1. The papers in the June 1986 special issue of the *European Economic Review* address some of the major current theoretical and empirical issues; see in particular the survey paper by Eaton *et al.* (1986) and the comments by Guesnerie (1986) and by Hellwig (1986). See also Ch. 2.
2. For a broader analysis and background relating to the Mexican economy in the 1970s and 1980s see, among others, Córdoba (1986), Dornbusch (1988), Ize (1989), Lustig and Ros (1987), Reyes Heroles (1990), and Ros (1987).
3. The domestic demand and private investment booms triggered a rapid growth of overall private indebtedness. In large private firms, the debt–capital ratio rose from 90% in 1978 to 120% in 1981, while the share of dollar-denominated liabilities in total debt increased from 30% to 63% over the same period (López 1985).
4. In oil-exporting Mexico, for example, a declining agricultural trade surplus and a persistent trade deficit in manufactures were the main sources of external imbalance. In contrast, the oil import bill was a major factor in the expansion of foreign debt in Brazil.
5. Thus, in principle, each sector's real financial surplus (deficit) refers to the change in the sector's real financial assets (liabilities). In this definition, the inflation adjustment involves correcting for the inflationary component of nominal interest flows as well as any real capital losses (gains) on monetary assets (liabilities). The data in Table 8.2 is not, however, adjusted for the effects of external inflation on the real value of assets denominated in foreign currency.
6. The debt crisis was made worse and more abrupt by the initial beliefs, on the part of both international lenders and the Mexican Government, that the increase in foreign interest rates was a temporary phenomenon while a high oil price in real terms would remain a lasting feature of the world economy. This initial stage, which explains the massive and continued expansion of debt over 1981 and part of 1982, was followed by a less optimistic outlook and the full realization of its implications.
7. The question of whether lenders' confidence refers to the Government's solvency (ability to pay) or to its willingness to pay is an important and debatable one, but only secondary to our main concern in this paper, i.e. its consequences on macroeconomic management. For a discussion of that question, see Eaton *et al.*, 1986.
8. The overall effects are similar if the fiscal expansion has been accompanied by an increase in bond sales abroad with unchanged levels of central-bank credit and bond sales to the domestic banking sector. In this case, the balance of international reserves improves because of foreign lending to the Government rather than to the corporate sector. The main difference with respect

to the previous case is that, depending on the parameters of the model, the process of economic expansion may be accompanied by private capital inflows or outflows. For example, if bank deposits expand rapidly in relation to the demand for bank loans, the expansionary fiscal policy will be accompanied by a private capital outflow.

9

Black Markets, Openness, and Central-Bank Autonomy

TARIQ BANURI

I. INTRODUCTION

Currency black markets open up the financial markets of a country to international forces, thus raising the costs and lowering the benefits of such conventional policies as exchange rate overvaluation and trade restriction. By weakening the effectiveness of capital controls, black markets can induce balance-of-payments problems which increase the costs of defending the exchange rate; at the same time they erode the effectiveness of alternative defensive policies, namely, restrictions on trade flows, by lowering the private cost of circumventing trade restrictions. In Third World countries, currency black markets have increased in size and sophistication because of a combination of institutional, technological, and policy factors. The greater amount of trade and travel between countries, the improvements in electronic communications systems, the emergence of large discretionary flows, mainly remittances, and inadequate policy responses to these changes are some of the major factors. Largely as a result of these factors, many governments have suffered an erosion in their ability to use commercial policy effectively, and have therefore shifted towards relatively less restrictive trade and exchange rate regimes in the last decade.[1]

That this happened does not mean that it was inevitable. It is the argument of this paper that if government policy in affected countries had been oriented towards 'governance' rather than 'control', and in particular if it had been sensitive to longer-run issues of institutional change, much of the most problematic developments would have been avoided. Governments were intent on maximization of benefits from foreign-resource inflows, and not on preserving the autonomy and effectiveness of policy-making. This allowed the emergence and strengthening of institutions which could challenge and undermine the very process of decision-making. Effective policy response may also have been hamstrung by the influence of ideological and political factors, such as IMF pressure, a shift in intellectual fashion from global Keynesianism to global neoclassicism (see Chapter 1), and the dominant (though misleading) interpretation of the experience of rapidly growing, newly industrialized countries (see Banuri 1991). These factors reinforced each other, in so far as ideological pressure diverted attention from pressing issues of institutional reform, while a particular type of institutional change, namely the emergence of black markets, made it more difficult for governments of affected countries to ignore the pressure.

This experience suggests that financial openness presents a country with a veritable Hobson's choice. On the one hand, if it tries to maximize the use of additional resources made available by openness, it will be forced to relinquish control over their allocation. On the other hand, if the retention of allocative control is an important objective, then a substantial fraction of the resource inflow may have to be left unutilized.[2] Most countries faced with this choice—including Pakistan, Turkey, Egypt, and Yugoslavia—appear to have opted for the former course, though not without a struggle. For a period of time, the major outstanding exception was India, which pursued prudent balance-of-payments policies throughout the 1970s and thus succeeded in retaining a degree of allocative control over incoming foreign resources. From 1984, however, the Indian Government, too, decided to opt for an expansionary strategy which sacrificed control in order to receive a larger volume of resource inflow. The result has been a similar decline in governance capacity in India.

The prescriptive content of the paper can be summarized in one word: restraint. The idea is quite straightforward, and derives from the notion of 'governance', which is central to Keynes's writing. The need for governance implies that the state must ensure orderly arrangements within which people can carry on their normal business of living. This involves maintaining some form of social control over sources of economic or political instability. Foreign-resource inflows have the potential to create instability, especially if the society becomes dependent upon them. In earlier times, when such inflows were small and originated mainly from other governments, Third World countries succeeded in minimizing instability by strict regulation of international trade and capital flows, and by the maintenance of fixed, stable, and often overvalued exchange rates. In recent years, however, as private flows have increased in magnitude and significance, capital controls have increasingly been bypassed through the establishment of strong and vibrant black markets for foreign currencies. The result is that, today, capital controls have lost all meaning, and so has the ability of the government to protect the economy and the polity from instability generated overseas.

This paper has as its premiss the theory that governments still wish to maintain the earlier protection. If this assumption is correct, financial openness calls for two types of policy response. First, by not using more than a fraction of the 'unstable' component of incoming resources, the government can ensure that society does not become overly dependent upon the continued inflow of the resources, and therefore that economic policy does not become hostage to the interests and beliefs of those who influence the inflow. Second, by avoiding policies which favour the expansion of black markets—endemically overvalued exchange rates, or a myriad of import restrictions—the government can inhibit their growth and thus retain autonomy in policy-making. This is a paradoxical result: if the government wishes to retain its power, it has to be willing not to use it to the fullest extent. Restraint in the use of power ensures that it will last; profligacy will result in its loss.

To analyse these issues, we shall begin with the case of Pakistan, where the rapid expansion of currency black markets was due to the sudden influx of worker remittances from the Middle East, and conclude with more summary descriptions of other remittance-receiving countries (Turkey, Egypt, Yugoslavia, and India) which bear out the central thesis of the paper. In Section II, we describe the history of currency black markets in Pakistan; this is followed, in Section III, by a theoretical analysis of the effect of black markets on capital flows and policy effectiveness; Section IV examines policy behaviour in Pakistan, Egypt, Turkey, Yugoslavia, and India; and Section V contains conclusions and suggestions for further research.

II. BLACK MARKETS FOR FOREIGN CURRENCIES

Black markets for foreign currencies (particularly dollars and sterling) are endemic in Third World countries.[3] However, various pieces of evidence indicate that recent years have witnessed a rapid and dramatic increase in the size of these markets in many developing countries. In order to examine this connection, we need to give a brief description of the history and internal structures of such markets.

Black markets develop in conditions of excess demand for a commodity subject to legal restrictions on sale, or to official price ceilings, or both. Foreign-exchange transactions in almost all Third World countries are usually subject to both kinds of restrictions (Cowitt 1985; also see Black 1976; Bhagwati 1978: ch. 2; Morgenstern 1974; and George and Giddy 1983: 56–63, which summarizes the information on capital controls in various countries). Legally, only a small network of closely monitored exchange-dealers (with small capital provisions) are permitted to engage in this trade; sale of foreign currencies is allowed only for specified purposes; and the exchange rate is pegged by the central bank. Consequently, as in the case of any other commodity, some of the supply is siphoned off to satisfy the excess demand, and sold at a black-market price higher than the official price as well as the theoretical equilibrium price.

II.1. Currency Black Markets in Pakistan

For obvious reasons, information on the functioning of black markets is neither readily available nor very reliable. As such, the specific magnitudes mentioned in the following description will have to be treated with a certain amount of caution. For our purposes, however, since we are concerned here primarily with the direction and not with the magnitude of changes in black markets, the absence of precise data is not an insurmountable problem. We shall discuss below the evolution and growth of currency black markets in Pakistan. However, as we argue later, many of the insights appear to be applicable to other countries in a similar situation.

Illegal exchange-trading in Pakistan[4] dates literally from Independence in 1947, and, as in all of South Asia, is linked directly to gold-smuggling.[5] Gold demand (for the 1–1.5 million weddings each year) has been increasing at a stable rate with increases in population and incomes; but since there is no domestic production or legal imports, the fresh demand can only be met with gold-smuggling. Given the high level of organization of the domestic gold market, it is not surprising that gold-smuggling took on an organized character very early in Pakistan's history, and helped influence the evolution of organized currency black markets.[6] Since the gold 'imports' have to be paid for in hard currency (or, initially, in Indian rupees), this also created a demand for illegal foreign exchange. Thus, the demand for illegally imported gold had an important institutional effect in Pakistan: it generated a demand for illegal currency, which in turn stimulated its supply, and led to the creation and establishment of a currency black market.

There is now an active black market for foreign exchange in almost every major city in Pakistan, run mainly by goldsmiths. The main centres of activity are the port city of Karachi, the northern city of Peshawar (close to Kabul, through which the currency is smuggled to Dubai to pay for the gold), and the 'tribal areas' adjoining the border with Afghanistan (where currency trading is semi-legal, as also is trade in smuggled goods). As in the case of most developing countries, the black market for foreign currencies, though illegal, appears to be surprisingly well tolerated by the authorities.[7] Although the exchange-dealers (except in the tribal areas) do not advertise their services, the market is substantially unified, and the prevailing price is common knowledge among all those with an interest in it.[8] Here is the classic case of demand stimulating supply and thus helping to establish a market, albeit illegal.

II.2. Demand for Illegal Currencies

While the currency black market may have come into existence (and have been unified) because of the substantial illegal imports of gold, it did not restrict itself to this task. High tariffs and quotas on consumer goods (luxury goods, durables, electronic goods, textiles, and alcohol) created strong incentives for smuggling, and thus a high demand for black-market currencies.[9] Similarly, shifts in investment climate (or expectations) induced capital flight, as also did the desire of public officials, as well as of businessmen, to maintain foreign assets (mainly, but not exclusively, Swiss bank accounts) as a hedge against adverse political changes (see e.g. Winston 1974); the low allowance for foreign travel caused potential tourists to finance their trips partly with illegally purchased dollars;[10] parents wishing to remit money to their children studying abroad were often to resort to the same method.

In Pakistan, it was easy for the smuggling operation to finance its needs from the already established black market, and this is indeed what happened. With the ending of the Korean War boom in Pakistan's jute and cotton exports, the country suffered a decline in foreign-exchange earnings, imposed strict trade controls, and thus created incentives for smuggling operations. This situation would itself have resulted in the establishment of a foreign-currency black market, and the fact that a well-organized market already existed no doubt facilitated the task of the smugglers. The smuggling operations developed somewhat slowly, in Karachi as well as in the tribal areas in the north. By 1970, the latter market was fairly well organized, and had a large inventory of consumer goods and textiles, as well as a reliable delivery system involving collusion with customs officials.

II.3. Supply of Illegal Currencies

Generally, the supply of black-market dollars has four possible sources: under-invoicing or smuggling of exports, over-invoicing of imports, foreign tourists, and worker remittances sent through non-official channels.[11] Although all four sources are likely to have been utilized in some degree, it turns out that, in the case of Pakistan, the most significant source before 1975 was the first, the smuggling of exports. Foreign tourism has never been a significant factor in the economy of Pakistan[12] (unlike, say, the case of Caribbean countries), and so it is unlikely to have played a determining role in the working of the black market. Nor was the magnitude of remittances before 1975 of any significance,[13] and the same observations would apply to them.

Similarly, with the possible exception of capital-goods imports, over-invoicing of imports is not likely to be a major source of illegal foreign exchange in a country like Pakistan. The reason is that this would be competitive only where the tariff rate on imported goods was sufficiently lower than the black-market premium. Since Pakistan has always had high tariff barriers on most privately imported goods, the price incentive is for *under*-invoicing (or smuggling *in*) of imports rather than for over-invoicing. The only exception, of course, would be in the case of capital-goods imports, where tariffs were generally lower than average, or even zero,[14] but such imports are generally quite strictly controlled by the Government. Bhagwati *et al.* (1974), using partner-country comparison, found Pakistan to be a net under-invoicer of imports in the 1960s (see Section II.4, particularly Table 9.1), despite large black-market premiums, and low tariffs on capital goods. Since then, however, the differentials between tariff rates and black-market premiums have shrunk, if anything.

Since most of the above observations would apply with equal force to a large majority of developing countries, it seems reasonable to assert that in most of these countries the major source of black-market dollars is the under-invoicing of exports, with the over-invoicing of (a subset of) imports running a distant second. The major exceptions to this are countries which receive a high influx of tourists,[15] or those which receive large amounts of remittances. We shall argue that the circumstances of such countries are unique and interesting.

Remittances and tourism differ from the conventional sources of black-market currencies (exports and imports) in a very important respect, in that they do not necessitate an *additional* illegal transaction. In general, neither the currency nor any goods have to be transported across a country's borders to generate the supply, with the result that real costs (in terms of clandestine transportation, pay-offs to officials, and risk of confiscation and of other legal penalties) are enormously reduced. Under-invoicing or smuggling of exports requires that the export good be illegally transported across the country's borders. Similarly, over-invoicing of imports requires that the actual amount of imports should not correspond to the import licence.[16] This means that the costs of procuring the supply of black-market dollars in this manner will have to be high enough to compensate the supplier for the higher risk as well as for higher real costs.[17]

II.4. Expansion of Black Markets

Available evidence suggests that the size of the black market for foreign currencies has expanded considerably since the early 1970s, because of an increase in supply. While it has also been associated with a reduction in the black-market premium, that issue does not lend itself to a mono-causal interpretation.

Two independent sources of evidence, one pertaining to the supply and the other to the demand for illegal dollars, indicate an expansion in the size of the black market: data on unrecorded remittances (which presumably end up in the black market) and partner-country data comparison of trade flows.

Unrecorded Remittances

Most observers of remittance-receiving countries remark that a substantial fraction of these flows use what are called 'informal', 'illegal', or 'non-banking' channels, thus providing foreign exchange to the currency black market rather than to the central bank, attempts by the latter to offset this tendency notwithstanding (see e.g. Serageldin *et al.* 1983: 90; Chandavarkar 1980; Bhagwati 1978: 71; Birks and Sinclair 1980: 39, 103; Ali *et al.* 1981: 94–6, Gilani *et al.* 1981: 110–13; Tsakok 1982: 321). The problems of central-bank control over these flows is compounded when (as in the case of Egypt) the home and host countries are geographically contiguous, and the reduced cost of transportation and frequent travel across the border further facilitate the flow of unofficial remittances.[18]

However, such impotence is not restricted to geographically contiguous countries. Financial intermediaries, linked to the network of currency black markets in the home countries, arise to provide a service to those wishing to remit their money home at a slightly higher rate. Pakistani migrants in the Middle East can buy an instrument called *hundi* or hand-payment (Gilani *et al.* 1981: 110–13) from informal exchange-dealers who generally set up shop outside the post office, the Pakistani embassy, or Pakistani banks, and advertise their rates quite openly. The customer often has a choice between getting a cheque drawn on a Pakistani bank or simply giving the name and address of his family members to the dealer, whose partner (in Pakistan) will then send them a cheque or money order for the right amount. The credibility of these exchange-dealers is quite good, and they seem to get a fair amount of business. In any event, since migrant workers form a community away from home, the exchange-dealers used by various people tend to be those connected one way or another to their personal network of friends and relations.

Gilani *et al.* (1981) note that, in 1979, as many as 14% of the Pakistani migrant workers in the Middle East remitted their savings to their families through non-banking channels, most commonly a *hundi*. Furthermore, 25% of the remaining remittances were stated to have been brought home by the worker himself on one of his visits; it is not entirely clear whether these workers surrendered their dollars at the airport or exchanged them at a premium in the black market, but the general presumption is that it was the latter. While this does not yield any firm estimates of the volume of illegal remittances, a figure anywhere between 15% to 35% of the recorded amount seems reasonable. This means an annual infusion (in 1983) of between \$450m. and over \$1bn. into the illegal market from remittances alone. This far exceeds Cowitt's (1985) figure of Re10–15m. of turnover in the black market per month (approximately $1m., which presumably relates to the size of the black market connected with the traditional gold-smuggling operation) and indicates the enormous expansion which must have taken place. To give an idea of the size of this infusion relative to the economy, it suffices to mention that in the same year Pakistan had a money supply of Re90bn., equivalent to approximately $5.6bn. when converted at the black-market exchange rate. Thus, the annual infusion of black-market dollars from remittances alone amounted to between 8% and 20% of the total money supply, not an insignificant increase in liquidity. This, of course, does not give any indication of the actual size of holdings of foreign currency in private hands, but it seems likely that the figure would be of the same order of magnitude.

A similar conclusion is provided by Ali *et al.* (1981) in the case of Bangladesh, where it was discovered that only 50% of the migrants relied exclusively on banks for remitting their savings, while 35% used private channels and another 9% used both. Those using private channels were predominantly from rural areas. They also found that non-bank channels were relatively more efficient, and that, on average, the money reached the recipients more quickly than through banking channels (Ali *et al.* 1981: 94–5).

Studies on other countries also show that a large volume of remittances is channelled into the black market, and that the Government is forever trying to provide incentives to remitters to use official channels. Swamy (1981: 58) reports a steadily rising volume of foreign-currency accounts held by Greek residents throughout the 1970s, with annual increases matching the inflow of recorded remittances. Similarly, Paine (1974: 207) shows that 65% of Turkish migrants remitted their money home through secret means or in person. Other examples of similar observations are found in Birks and Sinclair (1980: 39, 103), Bhagwati (1978: 71), Bruton, (1983: 686, 698–9), Serageldin *et al.* (1983: 89), and Granier and Marciano (1975: 163). Thus Pakistan or Bangladesh are not exceptional in this regard.

Partner-Country Data

On the demand side, the primary source of information is partner-country data on trade flows. Bhagwati (1978) used an innovative technique to demonstrate the existence of smuggling and capital flight in developing countries. He compared partner-country data on exports and imports to and from each other respectively, to find extensive evidence of under-invoicing of exports (to earn foreign exchange) as well as under-invoicing of imports (smuggling), with some cases of over-invoicing of imports thrown in.

TABLE 9.1. *LDC and OECD trade data, 1966*

Country	LDC exports 100(*M* – *X*)/*X*	Premium	LDC imports: 100(*M* – *X*)/*X* Total	SITC5-8	Share
Hong Kong	13.7	1	– 11.6	– 11.4	84.1
South Korea	– 4.6	0	– 0.4	– 10.0	67.4
Philippines	16.1	2	– 7.6	– 8.3	80.1
Taiwan	7.0	3	– 3.3	– 3.4	5.4
Thailand	6.4	0.6	+ 14.0	+ 11.0	88.5
Sri Lanka	20.1	94	– 5.7	– 11.0	71.2
Egypt	30.7	111	+ 8.3	+ 6.4	60.6
India	23.7	74	– 1.0	– 15.7	55.0
Iran	35.2	4	– 1.3	+ 0.8	90.7
Pakistan	14.3	74	– 1.3	– 7.6	77.4
Greece	27.9	4	– 0.2	– 0.2	81.7
Turkey	15.4	40	– 13.4	– 10.2	91.1
Yugoslavia	– 1.0	17	– 1.3	+ 6.2	72.6

Source: Bhagwati (1978: table 4. 1, p.73; table 4. 2, p.75).

Table 9.1 underscores this observation. The first column gives the percentage by which recorded values of various countries' imports from OECD countries exceeds the recorded values of corresponding exports from OECD countries to the LDCs. Column 2 gives the value of the black-market premium in 1966. Column 3 gives the percentage by which recorded OECD imports from each LDC exceeds the recorded value of exports from the sending country. Column 4 gives the same information for a subset of these exports, namely primary goods covered under Standard Industry and Trade Classifications 5–8.

An important correction to be borne in mind is that the export figures are f.o.b., while the import figures are c.i.f. Hence, imports will generally exceed exports by about 10%. If imports exceed exports by more than this amount, it indicates the existence of under-invoicing of exports. Similarly, if imports are less than exports (or exceed them by less than 10%), it indicates under-invoicing or smuggling of imports.

Notice that the black-market premiums for Pakistan, Turkey, India, and Egypt were among the highest in the world in 1966; all four countries showed evidence of under-invoicing of exports; and Pakistan and Turkey (though not Egypt) showed some under-invoicing of imports.

These data can be contrasted with Table 9.2, where the proportion of under-invoiced exports seems to be stable (or slightly reduced) and that of under-invoiced imports higher in all cases except India.[19] This is at the same time that the black-market premium has declined in all countries. With all the caveats about the weakness of the data, it is nevertheless difficult to reject the assertion that there must have been an expansion of supply of foreign currencies to the black markets. This is especially significant because average tariff rates declined in all three countries during this period, thus reducing the profitability of smuggling.[20]

TABLE 9.2. *LDC and OECD trade data, 1982*

Country	LDC exports $100(M - X)/X$	Premium	LDC imports $100(M - X)/X$
Egypt	+ 9.9	7.5	− 32.0
India	+ 9.9	11.1	+ 10.0
Pakistan	+ 5.3	24.6	− 23.2
Turkey	− 5.0	15.1	+ 3.2
Yugoslavia	− 4.1	18.4	− 0.8

Source: IMF, *Direction of Trade Statistics*; Cowitt (1985).

These observations can also be supplemented by looking at Table 9.3, which gives annual data on the black-market premium and Pakistani–USA trade, and Tables 9.4–9.8, which give annual partner-country data for the OECD and the five countries in which we are interested. Notice that both conventional sources of supply of black-market currencies have diminished in importance: over-invoicing of imports has completely disappeared, while under-invoicing of exports remains significant only in

TABLE 9.3. *Pakistan and US trade data, 1978–1987*

Year	Pakistan exports $100(M - X)/X$	Premium	Pakistan imports $100(M - X)/X$
1978	− 6.0	37.5	− 0.3
1979	+ 10.8	23.5	− 2.3
1980	+ 0.5	27.0	+ 17.1
1981	− 4.2	40.9	− 4.5
1982	+ 7.5	24.6	− 23.2
1983	− 4.8	30.6	− 37.7
1984	+ 2.1	20.2	− 41.8
1985	+ 9.0	15.1	− 21.1
1986	− 3.5	11.3	− 15.0
1987	− 5.3	9.7	− 25.4

Source: IMF, *Direction of Trade Statistics*.

Yugoslavia. On the other hand, the demand for foreign exchange, as expressed in the under-invoicing or smuggling of imports, is much larger in the 1980s than in the 1960s.

Once again, while partner-country comparisons are subject to various caveats, there is a presumption created here that the demand for foreign currencies has increased while conventional sources of supply have become less active. It is our argument that the new supplies of unrecorded remittances created a cheap source of black-market currency, which not only obviated the need for more expensive sources (such as export smuggling) but also eroded the effectiveness of capital controls and commercial policy.

TABLE 9.4. *Pakistan and OECD trade data, 1982–1987*

	Exports 100($M-X$)/X	Imports 100($M-X$)/X
1982	+ 14.10	− 4.66
1983	+ 5.03	− 9.52
1984	+ 0.64	− 13.10
1985	+ 10.49	− 7.60
1986	+ 3.67	− 9.26
1987	− 1.57	− 11.01
Average	+ 5.39	− 9.19

Source: IMF, *Direction of Trade Statistics.*

TABLE 9.5. *Egypt and OECD trade data, 1982–1987*

	Exports 100($M-X$)/X	Imports 100($M-X$)/X
1982	+ 133.69	− 32.72
1983	+ 127.61	− 25.16
1984	+ 142.57	− 26.65
1985	+ 128.28	− 23.85
1986	+ 9.97	+ 9.99
1987	+ 9.92	+ 9.98
Average	+ 92.01	− 14.66

Source: IMF, *Direction of Trade Statistics.*

TABLE 9.6. *Turkey and OECD trade data, 1982–1987*

	Exports 100($M-X$)/X	Imports 100($M-X$)/X
1982	− 1.62	+ 5.10
1983	− 5.09	+ 2.05
1984	− 17.05	− 0.97
1985	− 5.65	− 5.06
1986	+ 8.29	− 2.44
1987	− 0.69	− 5.99
Average	− 3.62	− 1.22

Source: IMF, *Direction of Trade Statistics.*

TABLE 9.7. *Yugoslavia and OECD trade data, 1982–1987*

	Exports 100$(M - X)/X$	Imports 100$(M - X)/X$
1982	+26.50	+16.39
1983	+27.52	−0.80
1984	+23.52	−0.91
1985	+35.45	−9.42
1986	+69.01	−25.49
1987	+20.89	+4.31
Average	+33.81	−2.65

Source: IMF, *Direction of Trade Statistics.*

TABLE 9.8. *India and OECD trade data, 1982–1987*

	Exports 100$(M - X)/X$	Imports 100$(M - X)/X$
1982	+9.61	+2.25
1983	+9.62	+9.95
1984	+9.59	+9.98
1985	+9.61	+9.99
1986	+9.59	+10.00
1987	+9.65	+9.99
Average	+9.61	+8.70

Source: IMF, *Direction of Trade Statistics.*

Expansion in Black Markets

The above assertions concerning the demand for illegal currencies are also supported by other available evidence on the issue. Cowitt (1985: 592) observed a sudden expansion in the size of smuggling operations and related markets in the mid-1970s in Pakistan. His explanation is that the rise in the international price of gold shifted gold-smugglers into other enterprises. This may be partially correct, but it was also at this time that the expanded black market began providing a cheap source of illegal currency. Both of these effects may have combined to create a tremendous boom in the tribal areas, with an entire new market town[21] being created to handle the expanded trade. Despite the subsequent reduction in tariff levels and quota restrictions this semi-clandestine market has continued to enjoy a sustained boom, and its offshoots have penetrated the 'settled' districts where the trade is ostensibly illegal but now increasingly tolerated.

Similarly, there has been a tremendous expansion in the number of Pakistanis travelling abroad every year. In part, of course, this expansion is the result of the increase in labour migration, but a significantly higher number of Pakistanis travel abroad for pleasure or business today than, say, in the early 1970s. Given the fact that the allowance for foreign travel has not risen in real terms since the 1960s, it seems reasonable to assume that Pakistanis are taking advantage of the easier availability of black-market foreign exchange for this purpose.

Since the late 1970s the major Pakistani business houses have become fairly active investors in various other countries, most particularly in the Persian Gulf. Thus, while capital flight has been endemic in Pakistan, it has increased in overall volume in recent years. However, the paucity of data means that not much can be said about short-run capital movements beyond the fact that they also appear to have increased somewhat in the last decade.

This concludes our description of currency black markets. We have argued that the size of these markets in Pakistan has expanded dramatically in recent years, mainly because unrecorded remittance inflows reduce the cost of procuring illegal funds. This assertion, commonly accepted by most observers, is supported by available data. We shall now turn to an analysis of the effect of such markets on the exchange rate.

III. BLACK MARKETS AND CAPITAL FLOWS

In this section, we shall argue that a large black market for foreign currency effectively undermines capital controls, and facilitates discretionary capital flows of a significant magnitude. Since capital controls seem to be necessary for maintaining any kind of restrictive trade policy, their erosion tends to decrease the effectiveness of such restrictions.

The effect of illegal transactions, including black markets in foreign exchange, has been explored by several authors. Those adopting a monetary approach view the black market as a financial phenomenon, emerging out of a macroeconomic disequilibrium in foreign-currency markets: Blejer (1978) assumes that the black market is simply a means of adjusting private portfolios in the face of capital controls. Similarly, Gupta (1980) sees illegal foreign currency as an alternate asset, whose relative price (the black-market premium) is determined by domestic money supply, real income, interest rate, the world price level, and the price of precious metals.

In contrast, there are partial-equilibrium models of the real economy, which see the black market simply as a sideshow. These include Sheikh (1974; 1976), who attempts to estimate the welfare consequences of smuggling and its connections to capital flight and the black market, and Culbertson (1975), who examines the link between purchasing-power parity and the black-market exchange rate. In this class are also the various welfare analyses of foreign-trade regimes by Bhagwati and collaborators (see Bhagwati, 1978, especially the chapters by Bhagwati and Hansen and Bhagwati and Srinivasan).

Lastly, there are general-equilibrium models, which attempt to incorporate the black market into a framework that includes real as well as financial considerations. De Franco (1985) attempts to construct a computable general-equilibrium model of the Nicaraguan economy in which the financial sector includes illegal currency markets. Dornbusch *et al.* (1983), while presenting a partial-equilibrium model of Brazil, use an underlying general-equilibrium framework: they abstract from consequences for the real sector because of the belief that in case of Brazil the black market is too small to have significant feedback effects. De Macedo (1982) has a more elaborate general-equilibrium model of the Egyptian economy, where the real and financial sectors are integrated. This paper uses many of the insights of the Dornbusch and de Macedo models. We see the interesting issues with regard to the black market for dollars as the following: (i) how do shocks in the real economy influence conditions in the black market? (ii) how is adjustment to these shocks helped or hindered by the existence and size of the black markets? and (iii) how does the black market constrain policy responses to shocks? But first, a few preliminary comments are in order.

III.1. Efficiency in Illegal Transactions

The existence of a black market for foreign exchange does not necessarily mean that the domestic currency is overvalued in a macroeconomic sense. (See, e.g., Gupta 1980: 237; also Culbertson 1975; Bhagwati 1978.) An excess demand for foreign currencies can be created for microeconomic reasons, namely selective restrictions on the importation of a particular good, service, or asset,[22] if the sale of legal foreign exchange is restricted to those buying for legitimate purposes.[23] This fact is important because it is easier for an existing black market to respond to additional excess demand generated by a temporary overvaluation—which might be created by inflation, terms-of-trade shocks, or fluctuation in relative demand for prohibited foreign assets—than if the market were to be created anew with each disturbance. As a result, the black market can endure and grow, even when the official exchange rate is in line with overall balance-of-payments considerations. An interesting corollary of this fact is the common observation that, despite repeated devaluations, the black market is consistently able to undersell the central bank.[24]

Related to the first point is the fact that there appear to be significant *economies of scale*, and *learning by doing* in these illegal institutions. Economies of scale are indicated by the sophistication of arrangements made for migrant workers in the Middle East. Such elaborate arrangements would not be possible unless the scale of operations were large enough to justify them. Similarly, the credibility of the exchange-dealers is also connected to their size in relation to the market, and the length of time they have been in business.

Apart from considerations of credibility, learning by doing is relevant in forming contacts with officials, acquiring knowledge of clandestine routes, etc. These considerations indicate that there are likely to be significant barriers to entry into these businesses. This is borne out by Cowitt's (1985) observation that the illegal gold trade is handled by one group in Pakistan and by a syndicate of two groups in India.

Finally, it also appears that the history of government controls is important because of the 'protection' these controls can provide to the formation of an illegal institution such as the black market. Once established, a black market can allow the controlling group or syndicate to strengthen its organizational structure and capability, and thus gain a measure of independence from the conditions which made its emergence possible in the first place. It can then diversify into other areas or take advantage of new profit opportunities, and it can create its own barriers to entry. This suggests the existence of 'hysteresis' in black market development.

To summarize, what is relevant for our purposes is that the increase in size and age of the market will tend to make it more sophisticated and efficient. A larger market will be in a better position to take advantage of temporary disturbances in global conditions or the domestic policy environment. This will be the case particularly if the larger market has existed for a significant length of time.

This observation can be approached through the traditional framework of the supply and demand for illegal foreign exchange. An increase in the size of the market will generally increase the short-run elasticity of the supply and demand for currency flowing into it. To see this point, note that the elasticity of supply depends on the willingness of exporters to smuggle out rather than to legally export their produce. Similarly, the elasticity of demand depends on the ability of smugglers to expand their operations to take advantage of a new source of disequilibrium. Both of these will depend on the response time of illegal traders in taking advantage of market conditions, which will in turn depend on the size of the market and the time it has been in operation.

Any fresh source of supply to the black market will expand the size of this market, and therefore of smuggling operations, leading indirectly to improvements in the efficiency of these operations. Furthermore, the longer the market has been in existence, the higher should we expect the efficiency to be. In other words, resource inflows through the black market (such as unrecorded remittances) increase the elasticity of supply and demand for illegal dollars from other sources as well. The obverse of this argument, noted by various authors, is that black markets increase the elasticity of *legal* exports and imports with respect to the exchange rate and restrictive policy as well.

The above argument, in a nutshell, is as follows. Black markets will exist in developing countries in 'normal' as well as in 'abnormal' times, with the turnover becoming larger in the latter. The responsiveness of the turnover to shocks depends on the elasticity of demand and supply of foreign exchange in the black market. Any economic or technological change which reduces the cost of supplying currencies to the black market will directly increase the supply elasticity. However, increasing the size of the black market during normal times will also increase the elasticity of supply of illegal foreign exchange from other sources, as well as the demand for such currencies. By the same token, it will increase the elasticity of supply and demand of *legal* foreign exchange by inducing it to shift into the illegal market.

III.2. A Model of Currency Black Markets

The above considerations can be incorporated into a simple model of currency black markets. We shall focus on the effect of remittances not only because they are important in Pakistan but also because they exemplify factors which lead to increases in the supply of currency to the black market.

Consider a country which has two markets for foreign currency: an official market, with turnover generated by exports X^*, remittances (or elastic foreign-resource inflows) R^*, and imports M^*;[25] and an unofficial (black) market with smuggled exports X, illegal remittances R, and smuggled imports M. There are capital controls in effect in the official market, with the result that the entire (incremental) demand for foreign assets F operates through the unofficial market. The official balance of payments B^* equals $X^* + R^* - M^*$, while the black market, which is assumed to be always in equilibrium, has a zero balance $B(= X + R - M - F)$.

To simplify the analysis, we shall make the following set of assumptions:

(1) The total (i.e. official plus unofficial) volume of exports and remittances is exogenous; while total (official plus unofficial) imports depend on the terms of trade and trade restrictions.

(2) The switching between the two markets depends only on p, the black-market premium; except in the case of imports, where it depends on the difference between p and the tariff rate t.

(3) The fractions of exports, imports, and remittances flowing through the unofficial market have a lower bound of zero, and an upper bound

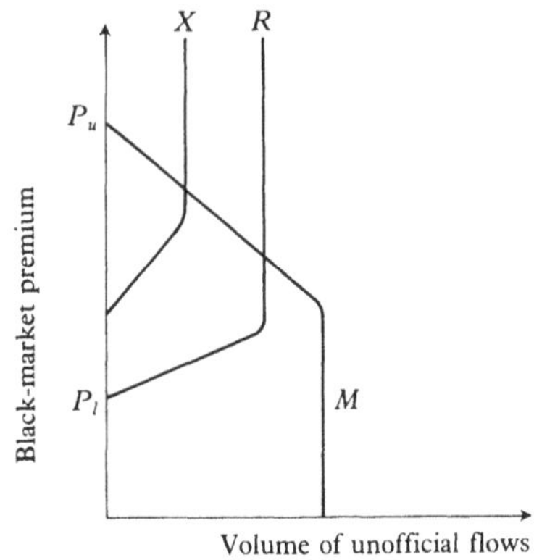

FIG. 9.1. Unofficial exports, imports, and remittances.

strictly less than unity. In other words, a significant fraction of these flows will always go through the official market, no matter how large or small the black-market premium.

(4) Illegal remittances are more responsive to changes in the premium rate, than illegal exports. This makes sense, since it is costlier and more risky to smuggle export goods across the border than to send unofficial remittances.

(5) The (illegal) demand for foreign assets F depends only on the black-market premium p, and on relative changes in asset returns discounted by expected exchange rate movements. The last are influenced by political or economic instability, the official current-account balance, government policies, and the premium rate itself.

Given these assumptions, it will be clear that, in the absence of increases in gross flows, changes in the volume of foreign assets dF will be exactly equal to changes in the official balance of payments dB^*. The rest of the analysis will focus on the determination of F.

Under these assumptions, the volume of smuggled exports, X, smuggled imports, M, and illegal remittances, R, is represented in Fig. 9.1. X and R are zero at their lower bounds, i.e. when the black-market premium is too low to elicit any flow into the illegal market. Note that the lower bound for remittances is below that for exports. Smuggling of imports M is zero when the black-market premium is higher than the tariff rate at the margin. (In the case of selective quotas or prohibitions on certain items, the black-market rate required to accomplish this may be very high indeed).

The other important feature of Fig. 9.1 is the region where market flows become completely inelastic with respect to the premium rate.

Clearly, this can happen either (as in the above case) when the premium falls below a lower bound, P_l, or rises above an upper bound, P_u. In the first case, the supply of currency to the black market will shrink to zero, and further declines in the premium will have no influence on the official market because the black market will be closed for all practical purposes. In the second case, the supply of currencies to the black market will reach a maximum, and any further increases in the premium will be unable to pull more resources out of the official sector.[26] In between these two extreme cases, a change in the black-market premium in either direction will give rise to a switching of flows from the official market to the black market, or vice versa.

Shifts in the three curves will occur mainly for two reasons: (i) an increase in the magnitude of total (unofficial plus official) flows due to changes in terms of trade or economic growth (we shall ignore this in our analysis); and (ii) an increase in the efficiency of black-market operations because of two factors, economies of scale and learning by doing. With an increase in the scale of operations, and with the passage of time, the black market gains credibility and legitimacy: it can increase the number of its outlets and the quality of its services (e.g. a quicker and more reliable delivery of money or an increase in the number and type of instruments), and reduce the spread between buying and selling rates. The result will be an increase in the number of people willing to use this channel in preference to the official one, and also in the number of those switching from one channel to the other.

The effect of an increase in market efficiency can be divided into three categories. Fig. 9.2 represents these for the supply of unofficial remit-

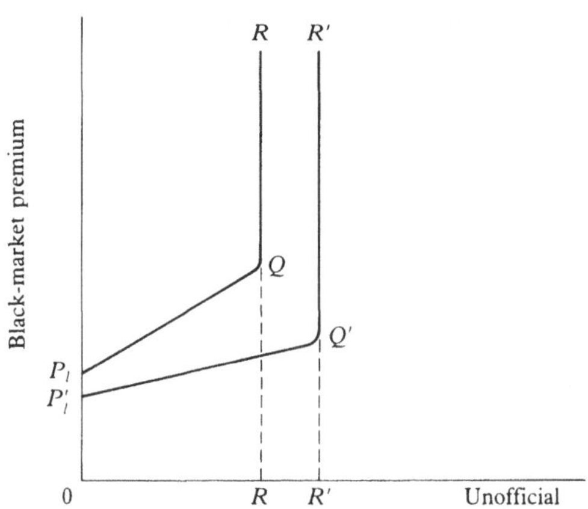

FIG 9.2. Changes in remittance flows due to improvements in (*a*) scale economies or (*b*) learning by doing.

tances R. The other two curves will be analogous to this. The three categories are:

(i) A reduction in the lower-bound premium rate, P_l, below which no flow takes place (in case of imports, it will be an upper bound). This means that people will need a smaller incentive to use the unofficial channel.

(ii) A reduction of the slope P_lQ, meaning that smaller changes in the premium rate will suffice to induce a switch between the two channels. In the case of imports and exports, it implies *inter alia* the discovery of clandestine routes for smuggling and a greater degree of collusion with surveillance agencies.

(iii) An increase in OR, the maximum volume of unofficial remittances. Again, this means the total number of people willing to use the unofficial channel has increased.

In addition to these effects, an increase in the size of the black market will also lead to an increase in the size and sophistication of the smuggling operations.[27] This will help increase the fraction of imports and exports going through the illegal channels at any level of the black-market premium, and will also make these fractions more responsive to variations in the premium. The net result of these influences will be to flatten out the curves X and M, and to shift them to the right.

We shall summarize the previous discussion in the form of a single graph, Fig. 9.3, which represents the market for foreign assets. The supply of resources to this market is the net value of illegal exports,

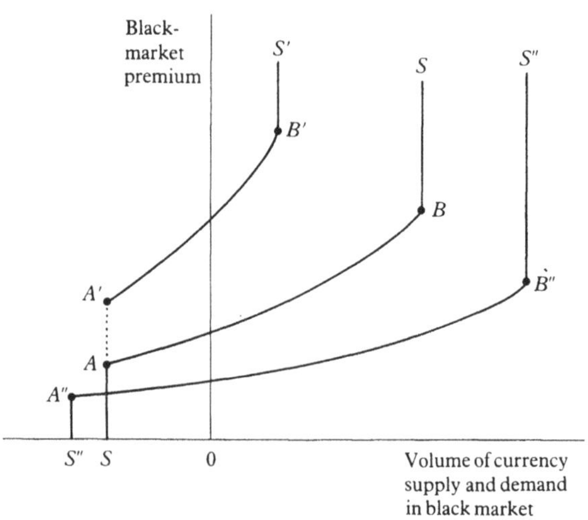

FIG 9.3. Total currency supplied to the black market (*a*) without remittances, (*b*) with remittances (short-run), and (*c*) with remittances (long-run).

smuggled imports, and unofficial remittances; and the demand is generated, as mentioned earlier, by expected movements in relative asset returns.

The supply curve, *SABS*, is the composite of the three curves, *X*, *R*, and *M*, of Fig. 9.1. In an economy without remittances, the curve would be *SA′B′S′*, where *AB* is steeper and *B*, the upper bound on total supply, much further to the left. On the other hand, an increase in efficiency of the black market would shift the curve to *S″A″B″S″*, the lower bound, *A*, shifting to the left and downwards, *B* shifting rightwards, and *AB* becoming flatter.

Finally, the equilibrium level of the premium rate, p^*, as well as F^*, the demand for foreign assets, will be determined by the intersection of the supply and demand for foreign assets, as depicted in Fig. 9.4. Changes in expectations, changes in relative asset returns, or political or economic instability would affect the demand for foreign assets, and thus the equilibrium premium rate.

As mentioned earlier, the counterpart of F^e is a reduction in resources available to the central bank, and thus an increase in the official payments deficit, B^*. A rightward shift of one of the two curves would result in a worsening of the official payments position.

III.3. Capital Flows and the Black Market

To interpret the results suggested by this framework, recall that the institution of capital controls is intended to insulate the economy from short-run changes in external conditions or market expectations (George

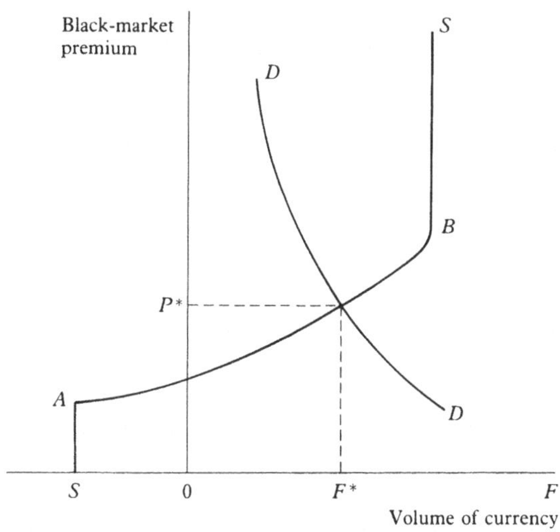

FIG 9.4. Equilibrium in the currency black market.

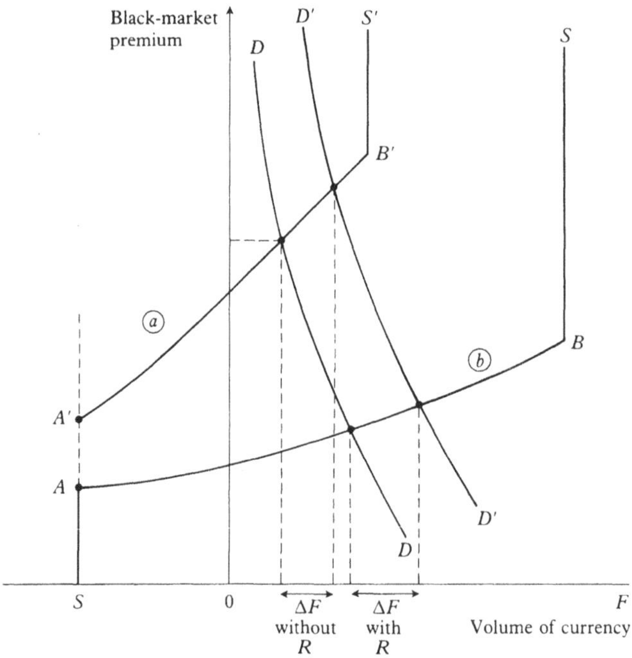

FIG 9.5. Effect of an increase in demand for foreign assets (*a*) without remittances, (*b*) with remittances.

and Giddy, 1983: s. 2.2.4–6). In our model, the insulation is represented by the fact that such considerations affect only the capital flows, *F*, which, being restricted to the black market, play no direct role in the official balance of payments. This is true, however, only if the black market is very small and does not pull a significant amount of inflowing resources from the official to the unofficial market. The first result from the above exercise is that elastic foreign-resource inflows, such as remittances, reintroduce capital flows into balance-of-payments considerations by expanding the volume of the black market.

> *Proposition 1*: An increase in remittance flows strengthens the connection between the black market for foreign currency and the real economy.

To see the connection, we look at Fig. 9.5, where the curves *SABS* and *SA'B'S'* represent the supply of black-market currencies, with and without remittances respectively.

As indicated in Fig. 9.5, an exogenous increase in the demand for foreign assets will shift the demand curve *DD* to the right, thus increasing the equilibrium level of the black-market premium as well as the volume of foreign resources in the black market. This in turn will affect the official market by withdrawing resources from it, the size of the withdrawal depending on two factors: the slope of the supply curve *AB* and the maximum potential supply $O\bar{R}$.

To see the reason for this, note that the black market functions to moderate the additional demand for foreign assets through two mechanisms: by raising the premium and thus reducing the attractiveness of foreign assets and by placing an upper bound on the volume of resources which can be withdrawn from the official market. The weaker this ability to moderate the demand, the greater will be the spill-over effect on the official market, as will be the connection between the unofficial and the official market. This ability is weaker the flatter the curve *AB* (which means that the shift in *DD* produces only a small change in *p*) and the longer the distance. As discussed earlier, remittance inflows increase the slope of the supply curve, and increase the maximum potential supply of resources to the unofficial market. Thus, they will help weaken the moderating effect of the black market on disturbances in the international capital market, with the result that the disturbance will be transferred almost intact to the official market.

> *Proposition 2*: A stronger link between currency black markets and the real economy erodes the effectiveness of capital controls.

Note that by disallowing capital flows (in order to insulate the economy from short-run changes in external economic conditions), the central bank effectively relegates these flows to the black market. With remittances flowing in, however, an increase in foreign-asset demand will produce only a small increase in *p*, leaving *F* almost unchanged, and thus shifting the entire excess demand onto the official market. Hence remittances help to erode the effectiveness of capital controls. This is just another way of saying that the official market, and therefore the economy, is no longer insulated from external shocks.

To summarize, an increase in remittance flows will make the official balance of payments more responsive to small changes in the black-market premium on foreign currencies, in addition to expanding the total volume of discretionary resources which can be switched between the two markets. The result will be the creation of larger fluctuations in the official balance of payments.

The erosion of capital controls creates a self-reinforcing spiral. The ability of foreign-asset demand to influence official payments balances will feed into exchange rate expectations, and so increases in the black-market premium, rather than dampening foreign-asset demand, may actually increase it, since the central bank may be forced to keep the official rate in line with the black-market rate to avoid excessive fluctuations in payments accounts.

III.4. Devaluation versus Trade Restriction

To introduce the next result, we can start by comparing various policies used to combat payment imbalances. A country faced with such a situation has three options: borrow abroad,[28] devalue its currency, or impose some form of trade restriction. Different circumstances will generally favour one or the other of such actions. For example, Sachs (1982) argues that, if the disturbance is expected to be temporary, it may be optimal to borrow to smooth consumption over time; on the other hand, permanent or long-lasting disturbances may necessitate structural adjustment, including currency devaluation and consumption-reducing policies. The case for trade restrictions is made on various grounds, including the perception that devaluation is an inegalitarian policy, creates political unrest (partly for the first reason), has an inflationary bias (and may therefore be self-defeating), and may not help restrict trade in the presence of short-run inelasticities of demand and supply of tradable goods (elasticity pessimism). Analysts have also noted that the latter policies are more often resorted to by 'inward-oriented' governments, or those with a bias towards direct interference in the economy (see e.g. Balassa 1984; Sachs 1985).

Be the above as it may, governments would tend to use the latter set of policies only if their results were the same as that of a devaluation, but without the attendant costs. The argument to be made here is that black markets reduce the effectiveness of trade restrictions relative to devaluation in combating balance-of-payments problems; among trade restrictions, the effect is to reduce the effectiveness of quotas relative to tariffs. Thus the net result is to shift the government's preference away from quotas towards tariffs, and away from tariffs towards devaluations.

> *Proposition 3*: Remittance inflows make trade restrictions less effective than exchange rate adjustments in combating balance-of-payments problems.

In order to demonstrate this proposition, note that *ceteris paribus* a devaluation will discourage official as well as unofficial imports, and thus lower the black-market premium. On the other hand, a tariff increase will serve mainly to switch imports from official to unofficial channels, and thus to *raise* the black-market premium. Thus, while a devaluation will reduce illegal remittances and smuggled exports, a tariff increase will raise them in order to meet the now higher demand for smuggled imports. In fact, under the assumptions of our model, if the change in the premium rate is small, the increase in smuggled imports and that in unofficial remittances and smuggled exports will cancel each other out, leaving no effect on the official balance of payments. In that case, the only difference between the two policies will be their varying impacts on the black-market premium.[29] However, the fact that the two policies will have differing effects on p becomes significant when we introduce other factors including capital flows.

Note that when the policy actions discussed above are called for, the black-market premium is likely to be high to begin with. The trade restriction policy will, then, worsen the disequilibrium situation in this market, where the devaluation will improve it.

Now, if expectations of the current exchange rate are partially based on the black-market rate, then an increase in the latter may lead to a higher demand for foreign assets; this will further increase the demand for black-market currency, put a greater upward pressure on the black-market rate, and possibly create a speculative spiral. If the restrictions imposed are perceived as a stop-gap arrangement, the expectations of the eventual devaluation may feed the spiral even more strongly, leading to even greater upward revisions in the black-market rate.

In the absence of remittances, when the maximum potential size of the black market is small, the upper limit may be reached rather quickly. In this case, the higher demand for foreign assets so created may not be able to induce a significant volume of resources to shift from the official to the black market. With remittances, however, the upper limit may not be approached so readily, and substantial capital flows may have to be accommodated by the central bank. Of course, this will show up in the official statistics as a sudden decline in reported remittances as well as in measured exports, worsening the balance-of-payments situation despite fresh trade restrictions.

Since one of the ideas behind imposing restrictions is to protect 'essential' imports, it is necessary for the success of this policy that the payments situation should not deteriorate too much. With remittances, this is likely to begin to happen with an excessive reliance of policy on trade restrictions instead of exchange rate management.

To summarize, the use of trade restrictions to combat payments imbalances is likely to generate discretionary (illegal) capital flows, which will have to be accommodated to a much greater degree by the official market if the country receives large amounts of discretionary liquid transfers. The problem will be more acute where the trade restrictions are perceived as a temporary arrangement, or where high black-market premiums signal future devaluations.

> *Proposition 4*: Currency black markets reduce the effectiveness of non-tariff barriers, by comparison with import tariffs, in combating payments disequilibria.

The argument behind this proposition derives from two premisses: first, that increases in government budget deficits stimulate capital flight because they help create expectations of future adjustments in tax and exchange rates. Second, that any system of non-price-rationing of imported goods will yield, in general, a larger excess demand for foreign exchange than an equivalent price-rationing scheme. This is likely to be so because the non-price system may exclude some people with higher marginal utilities for imported goods than the recipients.

Tariff barriers, in addition to moderating import demand, also support the government budget, and thus dampen inflationary expectations. As a result, they may help moderate the capital flight generated by an adverse payments situation.

Moreover, demand for smuggled imports under a tariff regime is viable only up to the point where the black-market premium is less than the tariff rate. Under a quota regime, the upper limit on the black-market premium will be higher. Both these problems will exacerbate the impact of induced capital flight on the official balance of payments.

IV. BLACK MARKETS AND COMMERCIAL POLICY

In this section, we shall present some evidence from Egypt, Turkey, Yugoslavia, Pakistan, and India in support of the propositions presented above. The main argument of this essay is that recent changes have increased the costs of controls on trade and capital flows, and therefore induced the governments and central banks to adopt market-type policies instead. This shift includes changes from rigid and overvalued exchange rates towards more flexible ones; from non-tariff towards tariff barriers on trade; across-the-board reduction of tariff levels; and increases in domestic interest rates to attract foreign savings.

This debate has been structured in terms of a conflict between two aims of commercial policy: increased volume versus increased allocative control over foreign resources. In earlier periods, most governments chose greater control for various reasons, including 'elasticity pessimism';[30] ready availability of foreign borrowing to mitigate the urgency of foreign-resource demand; and, most importantly, because greater control was a short-run problem with immediate political and economic consequences, while the question of volume of resources was a medium-run issue which could be left to the future.

The interesting point about financial openness is that it ends up reversing this order of priority. First, discretionary capital flows are highly elastic with respect to policy choices; remittance flows in particular have not only been as large as, or often even larger than, foreign-aid inflows, they have also led to increased borrowing capacity of countries. Second, it has been very difficult to direct the allocation of remittance resources into desired channels. Third, and most importantly, the short-run problem today concerns the volume of resources and not the question of allocation. As a result, it becomes more rational as well as more judicious to move policy towards the pursuit of increased resource inflows rather than to use it to control the allocation of an available level of resources.[31] This, in a nutshell, is the change in attitudes brought about by openness. The awareness of this change of attitude, however, is apparent only through hindsight. In actual practice, governments tried to achieve both objectives simultaneously, often with unpleasant results.

IV.1. Volume versus Control

There is a certain paradox in trying to pursue simultaneously the policies of increasing the volume of a certain resource and of controlling its disposition. The first requires the government to subsidize the producers, the second somehow to tax them. One response is to eschew control altogether, and to give incentives (possibly through subsidies) for increased production as well as for preferred allocative decisions.[32] Another option, which surfaces in many guises, is to try to discriminate between sub-marginal and marginal producers in order to tax the former and subsidize the latter.[33] Yet another possibility is to ignore the question of volume altogether and simply concentrate on controlling the allocation.[34]

Governments confronted with this question with regard to foreign-exchange inflows were often inclined to use the third type of policy; but before moving towards the first type they went through an intermediate phase, where various forms of the second option were tried out, only to be found wanting. The succeeding paragraphs will try to document this transition.

Unlike exports, which are often subject to fairly significant forms of taxation, no government has seriously attempted to tax remittance incomes.[35] Thus the object of policy has generally been to raise the amount of remittance inflows without interfering with the ability of the government to tax or control non-remittance inflows of foreign exchange. The classic policy was the use of a preferred exchange rate for remittances, while the other sellers had to use a lower rate.[36] Other discriminatory policies included the sale of assets or privileges to emigrants at subsidized prices.[37] However, like Serageldin (1983: 91), most writers find that 'unless general conditions in the labor exporting country are conducive to the transfer of remittances, no individual scheme can be successful in attracting more than a small proportion of migrants' earnings'. In the end, the countries discovered that a realistic, unified exchange rate is the most important incentive to attract remittances, and the only one which will work consistently (Chandavarkar, 1980). Given the above description, we now turn to a brief examination of the experience of some remittance-receiving countries in the recent past.

IV.2. Black-Market Premiums

Table 9.9 gives the figures on black-market premiums on the US dollar in four major remittance-receiving countries. The striking feature of these figures is the rapid decline from the high levels of the premium in the 1960s and early 1970s to the relatively lower levels in the late 1970s.

An important reason for this behaviour is that in the 1970s the large turnovers in the black market had become more costly, and corrective action was being instituted much sooner than in the past. Related to this is the point that reliance on partial devaluations and various multiple exchange rate schemes may have declined. This is certainly true of Pakistan, Turkey, and the Sudan, and, in a different manner, for Egypt.[38]

TABLE 9.9. *Black-market premiums on US dollars, 1962–1983 (%, end of year)*

	Turkey	Yugoslavia	Egypt	Pakistan
1962	43.2	195.0	—	—
1966	40.1	16.6	111.0	74.0
1970	6.0	9.4	109.1	120.6
1971	9.6	7.8	100.0	212.0
1972	4.3	4.5	75.6	29.5
1973	5.0	-2.2	10.4	13.6
1974	6.1	0.9	18.1	22.2
1975	11.2	5.6	19.7	16.7
1976	8.4	7.2	5.9	13.1
1977	35.0	1.9	0.0	33.3
1978	50.1	11.0	6.7	37.9
1979	52.8	9.1	7.5	23.7
1980	16.0	13.1	9.1	27.3
1981	19.0	11.9	5.0	40.9
1982	15.1	18.4	7.5	24.6
1983[a]	9.4	12.8	10.5	31.3

[a] Figures for 1983 are for the month of Sept.

Source: Cowitt (1985); *Pick's Currency Yearbook*, 1982; Bhagwati (1978: 73); Swamy (1981: 58).

IV.3. Egypt

Currency developments in Egypt have been interesting precisely because the Government has long been aware of its impotence in controlling capital flight, and has therefore instituted various actions to overcome this impotence.[39]

One of the earliest such developments was the creation of a 'tourist exchange rate' in July 1971 at $1.70/£E, a substantial discount over the official rate of $2.555/£E.[40] Since then the number of different exchange rates have proliferated as the Egyptian central bank strove unsuccessfully to compete with the black market. Besides the direct crackdown in 1972 on the so-called 'free shops', the centres of black-market activity, many indirect policies were attempted to reduce the influence of these markets. These included the *de facto* elimination of capital controls in 1975, as residents were increasingly permitted to import goods against their foreign-currency holdings,[41] and then the formal lifting of restrictions on ownership of foreign assets in August 1976. At this time, a 'free market rate' was also established for private-sector currency transactions and imports. This rate has followed the black-market rate quite closely since its advent, and is quoted by observers as *the* exchange rate. As *Pick's Currency Yearbook* remarked, in its usual cavalier tone, 'unable to beat the black market, the Egyptian Central Bank decided to join it'.

Today, Egyptians can own foreign securities as well as foreign currencies. They can maintain foreign-currency bank balances abroad or with Egyptian banks, and can use these accounts to finance foreign travel or private imports or to engage in currency transactions. However, export proceeds still need to be repatriated, and commercial imports are controlled through the rationing of foreign exchange rather than through licensing.

Because of these developments, the central bank has lost control over the exchange rate as well as the disposition of liquidity in the country.[42] The free market rate follows closely the interest rate on Euro-currency deposits (Bruton 1983: 699). Similarly, the volume of foreign resources held by commercial banks has grown rapidly without any semblance of central-bank control over it (ibid.). Lastly, it appears that, despite these changes, a large part of remittances are not available domestically.

Bruton (1983: 700) uses these observations to argue that the result of the economic changes of the last decade is an overvaluation of the domestic currency, reflected, not in exchange rate scarcity (since there is none), but rather in the shift of investment towards non-tradables, most notably construction.

IV.4. Turkey

The Turkish case is particularly interesting because in the mid-1970s the Government attempted to use conventional policies of import restriction and partial devaluation in order to control the adverse effect on the balance of payments of two significant events, the oil shock of 1973 and the invasion of Cyprus in 1974. The result of these policies was, however, to worsen the official balance of payments by shifting remittances (as well as tourist expenditures) into the black market. Short-term credits, which were used to finance the rapidly worsening situation, also dried up by 1977, and in September of that year the central bank suspended official foreign-exchange dealings, not to be restarted until August 1979. As a result, producers were forced to go to the black market for purchase of raw materials and supplies, and the rapid depreciation of the black currency soon led to an unprecedented bout of inflation, reaching a level of 100% before declining to more manageable rates in 1982. Remittances, which had stagnated during this period, picked up again when the central bank re-entered the foreign-currency market with a massive devaluation. However, the payments position continued to worsen with the rise in interest payments as well as the new oil shock.

The crisis was not resolved until after the military coup of September 1980, when, with IMF and consortium assistance, some measure of solvency was restored. Successive devaluations and import liberalization policies were used to reduce the size of the black market. Finally, in May 1981, the currency was placed on a controlled floating system, with the effective rate being determined daily. Capital controls have also been relaxed, and residents are now permitted to maintain foreign-currency accounts with Turkish banks, and even to purchase foreign securities with prior approval.

IV.5. Yugoslavia

Yugoslavia's experience is, in many ways, the mirror image of the Turkish one. Yugoslavia, which had fairly restrictive exchange rate and commercial policies during the 1960s, had started on the process of policy liberalization in the early 1970s. Following a much-awaited devaluation in early 1971, and two later ones in 1971 and 1973 with the devaluations of the dollar, the dinar was placed on a controlled, floating basis in July 1973.[43] Subsequently, the currency was devalued on a regular basis, and kept in line with the black-market rate, the premium ranging between 0% and 10% from 1973 to 1977, and between 10% and 20% thereafter.

One of the consequences of the early adjustment can be seen in the behaviour of official remittance flows. Despite the recession in the labour-importing countries, remittances to Yugoslavia managed to maintain their momentum, and the country seemed to have escaped the severe dislocation suffered by its neighbour to the east, Turkey.

Since 1979, however, Yugoslavia began facing payments problems of its own when it attempted to revive official currency markets in order to stem the rapid depreciation of the black-market dinar. These attempts have consisted in tightening foreign-currency controls, restrictions on foreign travel, reduction of duty-free allowances for returnees, and increases in import duties, in addition to various contractionary policies. Despite these policies, however, neither the inflation nor the payments position has been brought under control.

IV.6. Pakistan

Pakistan, like Turkey and Egypt, has often been singled out by writers on account of its extensive array of trade controls and exchange restrictions. Even today, unlike the other two countries, residents are not allowed to own foreign currencies or foreign securities, or to maintain bank balances abroad. All proceeds from exports or invisibles have to be surrendered, and all imports are subject to licensing.

Despite these restrictions, however, the experience of the 1970s and 1980s is quite different from that of the 1960s. Pakistan, like other South Asian countries, can be characterized in Pranab Bardhan's terms as 'inflation-sensitive' (see Bardhan 1984: 68). As such, there is a very strong resistance to devaluations, which are seen as being inflationary and, by that token, politically destabilizing. Nevertheless, in January 1982, in response to a persistent escalation of the black-market premium (and the consequent withdrawal of remittances from the official sector), the rupee was placed on a controlled floating rate pegged to an undisclosed basket of currencies. It has been devalued regularly ever since then. At the same time, import tariffs have been reduced, from an average level of 26% of the value of imports in 1973 to 18% in 1982. The number of items on the 'free list' of imports has been increased steadily since 1973, and now includes 435 items instead of 342.

Pakistan devalued its currency from Re4.76/$1 to Re11/$1 in December 1971, and at the same time abolished the complicated multiple exchange rate regime which had been built up to support the par rate. The subsequent devaluation of the dollar led to a revaluation of the exchange rate to Re9.90/$1 in 1973, where it remained until January 1982. After the 1971 devaluation, the payments position deteriorated somewhat in the mid-1970s, but devaluation as a means of structural adjustment was resisted by the Government. In the mean time, the inflow of remittances helped the balance of payments somewhat, as did buoyant exports in the late 1970s and the subsequent dose of US aid commitment. The interesting point of the story is that it was at this point of a strong current-account situation that the Government decided to opt for a devaluation. The reason seems to be that the temporary overvaluation of the currency in the fourth quarter of 1981 had caused a decline in remittance inflows, and a readjustment was recommended to avoid further deterioration in these flows. Before remittances became a major factor in the economy and the black market for dollars expanded its size and efficiency, such an action would have been seen as unnecessary and would have been strongly resisted by the Government.

From 1981, the rupee was devalued slowly but consistently, until by mid-1989 it had fallen from a level of Re9.90/$1 to Re21/$1. Much of this period was one where the dollar itself was depreciating with respect to other currencies; in other words, the depreciation of the rupee was even more pronounced with respect to Pakistan's other trade partners, in particular Japan and the EC.

In 1985, the central bank introduced another innovation which, for all practical purposes, opened up the capital market. This was a scheme called Foreign Exchange Bearer Certificates (FEBCs), in which remitters of foreign exchange were allowed to convert their remittances into special certificates, denominated in rupees, but freely convertible into foreign exchange. FEBCs are traded on the Stock Exchange at a premium, and even earn interest at 14% per annum. Being bearer certificates, they possess the virtue of anonymity, except for the first and last holder of the asset. The premium on FEBCs has, except for a short period in 1989, stayed below 10%, suggesting a minimal degree of overvaluation of the currency.

IV.7. India

Of all the countries on our list, India is the only one which has consistently pursued cautious exchange rate and commercial policies. It successfully resisted the temptation to increase its dependence on foreign resources—remittances as well as commercial credit—which had become available in larger quantities in the 1970s. Perhaps the best way of illustrating this policy stance is through an examination of the relative growth rates of exports and imports in five remittance-receiving countries (see Table 9.10).

TABLE 9.10. *Export and import growth rates, 1960–1985*

	1969–70		1970–80		1980–5	
	X	*M*	*X*	*M*	*X*	*M*
India	3.0	-0.9	3.7	2.8	4.6	2.1
Pakistan	8.2	5.3	1.2	4.3	2.4	3.9
Egypt	3.2	-1.1	-0.7	8.8	3.9	8.0
Turkey	1.6	5.5	1.7	3.3	25.3	10.1
Yugoslavia	7.7	8.8	3.9	3.9	2.1	-3.3

Source: World Bank (1984; 1987).

Note that import growth in India has consistently remained below the growth rate of exports even in the period when higher foreign resource availability could have relaxed this constraint. The other countries, too, had periods when exports grew faster than imports, but these were rare, and often triggered by some crisis, as in Turkey in the 1980s (actually beginning in 1978), or under balance-of-payments constraints, as in Yugoslavia in the same period.

Likewise, India refused to build up a high debt–GNP ratio, despite the ready availability of credit in the 1970s. In fact, India is one of the few countries where the debt–GNP ratio actually declined prior to the credit squeeze of the 1980s (and perhaps the only one where the decline was voluntary). The ratio fell from 14.9% in 1970 to 11.4% in 1982 (World Bank 1984). In the same period, Pakistan's debt–GNP ratio increased from 30.5% to 31.5%, Egypt's from 23.8% to 52.8%, Turkey's from 14.4% to 29.7%, and Yugoslavia's from 8.8% to 9.4% (ibid).

As a result, until 1984 we find very little evidence in India of exchange crises, frequent shifts in policy stance, debt-rescheduling, or other problems which have plagued remittance-receiving countries in recent years. Nor was the effectiveness of the Indian Government's policies seriously challenged in this period.

Beginning in 1984, however, the newly elected Rajiv Gandhi Government decided to opt for a liberalization strategy which involved an increase in levels of foreign debt, and the deregulation of domestic financial and industrial structures. Consequently, India's debt burden has doubled in five years, rising by 1990 to a level of $60bn., one of the highest in the world; this has harmed the creditworthiness of the country and created problems for commercial borrowing at a time when prospective increases in oil prices may make such borrowing necessary (*International Herald Tribune* 1990: 15).

V. CONCLUSIONS

The message of this paper is very simple and can be summarized fairly quickly. It stems from the suspicion that the market is not the answer to every economic problem that a country might face, and therefore that some form of 'governance' is necessary for the smooth functioning of the system. However, governance does not mean a blind reliance on government regulations or controls. It requires an intelligent discrimination between what can and what cannot be managed, and the establishment and nurturing of institutions which can facilitate such management. The present case study helps bring out some of the subtleties in this distinction.

Traditionally, a major economic problem—the vulnerability of the economy to external shocks—was handled through capital controls, fixed (and often endemically overvalued) exchange rates, and selective and regulatory controls on international trade. For a while this worked well. With the advent of remittances, however, the world changed completely; but policy approaches in many countries did not change at all. As a result, these countries found themselves in the unenviable position where their ability to protect the economy against externally generated disturbances had seriously deteriorated at the very moment when this ability was sorely needed.

In thinking about how matters might have turned out differently, two points can be made. First, it seems that governments should have tried to ensure that currency black markets do not develop or become sophisticated enough to render government policy ineffective. This would have required the abandonment of permanently overvalued exchange rates which diverted entrepreneurial investment into these channels. This is a very important point. It suggests that the objective of capital controls, or of exchange and commercial policies in general, is not to defend permanently overvalued exchange rates but to insulate the economy from external shocks, to reduce the vulnerability of the polity and society to external elements. Capital controls can allow a government to protect the economy against temporary fluctuations and short-run changes in international economic conditions, provided that these controls are not viewed as a means of defending permanent structural imbalances. By refusing to maintain defensible exchange rate parities, the government forfeited not only the ability to defend long-run overvaluation but also, and more importantly, the power to protect the economy against more volatile short-run fluctuations.

The second point is that a high degree of dependence on a potentially volatile source of foreign exchange, such as remittances, makes government policy hostage to that resource. Governments would have been well advised to ensure that they did not become dependent and thus lose their autonomy. As discussed above, the Indian Government's attitude until 1984 suggested that it had seen this problem, and had chosen the policy package consistent with its responsibility of managing the economy.

Economic policy is still a question of judgement and prudence. No simple formula will suffice to tell a government what to do in what circumstances. Whether the utilization of a resource will lead to an increase in dependence and vulnerability, or to rapid growth and therefore to a reduction of vulnerability, will depend upon the particular circumstances. Similarly, whether the task of governance calls for more regulation or less, and of what type, is not something which can be simply prescribed. Most governments that we examined pursued regulationary policies, not as pragmatic choices, but because of a mechanical adherence to certain rules. Today, the failure of this approach is leading the same governments to pursue another set of mechanical rules, this time tilted towards deregulation and liberalization. This time, too, the mindless adherence to a formula without a clear understanding of governments' responsibilities is not likely to be fruitful.

NOTES

1. In the 1970s, for example, Pakistan, Turkey, and Egypt shifted to quasi-flexible exchange rate regimes in the face of mounting balance-of-payments problems caused by unpredictable financial flows. These countries were particularly renowned for restrictive commercial policies (see Bhagwati 1978).
2. The frustration over this loss of control is expressed in government as well as non-government circles. See Lieberman and Gitmez (1974: 216–19); Serageldin *et al.* (1983: 90).
3. According to Cowitt (1985), such black markets existed in every Third World country except the high-income oil-exporters.
4. Except where stated otherwise, the following description relies mainly on Cowitt (1985) and George and Giddy (1983).
5. This indicates, as in most other instances, that the black market is directly linked to the assets market, since the demand for gold is really an asset demand in an economy where capital markets are weak.
6. See Cowitt (1985: 878–9). The entire gold-smuggling operation is controlled by a syndicate centred in Karachi, with close links to the 2 (formerly 3) groups who control the illegal trade in India. Gold is shipped mostly from Dubai, where 3 Swiss banks maintain a depository of gold bars. Payments to the banks have to be made in advance in US dollars or Swiss francs, but there are local intermediaries who accept (*hundis*—'hand-payments').
7. This seems to be the case in most countries. See e.g. Dornbusch *et al.* (1983) for the case of Brazil; Krueger (1974) for Turkey. In Pakistan, one never reads about an official crack-down on currency black markets, unlike, say, on black markets for commodities, or on merchandise-smuggling.
8. Most people who use the market appear to go through personal intermediaries, which may be a reason why the market seems so uniform. Nevertheless, given the minimal arbitrage possibilities in a clandestine arrangement, the level of uniformity is quite surprising. In Aug. 1981, while travelling in Pakistan, I happened to observe someone who contacted 7 different exchange-dealers over a period of 3 days, and got only *one* quotation out of line with the others, by about 1%.
9. For a general description of illegal transactions, see Bhagwati (1978: 64–81). Other descriptions can be found in Cooper (1974), Sheikh (1973), Winston (1974), and Bhagwati *et al.* (1974).
10. The legal allowance for foreign travel, $1000 every 2 years, has remained substantially unchanged in real terms for about 20 years.
11. See Dornbusch *et al.* (1983). In addition to the usual fare, there are various sophisticated currency-swap schemes used by multinationals to bypass official capital controls. See George and Giddy (1983: 2. 2. 49–55).
12. Tourist spending in Pakistan is estimated to have been of the order of $60m. in 1978 and $140m. in 1985, compared to a GNP of $30bn.
13. Remittances were below $150m. annually until 1973.
14. Winston (1974) discusses this case for 1966, when the import tariff on capital-goods imports to Pakistan was 34%, while the black-market pre-

mium was about 110%. He mentions a generally accepted figure of 10% over-invoicing of such imports, which would have been quite significant in comparison with the size of the black market.

15. Such as Caribbean countries. Note that this means high influx relative to the size of the economy, or the size of the black market. Thus, countries like India or Turkey may receive large numbers of tourists, but such numbers may still be small in relation to the economy.
16. As mentioned earlier, over-invoiced imports will also be subject to the legal tariff payments, raising the costs of procurement even more.
17. Some questions regarding economies of scale and learning by doing in goods-smuggling are relevant here. We shall return to these questions in Section III.1.
18. See e.g. Bruton, 1983. Also, for a similar discussion on the Sudan, see Serageldin *et al*, 1983: 89.
19. In Pakistan's case, some of the smuggling takes place through Afghanistan, which may not figure in either country's statistics.
20. Average tariff rates, i.e. tariff revenues divided by the value of imports, declined in Pakistan from a level of 26% in 1973 to 20% in 1980.
21. The town of Bara existed as a sleepy village and a military fort. However, since the mid-1970s, it has become a bustling market centre, attracting thousands of customers in search of relatively cheap imported goods.
22. This point has been made by many writers. See e.g. Gupta, 1980: 237. See also Culbertson, 1975; Bhagwati, 1978.
23. The good/asset mentioned in the text is gold. However, restrictions on foreign travel, contraband, or luxury goods (consumer goods, electronic gadgets, textiles, and clothing) or foreign assets may all lead to the establishment of a black market. This is the reason why the black market rate is often unconnected with purchasing power considerations.
24. Thus, many Western countries have restrictions on importation of certain goods (e.g. narcotics), but since they do not link these restrictions to the sale of foreign currencies, the policy will not generate a black market for foreign exchange. Third World countries, on the other hand, tend to use foreign-exchange dealings to enforce import restrictions, thus inducing the establishment of black markets even in 'normal' times.
25. Of course, this result is caused by the fact that the central banks are always willing to buy foreign exchange at the stipulated price, but sell only under restrictive conditions. Dornbusch *et al.* (1983) and Bhagwati (1978) mention instances where the black-market rate dropped below the official rate when the central banks (temporarily) refused to buy foreign exchange unless it was shown to be legitimate.
26. Throughout the model, terms with an asterisk denote a variable or parameter in the official market, while those without the prime denote the black market.
27. The black-market premium can indeed keep rising above this level on a speculative spiral. The only point is that these increases will not attract further resources out of the official market.
28. With the expansion of contacts, channels of operation, inclusion of new goods and services into the smuggling operations. An important aspect may

be the use of special dispensations of import licences for remitters abroad. On the demand side, foreign travel may become more responsive to the black-market conditions. Table 9.3 is instructive in this regard, since it shows an increase in estimated smuggling operations in Pakistan in the 1980s.

29. Or, equivalently, to run down foreign reserves.
30. The reasoning is obvious: equal proportional changes in v or p mean the same proportional change in the black-market exchange *rate*, so both will reduce smuggling demand; however, the latter also implies a higher *relative* rate in the black market, and will reduce smuggling demand even more.
31. This result follows directly from our assumption that a change in the black-market premium will only induce a switching of flows between the two markets but not a net increase in exports, imports, or remittances. For a model of real overall effects of the black market, see de Macedo (1982).
32. i.e. the belief that the amount of resources cannot be increased in the short run.
33. This point has also been made by Paine (1974: 45–6): 'The smaller the contribution of [remittances], the less the emigration country's policy is constrained to acquire them; the larger the contribution, the more the government has to concentrate on obtaining the expected repatriated earnings rather than earning or saving foreign exchange by other means.'
34. This, of course, is the 'market-type' solution to the problem, suggested by neoclassical economists. However, where the incentives produce unwelcome fluctuations, or create destabilizing uncertainty, most governments, particularly in the Third World, prefer to seek alternative solutions.
35. For example, the various multiple exchange rate schemes fall into this category. These schemes often tax supposedly inelastic 'traditional' export sectors, and subsidize the new producers. Windfall gains tax on old oil-producers was another such scheme, as also is the system whereby there is a graduated tax on income, with credits for investment.
36. This corresponds to the conventional 'elasticity pessimism' argument favouring high taxes on agricultural goods.
37. The only exception seems to be the abortive attempt made by the Government of Pakistan in 1976. This proposal, which sought to impose a 10% income tax on remittances, was hastily withdrawn when the resource inflow suffered an immediate and steep decline.
38. These policies were used by various countries, e.g. Turkey (1974–9), Sudan (1975–9), Bangladesh (1979–), Algeria (1972–), and Morocco (1972–).
39. These policies include the sale of subsidized urban land to emigrants (Pakistan, Bangladesh, Sudan); special high-interest rate bonds (Egypt, Jordan); joint co-operative ventures with the government in industry or services (Pakistan, Turkey, Egypt); concessionary import privileges for emigrants (Bangladesh, India, Pakistan, Turkey, and the Sudan); and even the Turkish proposal to reduce compulsory national-service requirement for male migrant workers for a fee.
40. Although not for Algeria or Bangladesh.
41. The Egyptian Government's policies to combat capital flight are described in various places. Cowitt (1985: 235-43) gives an overview. Other general descriptions are in de Macedo (1982) and Bruton (1983).

42. At this time tourism was the main source of black-market currencies in Egypt.
43. Despite the fact that these imports were technically illegal! In fact, a special exchange rate called the 'own import rate' was created for this purpose in 1975.

References

ABS (Australian Bureau of Statistics) (1987*a*), *Foreign Investment in Australia 1985–86* (Canberra).

—— (1987*b*), *Estimates of Capital Stock, 1985–86* (Canberra).

—— (1987*c*), *Australian National Accounts: National Income and Expenditure 1985–86* (Canberra).

ACTU (Australian Council of Trade Unions) (1983), Submission to the Review of the Australian Financial System.

Archer, R. (1991), 'The Australian Accord', in J. Pekkarinen, M. Pohjola, and R. Rowthorn (eds.), *Social Corporatism: A Superior Economic System?* (Oxford).

Argy, V. (1987), 'International Financial Liberalisation: The Australian and Japanese Experiences Compared', *Bank of Japan Monetary and Economic Studies*, 5.1.

Adams, C., and Greenwood, J. (1985), 'Dual Exchange Rate Systems and Capital Controls: An Investigation', *Journal of International Economics*, 18: 43–63.

Alchian, A., and Demsetz, H. (1972), 'Production, Information Costs, and Economic Organization', *American Economic Review*, 62: 777–95.

Alexander, G. J., and Eun, C. S. (1985), 'International Listings, Stock Prices and Capital Market Integration', Working Paper, Univ. of Maryland.

Ali, S. A. *et al.* (1981), 'Labour Migration From Bangladesh to the Middle East', World Bank Staff Working Paper No. 454 (Washington, DC).

Aliber, R. Z. (1977), *The International Money Game* (London).

Ayling, D. E. (1986), *The Internationalisation of Stockmarkets* (Aldershot, Hants.).

Bade, R., and Parkin, M. (1980), 'Central Bank Laws and Monetary Policy', mimeo, Univ. of Western Ontario.

Bagehot, W. (1978 edn.), 'Lombard Street', in *The Collected Works of Walter Bagehot*, ed. Norman St John-Stevas (London).

Balassa, B. (1984), 'Adjustment Policies in Developing Countries: A Reassessment', *World Development*, 12. 9: 955–72.

Banco de México (annual), *Indicadores Económicos* (Mexico City).

—— (1987), *Informe Annual, 1987* (Mexico City).

Banuri, T. (1991) (ed.), *Economic Liberalization: No Panacea: The Experiences of Latin America and Asia* (Oxford).

Bardhan, P. (1984), *The Political Economy of Development in India* (Oxford).

Basevi, G. (1985), 'Instruments for Preserving Economic Efficiency and International Capital Mobility', *Occasional Paper: Capital Controls and Foreign Exchange Legislation* (Milan).

Bhaduri, A., and Marglin, S. A. (1987), 'Conflict, Cooperation and Unemployment: A Keynesian Perspective', mimeo, Harvard Univ.

Bhagwati, J. N. (1974) (ed.), *Illegal Transactions in Foreign Trade* (Amsterdam).

—— (1978), *Anatomy and Consequences of Exchange Control Regimes* (Cambridge, Mass.)

Bhagwati, J. N., Krueger, A. O., and Wibulswasdi, C. (1974), 'Capital Flight From LDCs: A Statistical Analysis', in Bhagwati (1978).

Birks, J. S., and Sinclair, C. A. (1980), *International Migration and Development in the Arab Region* (Geneva).

BIS (Bank for International Settlements) (1986), *Recent Innovations in International Banking* (Basle).

—— (1987), *Fifty-Seventh Annual Report* (Basle).

Bitterman, H. J. (1973), *The Refunding of International Debt* (Durham, NC).

Black, S. W. (1976), 'Exchange Policies for Less Developed Countries in a World of Floating Rates', in D. M. Leipziger (ed.), *The International Monetary System and The Developing Nation* (Washington, DC).

Blejer, M. (1978), 'Exchange Restrictions and the Monetary Approach to the Exchange Rate', in J. Frenkel and H. Johnson (eds.), *The Economics of Exchange Rates: Selected Studies* (Reading, Mass.).

Block, F. L. (1977), *The Origins of International Economic Disorder: A Study of United States International Monetary Policy from World War II to the Present* (Berkeley, Calif.).

Bloomfield, A. (1959), *Monetary Policy Under the International Gold Standard* (New York).

Boddy, R., and Crotty, J. (1975), 'Class Conflict and Macro-Policy: The Political Business Cycle', *Review of Radical Political Economics*, 7: 1–19.

Boothe, P., Clinton, K., Cote, A., and Longworth, D. (1985), 'International Asset Substitutability: Theory and Evidence for Canada', Bank of Canada (Feb.) (Ottawa).

Bordo, M. D., and Schwartz, A. J. (1984), *A Retrospective on the Classical Gold Standard, 1821–1931* (Chicago).

Bowles, S., and Boyer, R. (1990), 'A Wage-led Employment Regime: Income Distribution, Labour Discipline, and Aggregate Demand in Welfare Capitalism', in Marglin and Schor (1990).

Bowles, S., and Gintis, H. (1986), *Democracy and Capitalism: Property, Community, and the Contradictions of Modern Social Thought* (New York).

—— and —— (1988*a*), 'Contested Exchange: Political Economy and Modern Economic Theory', *American Economic Review (Papers and Proceedings)*, 78. 2: 145–50.

—— and —— (1988*b*), 'Contested Exchange: The Political Structure of Competitive Markets', mimeo, Univ. of Massachusetts.

—— and —— (1990), 'Contested Exchange: New Microfoundations of the Political Economy of Capitalism', *Politics and Society*, 18: 165–22.

Brezis, E.S. (1988), 'Money Capital Flows and Protectionism', Ph.D. dissertation, Massachusetts Institute of Technology, Dept. of Economics.

British Invisible Exports Council (1986), 'International Information Flows', a report by the LOTIS Committee (London).

Brunello, G. (1988), 'The Economic Implications of Liberalizing Japanese Financial Markets', *Rivista Internazionale di Scienze Economiche e Commercili* 4–5: 409–36.

Bruton, H. (1983), 'Egypt's Development in the Seventies', *Economic Development and Cultural Change*, 31. 4: 679–704.

Bryant, R. C. (1980), *Money and Monetary Policy in Interdependent Nations* (Washington, DC).

—— (1987), *International Financial Intermediation* (Washington, DC).

Buchanan, J. M., Rowley, C. K., and Tollison, R. D. (1986) (eds.), *Deficits* (Oxford).

Calmfors, L. (1985), 'Exchange Controls Can Be Abolished!', *Skandinaviska Enskilda Banken Quarterly Review*, 4.

Campbell Committee (1981), *Australian Financial System Inquiry: Final Report*, (Canberra).

Cantor, D., and Schor, J. (1987), *Tunnel Vision: Labor, the World Economy, and Central America* (Boston).

Caprio, G. A., Jr., and Howard, D. H. (1984), 'Domestic Saving, Current Accounts, and International Capital Mobility', *International Financial Discussion Papers* (Board of Governors of the Federal Reserve System), 244 (Washington, DC).

Carland, D. J., and Valentine, T. J. (1982), 'The Relationship between Australian and Overseas Interest Rates', *Australian Financial System Inquiry: Commissioned Studies and Selected Papers*, p. 4 (Canberra).

Carron, A. (1983), 'The Australian Financial System', in R. Caves and L. Krause (eds.), *The Australian Economy: A View from the North* (Washington, DC).

Caves, R. (1976), 'The Welfare Economics of Controls on Capital Movements', in Swoboda (1976).

Chandavarkar, A. G. (1980), 'Use of Migrants' Remittances in Labor Exporting Countries', *Finance and Development*, 17. 2: 36–9.

Chandler, A. (1977), *The Visible Hand* (Cambridge, Mass.).

Chipman, J. S., and Kindleberger, C. P. (1980) (eds.), *Flexible Exchange Rates and the Balance of Payments: Essays in Memory of Egon Sohmen* (Amsterdam).

Chouraqui, J.-C., Jones, B., and Mortador, R. (1986), 'Public Debt in Medium-Term Perspective', OECD *Economic Studies* (autumn).

Cipolla, C. M. (1967), *Money, Prices and Civilization in the Mediterranean World: Fifth to Seventeenth Century* (New York).

Claassen, E.-M., and Wyplosz, C. (1982), 'Capital Controls: Some Principles and the French Experience', *Annales de l'Insee*, 47–8: 237–77.

Cole, A. H. (1929), 'Evolution of the Foreign Exchange Market of the United States', *Journal of Economic and Business History*, 1.3: 384–421.

Commission of the European Communities (1988), *European Economy*, 35 (Mar.).

Commonwealth Government *Budget Papers* 1987/88 (Canberra).

Cooper, R. N. (1971), 'An Assessment of Currency Devaluation in Developing Countries', in G. Ranis (ed.), *Government and Economic Development* (New Haven, Conn.).

—— (1974), 'Tariffs and Smuggling in Indonesia', in Bhagwati (1974).

—— (1986*a*), 'Towards an International Capital Market?', in *Economic Policy in an Interdependent World* (Cambridge, Mass.).

—— (1986*b*), 'Economic Interdependence and Coordination of Economic Policies' in *Economic Policy in an Interdependent World* (Cambridge, Mass.).

—— (1986*c*), 'The United States as an Open Economy', in R. W. Hafer (ed.), *How Open is the U.S. Economy?* (Lexington, Mass.).
—— (1987*a*), *The International Monetary System* (Cambridge, Mass.).
—— (1987*b*), *Trade, Development and the World Economy: Selected Essays of Carlos Diaz-Alejandro*, ed. A. Velasco (Oxford).
—— and Hollick, A. L. (1985), 'International Relations in a Technologically Advanced Future', in Anne G. Keatley (ed.), *Technological Frontiers and Foreign Relations* (Washington, DC).
Córdoba, J. (1986), 'El programa mexicano de reordenación económica, 1983–84', in SELA, *El FMI, el Banco Mundial y la crisis latinoamericana* (Mexico City).
Council of Economic Advisers (1988), *Economic Report of the President* (Washington, DC).
Cowitt, C. (1985) (ed.), *World Currency Yearbook* (Brooklyn, NY).
Crotty, J. R. (1983), 'On Keynes and Capital Flight', *Journal of Economic Literature*, 21. 1: 59–65.
CSO (Central Statistical Office) (annual), *United Kingdom's Balance of Payments* (London).
Culbertson, W. P. (1975), 'Purchasing Power Parity and Black Market Exchange Rates', *Economic Inquiry* (June), 287-296.
Cumby, R. E., and Obstfeld, M. (1984), 'International Interest Rate and Price Level Linkages under Flexible Exchange Rates: A Review of Recent Evidence', in J. F. O. Bilson and R. C. Marston (eds.), *Exchange Rate Theory and Practice* (Chicago).
Darrity, W. A., Jr., and Horn, B. (1988), *The Loan Pushers* (New York).
Datadisk (1989), Jan. (Cambridge).
Davis, K. (1987), 'Economic Policy: From Fraser to Hawke', Research Paper No. 182, Univ. of Melbourne, Dept. of Economics.
Davis, L., and Huttenback, R. (1986), *Mammon and the Pursuit of Empire: The Political Economy of British Imperialism, 1860–1912* (New York).
Dermine, J. (1990) (ed.), *European Banking in the 1990s* (Oxford).
Deutsche Bank Monthly Review (1985), 'Freedom of Germany's Capital Transactions With Foreign Countries', 37: 7.
Diaz-Alejandro, C. (1988), *Trade, Development and the World Economy: Selected Essays of Carlos Diaz-Alejandro*, ed. A. Velasco (Oxford).
Dooley, M. P., and Isard, P. (1979), 'The Portfolio-Balance Model of Exchange Rates', Federal Reserve Board, International Finance Discussion Paper No. 141 (Washington, DC).
—— and —— (1980), 'Capital Controls, Political Risk, and Deviations from Interest-Rate Parity', *Journal of Political Economy*, 88. 21: 370–84.
Dornbusch, R. (1980), *Open Economy Macroeconomics* (New York).
—— (1986*a*), 'Special Exchange Rates for Capital Account Transactions', *World Bank Economic Review*, 1. 1: 3–33.
—— (1986*b*), 'Equilibrium and Disequilibrium Exchange Rates', in R. Dornbusch, *Dollars, Debts, and Deficits* (Cambridge, Mass.).
—— (1986*c*), 'Flexible Exchange Rates and Interdependence', in R. Dornbusch, *Dollars, Debts and Deficits* (Cambridge, Mass.).

—— (1988), 'Mexico: Stabilization, Debt and Growth', mimeo, Massachusetts Institute of Technology.
Dornbusch, R. and Fischer, S. (1986), 'The Open Economy: Implications for Monetary and Fiscal Policy', in R. Gordon (ed.), *The American Business Cycle: Continuity and Change* (Chicago).
—— and Frankel, J. (1987), 'The Flexible Exchange Rate System: Experience and Alternatives', NBER Working Paper No. 2464 (Cambridge, Mass.).
—— *et al.* (1983), 'The Black Market for Dollars in Brazil', *Quarterly Journal of Economics*, 98. 1: 25–40.
Duck, N., Parkin, M., Rose, D., and Zis, G. (1976), 'The Determination of the Rate of Change of Wages and Prices in the Fixed Exchange Rate World Economy, 1956–1971', in M. Parkin and G. Zis (eds.), *Inflation in the World Economy* (Guildford, Surrey).
Eagly, R. V., and Kerry Smith, V. (1976), 'Domestic and International Integration of the London Money Market, 1731–1789', *Journal of Economic History*, 36. 1: 198–212.
Eaton, J., and Gersovitz, M. (1981), 'Debt with Potential Repudiation: Theoretical and Empirical Analysis', *Review of Economic Studies*, 48: 289–309.
—— Gersovitz, M., and Stiglitz, J. E. (1986), 'The Pure Theory of Country Risk', *European Economic Review*, 30. 3: 481–513.
Economía Aplicada (1989), *Cifras históricas* (Mexico City).
—— (1990), *Indicadores cíclicos de la actividad económica en México* (March) (Mexico City).
Edelstein, M. (1982), *Overseas Investment in the Age of High Imperialism: The United Kingdom 1850–1914* (London).
Eichengreen, B., and Lindert, P.H. (1989), *The International Debt Crisis in Historical Perspective* (Cambridge, Mass.).
—— and Portes, R. (1986), 'Debt and Default in the 1930's: Causes and Consequences', *European Economic Review*, 30. 3: 599–640.
Eizenga, W., Limburg, E. F., and Polak, J. J. (1988), *The Quest for National and Global Economic Stability: Essays in Honour of H. J. Witteveen* (Dordrecht).
Elton, E. J., and Gruber, M. J. (1984), *Modern Portfolio Theory and Investment Analysis*, 2nd edn. (New York).
Epstein, G. (1989*a*), 'Profit Squeeze, Rentier Squeeze and Macroeconomic Policy Under Fixed and Flexible Exchange Rates', Univ. of Massachusetts Working Paper No. 1989–12 (Amherst, Mass.).
—— (1989*b*), 'A Political Economy Model of Comparative Central Banking', mimeo, Univ. of Massachusetts.
—— and Gintis, H. (1988), 'An Asset Balance Model of International Capital Market Equilibrium', mimeo, Univ. of Massachusetts.
—— and Schor, J. B. (1986), 'The Political Economy of Central Banking', Harvard Institute for Economic Research, Discussion Paper No. 1281 (Cambridge, Mass.).
—— and —— (1988), 'The Determinants of Central Bank Policies in Open Economies', in B. Jossa and C. Panico (eds.), *The Political Economy of Central Bank Intervention* (Naples).
—— and —— (1989), 'The Divorce of the Banca d'Italia and the Italian Treasury: A Case Study of Central Bank Independence', in P. Lange and M. Regini

(eds.), *The State and Social Regulation: New Perspectives* (Cambridge).
—— and —— (1990*a*), 'Macropolicy in the Rise and Fall of the Golden Age', in Marglin and Schor (1990).
—— and —— (1990*b*), 'Corporate Profitability as a Determinant of Restrictive Monetary Policy: Estimates for the Post-War U.S.', in T. Mayer (ed.), *The Political Economy of American Monetary Policy* (Cambridge).
Ethier, W. J., and Marston, R. C. (1985) (eds.), *International Financial Markets and Capital Movements: A Symposium in Honor of Arthur I. Bloomfield*, Princeton Univ. International Finance Section, Essays in International Finance No. 157 (Princeton, NJ).
Euromoney (1986), *Australia: Economy*, special supplement (Feb.).
Fase, M. M. G. (1976), 'The Interdependence of Short-Term Interest Rates in the Major Financial Centres of the World: Some Evidence for 1961–72', *Kyklos*, 29: 63–96.
Feldman, R. A. (1986), *Japanese Financial Markets* (Cambridge, Mass.).
Feldstein, M. (1983), 'Domestic Saving and International Capital Movements in the Long Run and the Short Run', *European Economic Review*, 21: 129–51.
—— (1988) (ed.), *International Economic Cooperation* (Chicago).
—— and Horioka, C. (1980), 'Domestic Saving and International Capital Flows', *Economic Journal*, 90: 314–29.
——, Modigliani, F., Sinai, A., and Solow, R. (1988), 'Black Monday in Retrospect and Prospect', *Eastern Economic Journal*, 14. 4: 337–48.
Ferguson, T. (1984), 'From Normalcy to New Deal: Industrial Structure, Party Competition and American Public Policy in the Great Depression', *International Organization* (winter).
Fieleke, N. S. (1982), 'National Saving and International Investment', in *Saving and Government Policy*, Conference Series No. 25 (Boston).
Fischer, S. (1988), 'International Macroeconomic Policy Coordination', in M. Feldstein (1988), 11–43.
Fishlow, A. (1985), 'Lessons from the Past: Capital Markets during the Nineteenth Century and the Interwar Period', *International Organization*, 39. 3: 383–439.
Fleming, J. M. (1962), 'Domestic Financial Policies under Fixed and Floating Exchange Rates', *IMF Staff Papers*, 9: 369–80.
de Franco, M. (1985), 'An Analysis of the Black Market in Dollars in a Computable General Equilibrium Model for Nicaragua', dissertation prospectus, Univ. of Massachusetts Economics Dept.
Forbes (1976), 'Don't Blame the Oil Companies: Blame the State Department' and 'How the West Was Won', 15 Apr.
Frankel, J. A. (1979), 'The Diversifiability of Exchange Risk', *Journal of International Economics* (Aug.): 379–93.
—— (1982*a*), 'In Search of the Exchange Risk Premium: A Six-Currency Test Assuming Mean-Variance Optimization', *Journal of International Money and Finance*, 5: 255–74.
—— (1982*b*), 'A Test of Perfect Substitutability in the Foreign Exchange Market', *Southern Economic Journal*, 48: 406–416.
—— (1985), 'International Capital Mobility and Crowding Out in the U.S. Economy: Imperfect Integration of Financial Markets or of Goods Markets?',

NBER Working Paper No. 1773 (Cambridge, Mass.).

Frankel, J. A. (1987), 'International Capital Flows and Domestic Economic Policies', NBER Working Paper No. 2210 (Cambridge, Mass.).

—— (1989), 'Quantifying International Capital Mobility in the 1980s', NBER Working Paper No. 2856 (Cambridge, Mass.).

—— and MacArthur, A. T. (1987), 'Political vs. Currency Premia in International Real Interest Differentials: A Study of Forward Rates for 24 Countries', NBER Working Paper No. 2309 (Cambridge, Mass.).

Frenkel, J. (1986), 'International Interdependence and the Constraints on Macroeconomic Policies', in Hafer (1986).

——and Levich, R. M. (1975), 'Covered Interest Arbitrage: Unexploited Profits?', *Journal of Political Economy*, 83. 2: 325–38.

—— and —— (1977), 'Transaction Costs and Interest Arbitrage: Tranquil versus Turbulent Periods', *Journal of Political Economy*, 85. 6: 1209–26.

—— and —— (1981), 'Covered Interest Arbitrage in the 1970's', *Economic Letters*, 8. 3: 267–74.

—— and Razin, A. (1987), *Fiscal Policies and the World Economy: An Intertemporal Approach* (Cambridge, Mass.).

Frieden, J. (1984), 'Endeudamiento y fuga de capital. Los flujos financieros internacionales en la crisis de México, 1981–83', *Investigación Económica*, 170 (Mexico City).

Frieden, J. A. (forthcoming), 'The Economics of Intervention: American Overseas Investments and Relations with Underdeveloped Areas, 1890–1950', *Comparative Studies in Society and History.*

Fukao, M., and Hanazaki, M. (1982), 'Internationalization of Financial Markets and the Allocation of Capital', *OECD Economic Studies*, 8: 36–87.

Galbis, V. (1977), 'Financial Intermediation and Economic Growth in Less Developed Countries: A Theoretical Approach', *Journal of Development Studies*, 13. 2: 58–72.

Gardner, R. N. (1956), *Sterling–Dollar Diplomacy* (Oxford).

Genberg, H. (1988), 'Exchange Rate Management and Macroeconomic Policy: A National Perspective', paper written for the 90th Anniversary Symposium of the *Scandinavian Journal of Economics*, Hanasaari, Espoo/Helsinki, Finland, 12–14 June 1988.

George, A. M., and Giddy, I. H. (1983), *International Finance Handbook* (New York).

Giavazzi, F., and Giovannini, A. (1986), 'The EMS and the Dollar', *Economic Policy*, 2: 455–85.

—— and —— (1988), *Limiting Exchange Rate Flexibility: The European Monetary System* (Cambridge, Mass.).

—— and Pagano, M. (1985), 'Capital Controls and the European Monetary System', *Occasional Paper: Capital Controls and Foreign Exchange Legislation* (Milan), 19–38.

Gilani, I. *et al.* (1981), *Labour Migration from Pakistan to the Middle East and its Impact on the Domestic Economy*, Pakistan Institute of Development Economics, Research Report Series No. 126 (Islamabad).

Gilpin, R. (1987), *The Political Economy of International Relations* (Princeton, NJ).

Gintis, H. (1986), 'International Capital Markets and the Validity of National Macroeconomic Models', mimeo, Univ. of Massachusetts.
—— (1988), 'Savings, Investment, and the Interest Rate: Credit Rationing in Competitive Equilibrium', mimeo, Univ. of Massachusetts.
Glyn, A. (1987), 'The Case for Exchange Controls', mimeo, Univ. of Oxford.
Glyn, A. (1991), 'Corporatism, Patterns of Employment, and Access to Consumption', in J. Pekkarinen, M. Pohjola, and R. Rowthorn (eds.), *Social Corporatism: A Superior Economic System?* (Oxford).
—— Hughes, A., Lipietz, A., and Singh, A. (1990), 'The Rise and Fall of the Golden Age', in Marglin and Schor (1990).
—— and Sutcliffe, B. (1972), *Capitalism in Crisis* (New York).
Goldsmith, R. W. (1985), *Comparative National Balance Sheets: A Study of Twenty Countries, 1688–1978* (Chicago).
Goodhart, C. (1988), 'The Cost of Regulation' in *Financial Regulations—or Over-Regulation?* (London).
Gordon, D. M. (1988), 'The Global Economy: New Edifice or Crumbling Foundations?', *New Left Review* 168: 24–65.
Granier, R., and Marciano, J. P. (1975), 'The Earnings of Immigrant Workers in France', *International Labour Review*, 111. 2: 143–66.
Grauwe, P. de (1988), 'Exchange Rate Variability and the Slowdown in Growth of International Trade', *IMF Staff Papers*, 35. 1: 63–84.
——and de Bellefroid, B. (1987), 'Long Run Exchange Rate Variability and International Trade', in S. Arndt and J. D. Richardson (eds.), *Real-Financial Linkages among Open Economies* (Cambridge, Mass.).
—— and Peeters, T. (1983), *Exchange Rates in Multicountry Econometric Models* (New York).
Green, A., and Urquhart, M. C. (1976), 'Factor and Commodity Flows in the International Economy of 1870–1914: A Multi-Country View', *Journal of Economic History* (Mar.), 215–22.
Greenwood, J., and Kimbrough, K. P. (1985), 'Capital Controls and Fiscal Policy in the World Economy', *Canadian Journal of Economics*, 18. 4: 743–65.
Gros, D. (1987), 'The Effectiveness of Capital Controls: Implications for Monetary Autonomy in the Presence of Incomplete Market Separation', *IMF Staff Papers* 34. 4: 621–42.
Guesnerie, R. (1986), 'Comments on the Eaton, Gersovitz, and Stiglitz Paper', *European Economic Review*, 30. 3: 515–19.
Gupta, S. (1980), 'An Application of The Monetary Approach to Black Market Exchange Rates', *Weltwirtschaftliches Archiv* (June), 235–252.
—— (1981), 'A Note on The Efficiency of Black Markets in Foreign Currencies', *Journal of Finance* (June), 705–710.
Hafer, R. W. (1986) (ed.), *How Open Is The U.S. Economy?* (Lexington, Mass.).
Harper, I. R. (1986), 'Why Financial Deregulation', *Australian Economic Review* (1st quarter).
Hellwig, M. (1986), 'Comments on the Eaton, Gersovitz, and Stiglitz Paper', *European Economic Review*, 30. 3: 521–7.
Hicks, J. (1969), *A Theory of Economic History* (Oxford).
Herring, R. (1990), Comment on paper by E. Baltensperger and J. Dermine, in Dermine (1990).

Hirsch, F. (1967), *Money International* (London).

Historical Statistics of Canada, edn. (1983) (Ottawa).

HMSO (Her Majesty's Stationery Office) (quarterly), *Financial Statistics* (London).

—— (Aug. 1959), *Committee on the Working of the Monetary System* (London).

Hogan, W. P. (1987), 'Foreign Debt: Growth and Implications for Australia', Australian Chamber of Commerce/Westpac Discussion Paper 4.

Holmström, B. (1979), 'Moral Hazard and Observability', *Bell Journal of Economics*, 10. 1: 74–91.

Hughes, A., and Singh, A. (1980), 'Mergers, Concentration and Competition in Advanced Industrial Economies: An International Perspective' in D. C. Mueller (ed.), *Determinants and Effects of Mergers* (O.G.H. Publishers: Cambridge, Mass.).

—— and —— (1987), 'Takeovers and the Stockmarket', *Contributions to Political Economy*, 6 (March): 73–85.

IMF (International Monetary Fund) (annual), *International Financial Statistics*, data tape (Washington, DC).

—— (various years), *Direction of Trade Statistics* (Washington, DC).

—— (various years), *Balance of Payments Yearbook* (Washington, DC).

International Herald Tribune (1990), 'India Faces Crisis in Commercial Borrowing' (8 Aug.), 15.

International Monetary Fund (1950–87) *Annual Report on Exchange Arrangements and Exchange Restrictions*, Washington, D.C.

—— (1985), *Exchange Arrangements and Exchange Restrictions: Annual Report* (Washington, DC).

—— (1987), *World Current Account Discrepancy* (Washington, DC).

—— (1988*a*), *International Capital Markets* (Apr.) (Washington, DC).

—— (1988*b*), *World Economic Outlook* (Washington, DC).

—— (1988*c*), *International Financial Statistics* (Washington, DC).

Ito, T. (1986), 'Capital Controls and Covered Interest Parity Between the Yen and the Dollar', Economic Studies Quarterly, 37. 3: 223–41.

Ize, A. (1989), 'Savings, Investment and Growth in Mexico: Five Years After the Crisis', IMF Working Paper.

Jacquemin, A., and de Jong, H. (1976), *Corporate Behaviour and the State* (The Hague).

Kaletsky, A. (1985), *The Costs of Default* (New York).

Kasman, B., and Pigott, C. (1988), 'Interest Rate Divergences among the Major Industrial Nations', *Federal Reserve Bank of New York Quarterly Review* (autumn), 28–44.

Kenen, P. B. (1976), *Capital Mobility and Financial Integration: A Survey*, Princeton Univ. Dep. of Economics, Essays in International Finance No. 39 (Princeton, NJ).

—— (1985), 'Macroeconomic Theory and Policy: How the Closed Economy Was Opened', in R. W. Jones and P. B. Kenen, *Handbook of International Economics*, ii (New York).

—— (1987) (ed.), *International Monetary Cooperation: Essays in Honor of Henry C. Wallich*, Princeton: Princeton Univ. Dept. of Economics, Essays in International Finance No. 169 (Princeton, NJ).

Kennedy, P. (1988), *The Rise and Fall of the Great Powers: Economic Change and Military Conflict from 1500 to 2000* (New York).

Keohane, R. O. (1984), *After Hegemony: Cooperation and Discord in the World Political Economy* (Princeton, NJ).

Keynes, J. M. (1933), 'National Self-Sufficiency', *Yale Review*; repr. in Keynes (1980*a*).

—— (1936), *The General Theory of Employment Interest and Money* (New York).

—— (1980*a*), *The Collected Writings of John Maynard Keynes, xxi, National Self-Sufficiency*, ed. D. Moggridge (London).

—— (1980*b*), *The Collected Writings of John Maynard Keynes xxv, (Activities 1940–1944), Shaping the Post-war World: The Clearing Union*, ed. D. Moggridge (London).

Kharas, H. (1984), 'The Long-Run Creditworthiness of Developing Countries: Theory and Practice', *Quarterly Journal of Economics*, 98: 415–39.

Kindleberger, C. P. (1973), *The World in Depression, 1929–1939* (Berkeley, Calif.).

—— (1978), *Manias, Panics, and Crashes: A History of Financial Crises* (New York).

—— (1984), *A Financial History of Western Europe* (London).

—— (1985), *Keynesianism vs. Monetarism and Other Essays in Financial History* (London).

—— (1987), *International Capital Movements* (Cambridge).

Kletzer, K. M. (1984), 'Asymmetrics of Information and LDC Borrowing with Sovereign Risk', *Economic Journal*, 94: 287–307.

Kolko, G. (1988), *Confronting the Third World* (New York).

Kotz, D. M. (1978), *Bank Control of Large Corporations in the United States* (Berkeley, Calif.).

Krane, R. E. (1979) (ed.), *International Labour Migration in Europe* (New York).

Krueger, A. O. (1966), 'Some Economic Costs of Exchange Control: The Turkish Case', *Journal of Political Economy*, 74. 5: 466–80.

—— (1974), *Foreign Trade Regimes and Economic Development: Turkey* (New York).

Krugman, P. (1979), 'A Model of Balance of Payments Crises', *Journal of Money, Credit and Banking*, 11. 3: 311–25.

—— (1989), *Exchange Rate Instability* (Cambridge, Mass.).

Kurzer, P. (1987), 'Do Banks Matter? Economic Integration and Social Democracy in Four European Countries', mimeo, Harvard Univ. Center for European Studies.

Laffont, J.-J., and Maskin, E. (1982), 'The Theory of Incentives: An Overview', in W. Hildenbrand (ed.), *Advances in Economic Theory* (Cambridge).

Lambert, R. (1987), 'Deregulation Opens Doors', *Financial Times*, 21 Oct.

Lange, P., and Garrett, G. (1985), 'The Politics of Growth: Strategic Interaction and Economic Performance in the Advanced Industrial Democracies, 1974–1980', *Journal of Politics*, 47. 3: 792–827.

Lessard, D. R. (1986), 'Country Risk and the Structure of International Financial Intermediation', mimeo, Sloan School of Management, Massachusetts Institute of Technology.

Levich, R. M. (1987*a*), 'Economic Consequences of Innovations in International Financial Markets' (New York and Cambridge, Mass.).

—— (1987*b*), 'Financial Innovations in International Financial Markets', NBER Working Paper No. 2277 (Cambridge, Mass.).

Lewis, M. K., and Polasek, M. (1985), 'Foreign Exchange Markets and Capital Inflow', in M. K. Lewis and R. H. Wallace (eds.), *Australia's Financial Institutions and Markets* (Melbourne).

Lieberman, S. S., and Gitmez, A. S. (1979), 'Turkey', in Krane (1979).

Lindert, P. H. (1969), *Key Currencies and Gold: 1900–1913* Princeton Univ. Dep. of Economics, Studies in International Finance, No. 24 (Princeton, NJ).

—— and Morton, P. J. (1987), 'How Sovereign Debt has Worked', University of California at Davis Working Paper No. 45.

Lintner, J. (1965), 'Security Prices, Risk, and Maximal Gains from Diversification', *Journal of Finance* (Dec.), 587–615.

Lipson, C. (1985), *Standing Guard: Protecting Foreign Capital in the Nineteenth and Twentieth Centuries* (Berkeley, Calif.).

López, J. (1985), 'Balance de la economia mexicana' mimeo, UNAM (Mexico City).

Lustig, N., and Ros, J. (1987), 'Stabilization and Adjustment in Mexico: 1982–85', mimeo, WIDER.

McCloskey, D., and Zecher, J. R. (1984), 'The Success of Purchasing Power Parity: Historical Evidence and its Implications for Macroeconomics', in M. D. Bordo and A. J. Schwartz (eds.), *A Retrospective on the Classical Gold Standard, 1821–1931* (Chicago).

de Macedo, J. B. (1982), 'Currency Diversification and Export Competitiveness: A Model of the "Dutch Disease" in Egypt', *Journal of Development Economics*, 11. 3: 287–306.

Mackie, T., and Rose, R. (1982), *The International Almanac of Electoral History* (New York).

McKinnon, R. I. (1973), *Money and Capital in Economic Development* (Washington, DC).

—— (1981), 'The Exchange Rate and Macroeconomic Policy: Changing Postwar Perception', *Journal of Economic Literature*, 19. 2: 531–557.

—— (1982), 'Currency Substitution and Instability in the World Dollar Standard', *American Economic Review* (June), 320–33.

Mahajan, A., and Fraser, D. R. (1986), 'Dollar Eurobond and US Bond Pricing', *Journal of International Business Studies* (summer), 21–36.

Marglin, S. A. (1984), *Growth, Distribution, and Prices* (Cambridge, Mass.).

—— and Bhaduri, A. (1990), 'Profit Squeeze and Keynesian Theory', in Marglin and Schor (1990).

—— and Schor, J. B. (1990) (eds.), *The Golden Age of Capitalism: Reinterpreting the Post-War Experience* (Oxford).

Martin, A., (1986), 'The Politics of Employment and Welfare in Advanced Capitalist Societies: National Policies and International Independence', in K. Banting (ed.), *The State and Economic Interests* (Toronto).

Mayer, C. (1988), 'New Issues in Corporate Finance' *European Economic Review*, 32: 1167–1182.

Meade, J. E. (1951), *The Balance of Payments* (London).

de Ménil, G., and Gordon, R. J. (1986) (eds.), 'International Seminar on Macroeconomics', *European Economic Review* (June).

Minsky, H. (1982), *Can 'It' Happen Again?* (Armonk, NY).

Moran, M. (1984), *The Politics of Banking*, 2nd edn. (London).

Morgan, E. V. (1943), *The Theory and Practice of Central Banking 1797–1913* (Cambridge).

Morgenstern, O. (1959), *International Financial Transactions and Business Cycles* (Princeton, NJ).

—— (1974), 'On The Accuracy of Economic Observations: Foreign Trade Statistics', in Bhagwati (1974).

Morse, J. (1988), 'The Great Inflation and its Aftermath', in Eizenga *et al.* (1988).

Mundell, R. A. (1963), 'Capital Mobility and Stabilization Policy under Fixed and Flexible Exchange Rates', *Canadian Journal of Economics and Political Science*, 29. 4: 475–85.

—— (1968), *International Economics* (New York).

Naslund, B. (1984), 'Aktiekapitalets internationalisering', EFI Research Paper No. 6292.

National Academy of Sciences (1985), (ed.) *Technological Frontiers and Foreign Relations*, ed. A. G. Keatley (Washington, DC).

Neal, L. (1985), 'Integration of International Capital Markets: Quantitative Evidence from the Eighteenth to Twentieth Centuries', *Journal of Economic History* (June), 219–26.

—— (1987*a*), 'The Integration and Efficiency of the London and Amsterdam Stock Markets in the Eighteenth Century', *Journal of Economic History* (Mar.), 97–115.

—— (1987*b*), 'Was the South Sea Bubble Rational?', unpublished MS (Urbana, IU.).

Nicoll, Alexander, (1987), in *Financial Times Survey on Global Equity Markets*, 21 October.

Niskanen, W. A. (1988); *Reagonomics: An Insider's Account* (New York).

Norris, K. (1987), 'The Social Wage and Living Standards', mimeo, Murdoch Univ.

Nurkse, R. (1944), *International Currency Experience* (Geneva).

Obstfeld, M. (1985), 'Capital Mobility in the World Economy: Theory and Measurement', NBER Working Paper No. 1692 (Cambridge, Mass.).

—— (1986), 'Capital Mobility in the World Economy: Theory and Measurement', in K. Brunner and A. H. Meltzer (eds.), *The National Bureau Method, International Capital Mobility and Other Essays*, Carnegie–Rochester Conference Series on Public Policy, vol. 24 (Amsterdam).

OECD (quarterly) *Financial Market Trends* (Paris).

—— (1976, 1988) *National Accounts Statistics: Main Aggregates and Detailed Tables*, i (Paris).

—— (1984, 1987, 1988), *Australia: Economic Survey* (Paris).

—— (1987*a*), *Flows and Stocks of Fixed Capital* (Paris).

—— (1987*b*), *Structural Adjustment and Economic Performance* (Paris).

—— (1988*a*), *National Accounts Statistics: Main Aggregates and Detailed Tables*, ii (Paris).

—— (1988*b*), *Why Economic Policies Change Course* (Paris).

Okun, A. (1981), *Prices and Quantities: A Macroeconomic Analysis* (Washington, DC).

Paine, S. (1974), *Exporting Workers* (Cambridge).

Papademetriou, D. (1979), 'Greece', in Krane (1979).

Pastor, M., Jr. (1990), 'Capital Flight from Latin America', *World Development*, 18. 1: 1–18.

Payer, C. (1974), *The Debt Trap* (New York).

Pick's Currency Yearbook (Brooklyn, NY).

Platt, D. C. M. (1968), *Finance, Trade and Politics in British Foreign Policy 1815–1914* (Oxford).

Price, R., and Muller, P. (1984), 'Structural Budget Indicators and the Interpretation of Fiscal Policy Stance in OECD Economies', *OECD Economic Studies* (autumn), 28–71.

Pringle, R. (1966), 'The Expansion of American Banks Abroad', *Banker* (Oct.).

Reserve Bank of Australia, *Annual Reports* (Sydney).

—— *Monthly Bulletins* (Sydney).

—— (1979), *Evidence to Campbell Committee* (Sydney).

Reyes Heroles, J. (1990), 'Estabilización y crecimiento en México: Gestión de la deuda pública interna', *El Trimestre Económico*, 226 (Apr.–June).

Riley, B. (1987), 'Fund Management', *Financial Times*, 21 Oct.

Robinson, J. (1966), *Economics: An Awkward Corner* (London).

Rogerson, W. P. (1983), 'Reputation and Product Quality', *Bell Journal of Economics*, 14. 2: 508–16.

Rogoff, K. (1985), 'Can Exchange Rate Predictability Be Achieved Without Monetary Convergence?', *European Economic Review*, 28: 93–115.

Roosa, R. V., Atkinson, T. R., Casey, M., DeMarines, R. J., McVey, T., Morrison, M., Suro-Bredie, C., Swanson, D. H., and Yoffie, D. B. (1985), *Countertrade in the World Economy* (New York).

Ros, J. (1987), 'Mexico From the Oil Boom to the Debt Crisis: An Analysis of Policy Responses to External Shocks 1978–1985', in R. Thorp and L. Whitehead (eds.), *The Latin American Debt Crisis* (London).

Ross, S. A. (1976), 'The Arbitrage Theory of Capital Asset Pricing', *Journal of Economic Theory* (Dec.), 258–76.

Rowthorn, B. (1982), 'Demand, Real Wages, and Economic Growth', *Studi Economici*, 18: 3–53.

Sachs, J. (1982), 'The Current Account in the Macroeconomic Adjustment Process', *Scandinavian Journal of Economics*, 84. 2: 147–61.

—— (1984), 'Theoretical Issues in International Borrowing', *Princeton Studies in International Finance*, 54.

—— (1985), 'External Debt and Macroeconomic Performance in Latin America and East Asia', *Brookings Papers on Economic Activity*, 2: 523–64.

Salomon Brothers (1987), *Global Equity Market Review and Outlook—1987–88* (New York).

Sayers, R. S. (1952), *Modern Banking*, 3rd edn. (Oxford).

Schwartz, O. (1987), 'Foreign Listings of Stocks and Market Segmentation', mimeo, Stockholm School of Economics.

Serageldin, I. *et al.* (1983), *Manpower and International Labour Migration in the Middle East and North Africa* (Washington, DC).

Sharpe, W. F. (1964), 'Capital Asset Prices: A Theory of Market Equilibrium under Conditions of Risk', *Journal of Finance* (Sept.), 425–42.

Shavell, S. (1979), 'Risk Sharing and Incentives in the Principal and Agent Relationship', *Bell Journal of Economics*, 10. 1: 55–73.

Sheikh, M. A. (1973), *Economics of Smuggling: Theory and Application*, Ph.D. dissertation, Univ. of Western Ontario.

—— (1974), 'Smuggling, Production and Welfare', *Journal of International Economics*, 4: 355–86.

—— (1976), 'Black Market for Foreign Exchange, Capital Flows, and Smuggling', *Journal of Development Studies*, 3: 9–26.

Sieper, E., and Fane, G. (1982), 'Exchange Controls and Exchange Rate Policy', in *Australian Financial System Inquiry: Commissioned Studies and Selected Papers*, p. 2 (Canberra).

SPP (Secretaria de Programación y Presupuesto) (various years), *Sistema de Cuentas Nacionales, 1970–78, 1979–81, 1981–3, 1984* (Mexico City).

Stigler, G. (1971), 'The Theory of Economic Regulations', *Bell Journal of Economics and Management Science*, 2.1: 3–21.

Stiglitz, J. E. (1987), 'The Causes and Consequences of the Dependence of Quality on Price', *Journal of Economic Literature*, 25: 1–48.

—— and Weiss, A. (1981), 'Credit Rationing in Markets with Imperfect Information', *American Economic Review*, 71: 393–411.

Strange, S. (1986), *Casino Capitalism* (Oxford).

Swamy, G. (1981), 'International Migrant Workers' Remittances: Issues and Prospects', World Bank Staff Working Paper No. 481 (Washington, DC).

Swoboda, A. K. (1976) (ed.), *Capital Movements and Their Control: Proceedings of the Second Conference of the International Center for Monetary and Banking Studies* (Geneva).

—— (1980), *Credit Creation in the Euromarket: Alternative Theories and Implications for Control* (New York).

Syntec (1982), 'Exchange Controls', in *Australian Financial System Inquiry: Commissioned Studies and Selected Papers*, p. 2 (Canberra).

Tanic, Z. (1979), 'Yugoslavia', in Krane (1979).

Tatom, J. A. (1987), 'The Macroeconomic Effects of the Recent Fall in Oil Prices', *Federal Reserve Bank of St. Louis Review*, 69. 6: 34–45.

Taylor, L. (1985), 'A Stagnationist Model of Economic Growth', *Cambridge Journal of Economics*, 9. 4: 383–403.

Triffin, R. (1968), *Our International Monetary System: Yesterday, Today and Tomorrow* (New York).

Tsakok, I. (1982), 'The Export of Manpower From Pakistan to the Middle East, 1975–85', *World Development*, 10. 4: 319–25.

Uusitalo, P. (1984), 'Monetarism, Keynesianism, and the Institutional Status of Central Banks', *Acta Sociologica*, 27. 1: 31–50.

Wachtel, H. (1987), *The Money Mandarins* (New York).

Wallgren, J., and Karlsson, M. (1984) 'Why do Swedish Companies Issue Equity on Foreign Capital Markets? The Case of Esselte and Four Other Swedish Companies', Seminarieuppsats, Ak 6: 5. Handelshögskolan i Stockholm.

Wallich, H. C. (1985), 'U.S. Monetary Policy in an Interdependent World', in Ethier and Marston (1985).

Walter, N. (1976), 'Capital Controls and the Autonomy of National Demand Management: The German Case', in Swoboda (1976).

Watson, M., Mathieson, D., Kincaid, R., Folkerts-Landou, D., Regling, K., and Atkinson, C. (1988), *International Capital Markets, Developments and Prospects* (Washington, DC).

Whitman, M. von N. (1979), *Reflections of Interdependence* (Pittsburgh).

Williamson, J. (1985), 'Comment on Sachs', *Brookings Papers on Economic Activity*, 2: 565–70.

Williamson, O. E. (1985), *The Economic Institutions of Capitalism* (New York).

Winston, G. (1974), 'Overinvoicing, Underutilization, and Distorted Industrial Growth', in Bhagwati (1974).

World Bank (1984), *World Development Report* (Washington).

Wyplosz, C. (1986), 'Capital Controls and Balance of Payments Crises', *Journal of International Money and Finance*, 5: 167–79.

Yeager, L. B. (1984), 'The Image of the Gold Standard', in M. D. Bordo and A. J. Schwartz (eds.), *A Retrospective on the Classical Gold Standard, 1821–1931* (Chicago).

Zevin, R. B. (1983), *A Greater Good* (Boston).

Index

Index compiled by Frank Pert